THE RIGHT TO BEAR ARMS

A CONSTITUTIONAL RIGHT OF THE PEOPLE OR A PRIVILEGE OF THE RULING CLASS?

STEPHEN P. HALBROOK

Senior Fellow, The Independent Institute

BOMBARDIER BOOKS
An Imprint of Post Hill Press
ISBN: 978-1-63758-118-6
ISBN (eBook): 978-1-63758-119-3

The Right to Bear Arms:
A Constitutional Right of the People or a Privilege of the Ruling Class?
© 2021 by Stephen P. Halbrook
All Rights Reserved

Cover art by Tiffani Shea

Post Hill Press
New York • Nashville
posthillpress.com

Published in the United States of America

ALSO BY STEPHEN P. HALBROOK

The Founders' Second Amendment (2008, 2019)

Securing Civil Rights: Freedmen, the Fourteenth Amendment, & the Right to Bear Arms (1998, 2021)

Firearms Law Deskbook (2020)

That Every Man be Armed: The Evolution of a Constitutional Right (1984, 2013)

A Right to Bear Arms (1989)

Gun Control in the Third Reich: Disarming the Jews and "Enemies of the State" (2013)

Gun Control in Nazi-Occupied France (2018)

The Swiss and the Nazis (2016)

Target Switzerland: Swiss Armed Neutrality in World War II (1998)

A Government resting on a minority, is an aristocracy, not a Republic, and could not be safe with a numerical [and] physical force against it, without a standing Army, an enslaved press, and a disarmed populace.

–JAMES MADISON

Table of Contents

PART FOUR:

HISTORY MARCHES ON

Foreword

Renée Lettow Lerner
Donald Phillip Rothschild Research Professor of Law
George Washington University Law School

Let me transport you back in time a little over five decades. In the late 1960s, rates of violent crime were skyrocketing. In large American cities, in the decade between 1960 and 1970, reports of robberies to the police rose over 400 percent. Homicides nearly doubled. American cities, which had before been safe for women and children to navigate freely, even alone and at night, became hazardous. American urban life was transformed; crime seemed to be spiraling out of control.

In an effort to stem the violence and fear, officials and legislators in cities and states hit upon the idea of restricting guns. They got encouragement from former U.S. Attorney General Ramsey Clark's 1970 book *Crime in America*. Clark had launched his anti-gun campaign while in office in 1968. Handgun ownership, and especially carrying a gun in public, was forbidden for many law-abiding citizens. This policy was and is called "liberal." Nothing could be further from the truth. The true liberal thinkers—John Locke, Cesare Beccaria, William Blackstone, and Adam Smith—uniformly supported widespread gun ownership and carry for self-defense. The misappropriation of the term "liberal" to describe policies that are actually statist is a public relations triumph of exactly the kind that Orwell warned against.

Courts acquiesced to the new gun restrictions. Courts were not blameless in the rise of violent crime. The criminal procedure revolution of the 1960s, led by the Warren Court, increased the costs and uncertainties of accurately investigating crimes, arresting offenders, trying them, and punishing them. These novel judicial requirements burdened criminal justice systems and lowered deterrence, just at the time those systems needed to be more efficient and deterring. (The problem has since been "solved" by applying ever-greater pressure on defendants to plead guilty. Many courts and lawyers have prided themselves on their compassion while disregarding unintended, but foreseeable, consequences.) Courts put up no resistance to gun restrictions. Focusing on guns conveniently deflected attention from the effects of courts' decisions on criminal procedure. Meanwhile, legal scholars almost wholly ignored the Second Amendment right to keep and bear arms, except to dismiss it as a collective right, to be curtailed at the states' or the federal government's pleasure.

Predictably, gun restrictions failed. Not only did violent crime not fall, it rose—substantially. From 1960 to 1980, homicides in the largest American cities nearly tripled. As Beccaria explained two and a half centuries ago, gun prohibitions only disarm law-abiding persons. Someone who is willing to commit armed robbery or murder is not likely to obey laws restricting guns. As a result of gun restrictions, criminals had an easier time wreaking havoc, intimidating, and making our cities even more unlivable. Police were overwhelmed.

By the early 1980s, the failure of gun restrictions—together with the failure of other so-called "liberal," but really statist policies—had become manifest. Thoughtful persons started to see the importance of returning to true liberal principles, of rediscovering fundamental truths. It was, in some sense, a new birth of freedom.

One of the first signs of this new birth of freedom was Stephen Halbrook's 1981 article in the *George Mason University Law Review* (now the *George Mason Law Review*), "The Jurisprudence of the Second and Fourteenth Amendments." Many works are called groundbreaking, but this one deserves the title. Steve argued that the Second Amendment guarantees an individual right to arms, and that the Fourteenth Amendment was intended to make the Second Amendment enforceable against the states. At the time, those arguments were outliers to the point of being shocking in academic and legal circles. But Steve's work, and the work of other scholars, steadily revealed a sure foundation for these positions. Decades later, the U.S. Supreme Court confirmed both of those principles in *District of Columbia v. Heller* (2008) and *McDonald v. Chicago* (2010).

Steve had a combination of training and interests that fitted him perfectly for the job of pioneering Second Amendment scholarship. He was at once a lawyer, trained philosopher, and historian. Steve brought all these skills to bear in his monumental 1984 book, *That Every Man Be Armed*. That book delved deeply into the history and original meaning of the Second Amendment. Steve examined eighteenth century English constitutional history, understandings of rights to firearms during the American founding, and the later American history in the antebellum period, reconstruction, and twentieth century. This was the first significant book-length treatment of the Second

Amendment. It laid the foundation for the next four decades of scholarship and debate concerning the Amendment.

In the 1980s and 90s, Steve was joined by other important scholars working on the right to keep and bear arms. Two of the first were Joyce Lee Malcolm, who revealed the earlier English history, and Don Kates, who had learned the importance of carrying a firearm during his civil rights work in the 1960s in the South. Daniel Polsby teamed up with Don to write several influential empirical studies of the effects of gun prohibitions, and provided his own robust arguments for the importance of gun ownership and carry. Nelson Lund has elegantly illuminated the philosophic basis of the right. Robert Cottrol and Raymond Diamond have used their knowledge of history, race relations, and civil rights to emphasize the importance of firearms for securing the liberties of black Americans. In 2012, Nicholas Johnson, David Kopel, George Mocsary, and Michael O'Shea wrote the first law school textbook on the Second Amendment, now in its second edition. The field had come of age, and flourishes today, with articles pouring out every year on all sides of the debate.

All of them need to address Steve's work. In article after article, and book after book, Steve has continued to make invaluable contributions to the field he essentially founded. By the mid-1980s, journals were holding symposia on the Second Amendment. For the 1986 symposium in *Law and Contemporary Problems*, Steve wrote a detailed analysis of the language of the Second Amendment entitled "What the Framers Intended: A Linguistic Analysis of the Right to 'Bear Arms.'" After several more articles, in 1989, he produced another book, *A Right to Bear Arms: State and Federal Bills of Rights and Constitutional Guarantees*. That book meticulously documents the various state constitutional provisions that influenced the drafting and ratification of the Second Amendment.

Steve moved forward in time with his next book, first published in 1998, called *Freedmen, the Fourteenth Amendment, and the Right to Bear Arms, 1866-1876*. This is an exhaustive, carefully researched study of the struggle of newly-freed black Americans to secure the equal benefit of the right to keep and bear arms. The book made a huge contribution to our understanding of the importance of the Second Amendment during the postbellum period, and of the fundamental and enduring link between the right to keep and bear arms, and social and civil equality.

As if these were not enough, Steve's 2008 book, *The Founders' Second Amendment*, remains the definitive account of the founding-era history of the Amendment's origins, drafting, and ratification.

Steve's body of scholarship is so vast that I have only been able to mention some of it here. All of his work shows his historical acumen and penetrating legal analysis. His work is influential and widely read not only among academics, but among judges as well. The U.S. Supreme Court repeatedly cited and relied on his work in both *District of Columbia v. Heller* and *McDonald v. City of Chicago*. Federal courts have cited his work in 122 other decisions (and counting). In addition to his scholarship, Steve is an active litigator. He has been deeply involved in many Second Amendment cases, including *Heller* and *McDonald*.

In this new book, Steve turns to the history of the right to carry firearms outside the home. His topic couldn't be more timely. This is a question of enduring importance, but with special salience now. The federal courts have split over the extent to which the Second Amendment applies outside the home, the U.S. Supreme Court dodged the issue in the 2019 Term, and that Court is likely to face the question again in the near future.

Recent political and social unrest underscores the importance of this topic. The events of 2020 have emphasized to many, if they did not notice it before, that every citizen is his or her own first responder. In American cities, homicide rates have ballooned. In 2020, in a sample of 57 large and medium-sized cities, murder rose 37 percent. The numbers for individual cities are even more staggering: a 95 percent increase in Milwaukee, 74 percent in Seattle, 72 percent in Minneapolis, 58 percent in Atlanta, 55 percent in Chicago. The COVID epidemic has prompted many state and local governments to release convicted criminals from prison. Faced with growing public hostility, police have backed down and ceased active policing, such as patrolling areas. In many places today, because of police passivity, officers are no longer an effective deterrent to crime. They appear only when called for, after a shooting has occurred. And in many cities, the majority of serious crimes—even homicides—go unpunished. In 2020, clearance rates for homicides fell. Chicago's clearance rate, for example, fell 6 percentage points to a mere 46 percent. Greater reluctance to cooperate with the police, mask wearing, and fewer police on the job because of contracting COVID have all contributed to the slip in clearance rates for the most serious crimes. In some cities, clearance rates are dismal even in ordinary years. In 2019, Baltimore's clearance rate for homicides was 32 percent. In 2016, Detroit's was less than 15 percent.

Across the country, government officials charged with protecting public safety in our cities—from Minneapolis to New York, Kenosha to Atlanta—failed spectacularly. For weeks, officials in Portland ceded all control over a swath of the city's downtown to rioters and anarchists. Looting, intimidation, and murders occurred. Just ask a small business owner in Kenosha, or a single mom living in Seattle's "Capitol Hill Autonomous Zone," whether the right to keep and carry firearms for self-defense is an outdated relic in our society.

Actually, we don't have to ask them. Americans by the millions, of all races and in all areas, are showing by their actions what they think about the right to keep and carry arms. They are doing it. Gun sales have been soaring, especially to first-time buyers. The FBI's figures show that American gun sales surged in 2020, with nearly 23 million firearms purchased that year—a 65 percent increase over 2019. Sales for the month of July 2020 alone were at least 1.8 million, a 122 percent increase over July 2019. And the trend has continued into 2021: the FBI processed nearly 4.3 million background checks for gun buyers in January, up from 2.7 million in January of 2020.

Now 40 percent of first-time buyers are women. And a survey of gun retailers reports that, for the first half of 2020, sales to black Americans were up 58.2 percent, the largest increase for any demographic group. More and more Americans understand that the professional police simply cannot prevent all violent crimes from occurring, and that their wisest course is to provide the means to defend themselves.

In this book, Steve brings his characteristic blend of acute legal analysis and thorough historical learning to bear on the question of the right to carry. He demonstrates that the right to carry a firearm freely outside the home was well-accepted at the founding. He shows its roots in England. And he demonstrates that the right to carry continued to be well-accepted throughout most of the nineteenth century. In the process, Steve dispels myths and misinterpretations about the history of the right to bear arms that have muddied recent debate. These include the notion that the Founders understood the 1328 Statute of Northampton to generally prohibit carrying arms in public. And the idea that the acceptance of the right to carry was limited to the slaveholding South.

Like Steve's earlier work, this book promises to become a definitive account—in this case, of the history of the right to carry. As the debate continues, Second Amendment scholars of all views will have to grapple with the arguments in this book.

Renée Lettow Lerner
Donald Phillip Rothschild Research Professor of Law
George Washington University Law School

Introduction

The Second Amendment to the United States Constitution provides: "A well regulated militia, being necessary to the security of a free state, the right of the people to keep and bear arms, shall not be infringed." Whether that protects the right to carry a firearm outside the home and in public is a festering issue among the courts, historians, and members of the public.

Over forty states allow law-abiding citizens to exercise their right to carry firearms in public, either with or without a license. Only a handful of states prohibit the bearing of arms by virtually all of their citizens by limiting their licenses to carry to a select few individuals who, in the subjective eyes of the police or other government officials, have a special "need" to do so.

Most states do not restrict the carrying of a firearm openly, such as a handgun carried exposed in a holster. Carrying a handgun concealed means having clothing over the handgun such that it is not visible to common observation. Because of their size, rifles and shotguns are normally carried openly, although they are not typically carried in public, outside of the contexts of hunting and target shooting. Handguns are most frequently carried for self-defense.

During oral argument in the seminal case of *District of Columbia v. Heller* (2008),[1] Supreme Court Justice Anthony Kennedy asked the

---

[1] *District of Columbia v. Heller*, 554 U.S. 570 (2008).

lawyer for the District whether the Second Amendment's reference to "the right of the people to keep and bear arms" concerns something besides the militia. When counsel replied that those words refer only to "a military context," Justice Kennedy then asked the further question: "It had nothing to do with the concern of the remote settler to defend himself and his family against hostile Indian tribes and outlaws, wolves and bears and grizzlies and things like that?"[2] This question suggested that Justice Kennedy read the Amendment to protect an individual right to carry arms for self-defense outside the home, where unfriendly humans and wild animals would be encountered.

While the right had obvious utility in frontier society, one might ask what relevance does the right to carry a gun outside the home have in today's modern society? Richard Posner, a prominent law professor and longtime federal judge, answered that "a Chicagoan is a good deal more likely to be attacked on a sidewalk in a rough neighborhood than in his apartment on the 35th floor of the Park Tower."[3] The murder rate in today's Chicago far exceeds that of any cattle town in the Wild West. And, of course, the riots and social unrest of 2020 further put to rest any suggestion that Americans do not need the means of self-defense on our streets today.

On April 19, 1775, American patriots bearing their own firearms stood outside under a bright sun before a contingent of British Redcoats representing the greatest military power on Earth. These Americans did not bear arms in their living rooms or before their fireplaces, but carried and bore their private firearms prominently in public—on the town

---

[2] Transcript of Argument at 8, *District of Columbia v. Heller*, Mar. 18, 2008 (No. 07-290).
[3] *Moore v. Madigan*, 702 F.3d 933, 937 (7th Cir. 2012).

common of Concord, Massachusetts. In Ralph Waldo Emerson's words: "Here once the embattled farmers stood / And fired the shot heard round the world."[4] Thus, privately-owned firearms, publicly borne by citizens, launched the American Revolution, and, before long, a new country that became the United States of America.

The Founders who drafted the Bill of Rights in 1789 recalled the British efforts to confiscate private firearms from the American colonists and knew that firearms helped to win the American Revolution. They also knew that the same firearms could be used for protection against persons and wild animals that would do harm. This was all in addition to the Founders' understanding of world history, which taught them the great dangers posed to an unarmed citizenry by tyranny. They would thus enshrine the right to bear arms in the Second Amendment.

Yet today, there has developed a cottage industry of advocates who seek to write out of American history these basic facts found in elementary school books. Their objective is to establish that, in contravention of the Second Amendment's clear text and America's Founding history, individual Americans actually have *no* right to bear arms.

This book seeks to address and rebut such assertions. It demonstrates that the Second Amendment guarantee that "the right of the people to…bear arms, shall not be infringed" protects the individual liberty to carry firearms outside the home for self-defense and other lawful purposes. It is based on the Amendment's text, history, and tradition. This book should not be necessary to show that "the people"

---

[4] Ralph Waldo Emerson, *Concord Hymn* (1837).

have an individual right to "bear arms," but because the explicit text and its surrounding history have been so obstructed and distorted by some, this work is indeed warranted.

Today, the overwhelming majority of states recognize a right to carry a handgun in public, either with or without a license. Only eight states—California, Delaware, Hawaii, Maryland, Massachusetts, New Jersey, and New York, and Rhode Island—grant discretion to the government to restrict that right only to those few persons it decides "need" or have "good cause" to carry a firearm. These outlier states make it a serious crime to bear arms for self-defense, without first receiving permission to do so from the government, and routinely incarcerate their own citizens and unsuspecting travelers for gun possession on the basis that, to put it colloquially, "Your papers are not in order!" These discretionary licensing schemes have become a major issue in Second Amendment litigation, with some federal circuits upholding such laws and others invalidating them.

As examples, Florida will issue a license to carry a concealed handgun to a resident or nonresident who demonstrates competence with a firearm and has not been convicted of a felony, committed to a mental institution, or otherwise disqualified.[5] Florida also recognizes and honors conceal carry licenses issued by many other states; this allows those out-of-state residents, holding their home state licenses, lawfully to carry handguns in Florida.

In stark contrast, New Jersey requires that a person have "a justifiable need to carry a handgun" in the form of "a special danger to

---

[5] Fla. Stat. § 790.06.

4

the applicant's life"; "[g]eneralized fears for personal safety are inadequate."[6] In practice, New Jersey's government rarely finds that individuals have proven an adequate need to carry firearms in that state. And New Jersey, unlike Florida and many other states, does not recognize carry licenses issued by any other state.

One would think from the clear text of the Second Amendment that courts would presume a general right to carry and closely scrutinize restrictions. But the starting point for those courts upholding carry restrictions appears to be an outright denial of the existence of the right.

This book begins by analyzing the text of the Second Amendment. What could be confusing about the prohibition on the infringement of "the right," not the privilege, of "the people," not a tiny elite, to "bear arms"? Especially such a right found expressed at the top of the American Bill of Rights. Plenty, if one muddies the water enough.

Next, the English origins of the right to bear arms are traced. The Statute of Northampton of 1328, cited by some today as somehow overriding America's Second Amendment, was actually construed as prohibiting one from going armed in a manner to terrify one's fellow subjects. The leading precedent construing this medieval statute is the 1686 case of *Rex v. Knight*,[7] a prosecution against a Protestant activist who carried arms for self-defense against attacks by Catholic partisans. The Catholic King James II increasingly resorted to disarming his Protestant political opponents, prompting his removal in the Glorious Revolution of 1688.

---

[6] N. J. Stat. § 2C:58–4(c); N.J. Admin. Code § 13:54–2.4; *In re Preis*, 118 N.J. 564, 571, 573 A. 2d 148, 152 (1990).

[7] *Rex v. Sir John Knight*, 90 Eng. Rep. 331, Comberbach, 4 (1686).

The Declaration of Rights of 1689 recognized the right of English Protestants to "have Arms for their Defence" as allowed by law. The right was not accorded to Catholics, particularly the majority of Ireland's population, who were also denied the benefit of other civil rights then available to Protestants.

The right to bear arms continued to be recognized in England, even in tumultuous times. What was seen as a universal right in England was reversed in oppressed Ireland. It was not until 1870 that a license to carry a gun was required in England; even then, anyone could buy the license at a post office. Only beginning in 1920 was an Englishman required to show a "need" to the authorities for a gun license, representing the loss of the right to bear arms.

The American settlers would insist on, and expand, their already existing rights as Englishmen. In the colonies, carrying arms was generally an unchallenged right, a practical necessity, and sometimes a legal duty. When the Stamp Act and other oppressive measures were imposed in 1765, the Sons of Liberty protested. They often carried arms openly or concealed at will. In the 1770 homicide trials arising out of the Boston Massacre, both the prosecution and the defense agreed that individuals in the colonies had a right to carry weapons for self-defense.

While the British began to cut off the supply of arms and ammunition to the colonies, the royal administration in the colonies recognized that it had no legal power to seize arms from those who were carrying or transporting them. But once armed conflict erupted at Lexington and Concord, British commander Thomas Gage demanded that Bostonians surrender their firearms in exchange for safe passage to leave the city. He then confiscated the firearms and reneged on his promise. The Revolution was on, and the independent states began adopting constitutions and bills of rights, including recognition of the preexisting right to bear arms.

When the Constitution was proposed for the United States, the alarm went out that it had no bill of rights. Recognition of the right to bear arms was demanded along with freedom of speech. James Madison proposed what became the Second Amendment with its familiar wording, and the Bill of Rights was ratified by the states in 1791. The right to bear arms for self-defense was taken for granted as a legal right and necessary practice. The federal Militia Act of 1792 required able-bodied males to arm themselves. The Founders personally carried arms and defended the right to do so.

At the beginning of the early Republic, citizens were at liberty peaceably to carry arms outside the home in public, openly or concealed, without any restrictions. Legal commentators acclaimed the constitutional right to bear arms as the palladium of liberty of a free state.

By statute or judicial decisions, some states prohibited going armed in a manner that would terrorize others, and required violators to find sureties to keep the peace. In 1813, over two decades after ratification of the Second Amendment, two states banned one method of carrying firearms, i.e., the carrying of concealed weapons; a handful of other states followed. Courts upheld these restrictions because one could bear arms openly. Most states, however, continued to allow arms to be carried openly or concealed.

The slave codes provided the great exception to the right to bear arms, as well as to other recognized constitutional and civil rights.

Slaves were virtually prohibited from firearms possession, while free blacks—unlike free whites—were required to obtain a license to carry a firearm. Like today, in America's "may issue" carry states, licenses were subject to the discretion of the government's issuing authority.

In considering the history of the Second Amendment, the Supreme Court has placed an emphasis on text and history. The history is important to illuminate the public understanding of the text when it was adopted in 1791. Logically, at some point, the history becomes sufficiently remote in time from the Amendment's adoption that it no longer has relevance to constitutional adjudication. Although we cannot pinpoint with precision the time at which the history becomes irrelevant, certainly the death of the leading Founders by the 1820s is a logical stopping point for purposes of trying to understand the meaning of the Second Amendment; John Adams and Thomas Jefferson both died on the fiftieth anniversary of the Declaration of Independence in 1826. Nevertheless, this book is intended to give a full history of carriage in America through the centuries, and thus does not terminate in the early 19th century.

When slavery was abolished in 1865, the Southern states reenacted the slave codes as the black codes, a prominent provision of which was the requirement that African Americans must obtain a license, subject to official discretion, to possess and carry firearms. Congress sought to prohibit the confiscation of unlicensed firearms from the newly-freed slaves through passage of the Civil Rights and Freedmen's Bureau Acts of 1866. The Fourteenth Amendment was proposed and ratified intending, in part, to protect the right to bear arms from state violation, and the Civil Rights Act of 1871 provided for enforcement of that and other rights. The courts responded with mixed results to the carry restrictions that were enacted in a handful of states during Reconstruction.

The U.S. Supreme Court weighed in with two decisions in the last quarter of the nineteenth century. *United States v. Cruikshank*[8] held that the rights peaceably to assemble and to bear arms for a lawful purpose preexisted the Constitution, but no basis existed for the federal prosecution of private individuals for violation of the exercise of those rights by African Americans. And in *Presser v. Illinois*,[9] the Court held that the requirement of a license to parade with arms in cities, which was passed during a period of labor unrest, did not infringe on the right to bear arms. Both of these decisions pre-dated the Supreme Court's adoption of the "incorporation doctrine" of the Fourteenth Amendment, which began in 1897.

Before and after the turn of the century, restrictions were sporadically enacted against the bearing of arms in unique contexts not shared by most of America. Far from being predominant or longstanding, these laws were needles in a haystack. Some "Wild West" cattle towns disallowed the carrying of firearms, although statehood and court rulings invalidated some of the bans. Jim Crow-inspired licensing requirements and fees essentially prohibited blacks from exercising the right to bear arms in some states. And New York's Sullivan Law of 1911, named after a politician with ties to organized crime, sought to ensure that Italians and other immigrants went to prison if they dared to carry a gun for self-defense.

In the twentieth century and beyond, the state courts upheld the right to bear arms under state constitutional guarantees. The U.S.

---

[8] *United States v. Cruikshank*, 92 U.S. 542 (1875).
[9] *Presser v. Illinois*, 116 U.S. 252 (1886).

Supreme Court upheld the common law right to be armed in self-defense, opined in dictum that restrictions on concealed carry did not violate the right to bear arms, and in *United States v. Miller*,[10] held that militia arms are protected by the Second Amendment.

Finally, in *Heller*, the Court held that the District's handgun ban violated the individual right to keep and bear arms. The opinion clarified that to "bear arms" means to carry arms and has no exclusive militia context. And it rejected the view that the right could be dismissed or diminished by judge-made interest-balancing tests. That was followed by the Supreme Court's *McDonald v. Chicago* decision in 2010,[11] which held the right to arms to be fundamental and protected from state violation by the Fourteenth Amendment.

After that, the Supreme Court in *Caetano v. Massachusetts*[12] in 2016 remanded a state court decision that misapplied *Heller*'s broad test for protected arms; the decision was premised on the right to bear arms outside the home, as the case involved a stun gun carried in public. At the time of this writing, the Court has not weighed in on the merits of a Second Amendment case since then.

Since *Heller* and *McDonald* were decided, state carry bans have been litigated in the lower federal courts. Some federal circuits have found discretionary issuance laws to violate the right of the public at large to bear arms. Other circuits have upheld the denial of the right to ordinary citizens, typically under a watered-down version of intermediate scrutiny that allows judges to balance away the right.

---

[10] *United States v. Miller*, 307 U.S. 174 (1939).
[11] *McDonald v. Chicago*, 561 U.S. 742 (2010).
[12] *Caetano v. Massachusetts*, 136 S. Ct. 1027 (2016).

One extreme example of a restriction and of a judicial decision to uphold it was New York City's rule prohibiting the transport of a handgun from one's licensed premises (a home or business) to other locations. The Second Circuit upheld the rule because a single police official opined that such transport would threaten public safety. After the Supreme Court granted certiorari to review that decision, the supposed grave public safety concerns addressed by the law dissolved. The City revised the law in an effort to moot the case. The Supreme Court then held that the case no longer presented a live case or controversy, and thus made no ruling on the merits.[13]

* * *

This book ends with an afterword that puts the right to bear arms outside of the home into perspective. This book does not engage in argument about whether the right to bear arms is good or bad policy, and instead seeks to establish what the Constitution means and requires. Criminologists debate whether various restrictions on the right work or don't work, yet as the Supreme Court stated in *District of Columbia v. Heller*: "But the enshrinement of constitutional rights necessarily takes certain policy choices off the table."[14]

Today, the overwhelming majority of states recognize the right to bear arms, with variations about open and concealed carry and about whether carry permits are required. Only eight states are "may issue," i.e., government officials may issue a permit, but are not required to do so, if they decide a person "needs" to carry a firearm. Litigation over the issue of what the Second Amendment means and requires is mostly

---

[13] *New York State Rifle & Pistol Association, Inc. v. City of New York*, 140 S. Ct. 1525 (2020).
[14] *District of Columbia v. Heller*, 554 U.S. 570, 636 (2008).

limited to those states. And it is those states' restrictions that have raised the issue about whether Congress has authority to require states to recognize the carry permits of other states, in the same way that states recognize and honor one another's driver's licenses.

The way and extent to which the right to bear arms is exercised may vary with societal changes, uncertainties, and disasters. The year 2020 exemplified that, with record gun sales being prompted by political transformations resulting in greater restrictions in certain states, fewer restrictions in other states, the arrival of the coronavirus and its devastating impact, and the sparking of rioting and pullback of law enforcement nationwide.

Whatever the future holds, the Second Amendment and the ongoing love affair of Americans with private firearms ownership have endured for well over two centuries. If some politicians and judges are mystified by the meaning of the words "the right of the people to...bear arms," most Americans are not. The Bill of Rights is not just ten commandments that tell the government what it cannot do, but is a testament to instruct the people as to their rights so they can protect them.

Prologue

"THE RIGHT OF *THE PEOPLE* TO...*BEAR* ARMS"

The Second Amendment unequivocally guarantees the right of "the people" to "bear arms": "A well regulated Militia, being necessary to the security of a free State, the right of the people to keep and bear Arms, shall not be infringed."[15] What did those words mean in ordinary English when the Amendment was ratified in 1791, and do they mean anything different today?

The Bill of Rights was intended to inform the ordinary citizen of his or her rights. Understanding its meaning is not a legal monopoly of the very same governmental entities whose powers it was intended to limit. St. George Tucker said it best in his 1803 treatise, the first ever published on the Constitution, as follows:

> A bill of rights may be considered, not only as intended to give law, and assign limits to a government about to be established, but as giving information to the people. By reducing speculative truths to fundamental laws, every man of the meanest capacity and understanding may learn his own rights, and know when they are violated....[16]

---

[15] U.S. Const., Amend. II.
[16] 1 William Blackstone, *Commentaries*, St. George Tucker ed., App. 308 (Philadelphia: William Young Birch and Abraham Small, 1803).

The text should be read while keeping in mind the words of Justice Felix Frankfurter: "To view a particular provision of the Bill of Rights with disfavor inevitably results in a constricted application of it. This is to disrespect the Constitution."[17] Since the 1960s, the Second Amendment has suffered more than its share of disrespect.

"The Right of the People"

The Second Amendment refers to "the right of the people." The term "people" was defined as "persons in general" in Webster's 1806 dictionary,[18] and "the people" was defined as "the commonalty, as distinct from men of rank" in his 1828 dictionary.[19] Noah Webster was a prominent Federalist spokesman in the debates on the Constitution in 1787, and his latter dictionary was adopted as the standard by Congress and the American people.[20]

In the constitutional lexicon, only "the people" or "persons" have "rights," while governments have "powers."[21] Although the term "States' Rights" came into colloquial use in the early Republic, the States have powers, not rights, and only persons have "rights." Webster defined "right" in pertinent part:

> Just claim; immunity; privilege. All men have a right to the secure enjoyment of life, personal safety, liberty and property. We deem the

---

[17] *Ullmann v. United States*, 350 U.S. 422, 428-29 (1956).

[18] Noah Webster, *A Compendious Dictionary of the English Language* 220 (New Haven: Sidney's Press, 1806).

[19] Noah Webster, *An American Dictionary of the English Language* (New York: S. Converse, 1828) ("people," 3).

[20] Noah Webster, *On Being American: Selected Writings, 1783-1828*, Homer D. Babbidge Jr. ed., 166 (New York: Frederick A. Praeger, 1967).

[21] E.g., U.S. Const., Art. I, § 8 ("Congress shall have power"); Art. II, § 1 ("The executive Power shall be vested in a President"); Amend. X ("The powers not delegated to the United States…are reserved to the States respectively, or to the people.").

right of trial by jury invaluable, particularly in the case of crimes. Rights are natural, civil, political, religious, personal, and public.[22]

Thus, "the right of the people" refers to a just claim or freedom by persons at large, not an authorization granted by government to privileged persons. The phrase "the right of the people" appears in the First Amendment: "Congress shall make no law…abridging the freedom of speech, or of the press; or *the right of the people* peaceably to assemble, and to petition the government for a redress of grievances." After the Second Amendment's reference to "*the right of the people* to keep and bear arms," the Fourth Amendment guarantees: "*The right of the people* to be secure in their persons, houses, papers, and effects, against unreasonable searches and seizures, shall not be violated.…"

The Ninth Amendment uses the same phraseology, only in the plural rather than the singular: "The enumeration in the Constitution, of certain *rights*, shall not be construed to deny or disparage others retained by *the people*." Whatever those rights are, they extend to the people at large and may not be denied or disparaged to all except an elite chosen by government.

The word "the" used twice in the phrase "*the* right of *the* people" is significant. The term "the right" expresses a preexisting right, not a new right invented for the Bill of Rights. To declare that "the right" to do or be free of something shall not be abridged, infringed, or violated presupposes that the right already exists.

The unitary phrase "the right of the people" appears in the First, Second, and Fourth Amendments. No one would suggest that exercise

---

[22] Webster, *An American Dictionary* ("right," 10).

15

of the right to assemble and petition the government for a redress of grievances, and security from reasonable searches and seizures, are not a "right of the people," but may be limited to a select few individuals determined by government officials to have a special "need." So too, "the right of the people to...bear arms" extends to the populace at large, and is not restricted as a "privilege to bear arms" reserved to a handful of societal elites, all receiving the blessing of their friends in government.

All four of the above Bill of Rights guarantees protect individuals from government action; none of them delegate or reserve powers to governmental bodies.

The term "the right" also appears in the Bill of Rights in reference to a subclass of private individuals constituting less than "the people" at large. The Sixth Amendment provides that "in all criminal prosecutions, the accused shall enjoy *the right* to a speedy and public trial, by an impartial jury...." The Seventh Amendment states in part: "In suits at common law, where the value in controversy shall exceed twenty dollars, *the right* of trial by jury shall be preserved...." In every instance where it is used, the term "right" is a guarantee to individuals against governmental action.

The Militia Clauses

The Tenth Amendment concerns "powers," not "rights," and distinguishes "the States" from "the people": "The powers not delegated to the United States by the Constitution, nor prohibited by it to the States, are reserved to the States respectively, or to the people." The "right of the people" to bear arms was not a secret code for "the power of the States" to maintain militias.

16

When a subset of "the people" is intended, the Bill of Rights is clear. The Second Amendment itself distinguishes "the people" from the subset "well regulated militia." A subset of the militia appears in the Fifth Amendment as follows: "No person shall be held to answer for a capital, or otherwise infamous crime, unless on a presentment or indictment of a grand jury, except in cases arising in the land or naval forces, or in *the militia, when in actual service in time of war or public danger....*"

The militia would be in active service when called forth "to execute the laws of the Union, suppress insurrections and repel invasions."[23] The distinction is thus made between "the people" at large (who have the "right" to bear arms), the general "well regulated militia," and that part of the militia "when in actual service."

If keeping and bearing arms was a "right" only of "the militia, when in actual service," the Framers certainly would have so stated. It would have been odd, when guaranteeing "the right of the people to keep and bear arms," had the Framers really meant "the right of the militia to keep and bear arms when authorized and activated by the government."

Moreover, the power of a State to maintain and call out the militia is just that—a power, not a right. But does a person have a "right to bear arms" in the militia? When not in actual service, a militia member has as much of a right to bear arms as any other person. But when in actual service, a militia person has no "right" to bear arms unless ordered to do so, in which case bearing arms is a duty, not a right.

---

[23] "The Congress shall have power...To provide for calling forth the militia to execute the laws of the Union, suppress insurrections and repel invasions." U.S. Const., Art. I, § 8, cl. 15.

Indeed, a person "in the land or naval forces, or in the militia, when in actual service in time of war or public danger" may not only be subject to trial by a military tribunal rather than upon an indictment by a grand jury, but also must obey all lawful commands, even those precluding exercise of rights such as speech, assembly, and bearing arms.

Moreover, whether a person is conscripted into or volunteers for service in a militia, there is no constitutional "right" to join or be in the active militia of a state or the federal government. Once in a militia, a person has no "right" to keep, bear, use, or otherwise have access to arms, but may do so only subject to the command of superior officers. To speak of the "right to bear arms in the militia" is an oxymoron.

Similarly, "the right of the people" to bear arms is not limited only to those appointed to do so by a state. It is not analogous to the militia clause of the Constitution, which reserves to the states respectively "the Appointment of the Officers."[24]

In short, "the right of the people" to assemble, to bear arms, to be secure from unreasonable searches, and to retain nonenumerated rights is not limited to a subset of the people chosen by the government to enjoy special privileges. These are rights reserved for all the people.

To Keep and Bear Arms

The Second Amendment refers to two separate but related rights, i.e., the right to keep "and" to bear arms. Keeping implies passive possession, actual or constructive, while bearing implies active carrying on the person. The two words in this clause have different

---

[24] "The Congress shall have Power...To provide for organizing, arming, and disciplining, the Militia,...reserving to the States respectively, the Appointment of the Officers...." U.S. Const., Art. I, § 8, cl. 16.

meanings, just as do the two words in the other constitutional clauses such as "search and seizure" in the Fourth Amendment, and "cruel and unusual" in the Eighth Amendment.

Textually, the right to keep and bear arms is no more restricted to the home than are the First Amendment rights to the free exercise of religion, freedom of speech and the press, and "the right of the people peaceably to assemble, and to petition the government for a redress of grievances." If nothing more is meant than keeping arms in the home, there would be no point in including a right to bear arms.

> Webster defined "keep" in part as:
>
> 1. To hold; to retain in one's power or possession; not to lose or part with; as, to *keep* a house or a farm....
>
> 2. To have in custody for security or preservation....
>
> 3. To preserve; to retain.[25]

Webster's following further definition seems particularly apropos to the right to keep arms: "To have in the house...."[26]

The term "bear," according to Webster, meant "to carry" or "to wear; to bear as a mark of authority or distinction; as, to *bear* a sword, a badge, a name; to *bear* arms in a coat."[27] Consistent with the meaning of "bear arms" as carrying weapons on the person, Webster defined "pistol" as "a small fire-arm, or the smallest fire-arm used.... Small pistols are carried in the pocket."[28]

---

[25] Webster, *An American Dictionary of the English Language* ("keep").
[26] *Id.* ("keep," 18).
[27] *Id.* ("bear," 2 and 3).
[28] Webster, *An American Dictionary of the English Language* ("pistol").

As will be seen in this work, the term "bear arms" was used countless times to refer not just to military activity, but also to carrying arms for self-defense, hunting, and resistance to tyranny. When coupled with "the right of the people," the term "bear arms" always refers to individuals carrying arms and never refers to military service, in which persons are subject to commands by their senior officers rather than being entitled to rights. The term was also used in regard to restrictions on slaves: "Let no Negroe or mulattoe be capable...of keeping, or bearing arms...."[29] That too had no militia nexus.

A purportedly brand new method of bean counting called Corpus Linguistics asserts that, in the eighteenth century, the term "bear arms" most often appeared in a military context, and then makes the illogical leap to claim that it *always* has that meaning. Besides disregarding the context in which the *right* to bear arms was actually discussed by the Founders, proponents of the theory use the overly broad search term "bear arms" rather than the more narrow term at issue, the "right to bear arms," which could not have meant being *required* to serve in the militia.[30]

Neither the First nor the Second Amendment limits exercise of the rights declared therein to the home or other private places. The "free exercise" of religion, "the freedom of speech, or of the press," and "the right of the people peaceably to assemble, and to petition the government for a redress of grievances" are all activities that may be

---

[29] St. George Tucker, *A Dissertation on Slavery: With a Proposal for the Gradual Abolition of it, in the State of Virginia* 93 (Philadelphia: Mathew Carey, 1796).
[30] Neal Goldfarb, *A (Mostly Corpus-Based) Linguistic Reexamination of D.C. v. Heller and the Second Amendment* (2020).
https://papers.ssrn.com/sol3/papers.cfm?abstract_id=3481474. But see Josh Blackman & James C. Phillips, "Corpus Linguistics and the Second Amendment," *Harvard Law Review Blog* (Aug. 7, 2018). https://blog.harvardlawreview.org/corpus-linguistics-and-the-second-amendment/.

conducted in public. By the same token, the right to "bear arms" is an activity, not just a passive right, and nothing in the text restricts it from being exercised in public. It would be bizarre to limit the term "bear arms" to carrying a weapon from one's kitchen to the living room.

When a provision of the Bill of Rights applies only to a house, it says so; the Third Amendment's restrictions on quartering soldiers "in any house" do not apply to buildings that are not houses.[31] The Fourth Amendment protects the right to be secure from unreasonable searches and seizures not only in houses, but also in persons, papers, and effects.

What are the "arms" that the people may keep and bear? According to Webster, "arms" are "weapons of offense, or armor for defense and protection of the body."[32] Citing Blackstone, Webster noted: "In *law*, arms are any thing which a man takes in his hand in anger, to strike or assault another."[33]

The Second Amendment ends by stating that the right to bear arms "shall not be infringed." For the breadth of the term "infringe," Webster's definition of that term indicates the following direct and indirect transgressions:

> 1. To break, as contracts; to violate, either positively by contravention, or negatively by non-fulfillment or neglect of performance. A prince or private person infringes an agreement or covenant by neglecting to

---

[31] U.S. Const., Amend. III ("No soldier shall, in time of peace be quartered in any house, without the consent of the owner, nor in time of war, but in a manner to be prescribed by law.").

[32] Webster, *An American Dictionary of the English Language* ("arms," 1).

[33] *Id.* ("arms," 4).

perform its conditions, as well as by doing what is stipulated not to be done.

2. To break; to violate; to transgress; to neglect to fulfill or obey; as, to infringe a law.

3. To destroy or hinder; as, to infringe efficacy.34

Like the First Amendment's command that Congress shall make no law "abridging the freedom of speech," the Second Amendment proscribes any infringement, not just "unreasonable" infringement. By contrast, the Fourth Amendment proscribes only "unreasonable" searches and seizures.

By the plain language, surely it would be an infringement of the right of the people to bear arms for a law to prohibit the bearing of arms to the people at large and to allow only privileged persons to bear arms whom the government decides have a "need" to do so. Nor would the infringement be justified if another branch of the government—the courts—decides, based on a doctrine invented by those same courts, that an asserted governmental interest overrides the constitutional right.

We live in an age in which courts have recognized—perhaps invented—rights that have no specific mention in the Constitution. Yet, as detailed later in this work, some courts sweep the right to bear arms under the rug. As the Supreme Court has stated, there is "no principled basis on which to create a hierarchy of constitutional values,"[35] and "the Second Amendment is not "a second-class right, subject to an

---

[34] Webster, *An American Dictionary of the English Language* ("infringe").
[35] *Valley Forge Christian Coll. v. Ame's United for Separation of Church and State, Inc.*, 454 U.S. 464, 484 (1982).

entirely different body of rules than the other Bill of Rights guarantees...."[36]

The Supreme Court has explained that, when determining the meaning of the Second Amendment, the relevant inquiry is "the public understanding in 1791 of the right codified by the Second Amendment."[37] James Madison wrote to Henry Lee in 1824:

> I entirely concur in the propriety of resorting to the sense in which the Constitution was accepted and ratified by the nation. In that sense alone it is the legitimate Constitution. And if that be not the guide in expounding it, there can be no security for a consistent and stable, more than for a faithful exercise of its powers. If the meaning of the text be sought in the changeable meaning of the words composing it, it is evident that the shape and attributes of the Government must partake of the changes to which the words and phrases of all living languages are constantly subject. What a metamorphosis would be produced in the code of law if all its ancient phraseology were to be taken in its modern sense.[38]

The above analysis of the text of the Second Amendment is confirmed by its history and tradition, from its English origins, adoption by the Founders, and custom and practice in the early Republic. The literal meaning of the right to bear arms, while denigrated by detractors, has persisted through today.

---

[36] *McDonald v. Chicago*, 561 U.S. 742, 780 (2010).

[37] *Gamble v. United States*, 139 S. Ct. 1960, 1975 (2019).

[38] James Madison to Henry Lee, June 25, 1824. 3 *Papers of James Madison, Retirement Series*, ed. David B. Mattern et al., 338-39 (Charlottesville: University of Virginia Press, 2016).

Part One

ENGLISH ORIGINS OF THE INDIVIDUAL RIGHT TO BEAR ARMS

Chapter One

TO GO ARMED

The impetus for recognition of the Second Amendment right to bear arms goes far further back than King George III's attempt to disarm the American colonists, which helped to spark the American Revolution. While it is a universal law of history that tyrants attempt to disarm their subjects, the Americans were cognizant of the disarming measures taken by kings in seventeenth century England. Those measures took various forms, from laws imposing property qualifications to possess firearms to searches for and confiscation of firearms.

In the famous prosecution of Sir John Knight, the Catholic King James II sought to prosecute a Protestant political enemy for carrying arms under the all-but-forgotten medieval Statute of Northampton. It backfired when the court ruled that the law applied only to persons going armed in a manner to terrify others.

In the controversy over the Second Amendment today, it is argued by some that the Statute of Northampton criminalized even the peaceable carrying of arms, that the early Statute somehow overrides the later constitutional right to bear arms, and thus that the government may prohibit the people from bearing arms outside the home and in public. Some even argue that Sir John Knight was not really acquitted because he carried arms without evil intent, but (so the theory goes) because he acted as a government agent.

It seems farfetched to claim that an obscure medieval English statute negates an American constitutional right. This chapter tells the complete, accurate story of the Statute, the *Knight* case, and how the English common law forbade the carrying of arms only if one did so intending to terrorize his fellow subjects.

A) From the Statute of Northampton to Restoration of the Stuarts

Three Edwards attempted to rule England with an iron hand in the years 1272 to 1377. That required arming the monarch's forces and disarming and suppressing any potential opponents and unruly serfs. One form of doing so was to issue orders to sheriffs to prohibit subjects from going armed without "the license of the King." Such diktats were rendered by Edward I Longshanks,[39] one of the most ruthless kings who is best known today for his cruelty toward the Scots (he ordered the indescribably gruesome execution of William Wallace of "Braveheart" fame). Similar commands were issued by his son Edward II, who fought against reforms by the barons and was eventually forced to abdicate, after which he was murdered.[40]

Under the above, the King and his minions had the arbitrary power to decide who could be licensed to keep or carry arms and who could

---

[39] 4 *Calendar Of The Close Rolls, Edward I, 1296–1302*, at 318 (Sept. 15, 1299, Canterbury) (H.C. Maxwell-Lyte ed., 1906); 5 *Calendar Of The Close Rolls, Edward I, 1302–1307*, at 210 (June 10, 1304, Stirling) (H.C. Maxwell-Lyte ed., 1908).
[40] 1 *Calendar Of The Close Rolls, Edward II, 1307–1313*, at 52 (Feb. 9, 1308, Dover) (H.C. Maxwell-Lyte ed., 1892); *id.* at 257 (Mar. 20, 1310, Berwick-on-Tweed); *id.* at 553 (Oct. 12, 1312, Windsor); 4 *Calendar Of The Close Rolls, Edward II, 1323–1327*, at 560 (Apr. 28, 1326, Kenilworth) (H.C. Maxwell-Lyte ed., 1892).

not. As Parliament began to gain more power, such monarchal decrees, not based in the rule of law, began to recede somewhat. Obviously, they were not part of the English heritage that the Americans would adopt centuries later.

The Statute of Northampton was passed in 1328, over a decade before the birth of Geoffrey Chaucer of *The Canterbury Tales* fame and over four-and-a-half centuries before adoption of the American Second Amendment. This was the second year of the rule of Edward III as King of England. War and political violence characterized the era. The Statute sought to protect the regime's supremacy and repress disorder as follows:

> Item, it is enacted, that no man great nor small, of what condition soever he be, except the King's servants in his presence, and his ministers in executing of the King's precepts, or of their office, and such as be in their company assisting them, and also [upon a cry made for arms to keep the peace, and the same in such places where such acts happen,] be so hardy to come before the King's justices, or other of the King's ministers doing their office, with force and arms, nor bring no force in affray of the peace, nor to go nor ride armed by night nor by day, in fairs, markets, nor in the presence of the justices or other ministers, nor in no part elsewhere, upon pain to forfeit their armour to the King, and their bodies to prison at the King's pleasure.[41]

What did the awkward and archaic language mean to "bring no force in affray of the peace, nor to go nor ride armed"? As read in the handful of English judicial decisions that were rendered on the Statute, essential elements of the crime included not just going or riding armed, but also doing so in affray of the peace. The term "affray" generally entails the creation of great fear in the minds of others. And what

---

[41] 2 Edw. III c. 3 (1328).

ultimately matters is not some purportedly original meaning of the medieval Statute, but the understanding of what was recognized as a crime at common law when the United States was founded and the Bill of Rights adopted.

That the Statute was not aimed at single, peaceable subjects just going about their business was made clear in orders given by Edward III to sheriffs the same year, "to cause the statute made in the late parliament at Northampton prohibiting men coming armed before justices or other ministers of the king, or going armed, etc., to be observed," and to investigate "the malefactors who have made assemblies of men-at-arms or have ridden or gone armed in his bailiwick, contrary to the statute and the king's proclamation...."[42] He further ordered sheriffs "to take all those whom he shall find going armed, with their horses and armour, and to cause them to be imprisoned, and their horses and armour to be kept safely until otherwise ordered...."[43]

In 1332, officials in Northumberland were instructed about "malefactors and felons, who made assemblies in excessive number and daily perpetrated many crimes openly," and were ordered "to pursue, arrest and take them and all persons riding or going armed to disturb the peace...."[44] Similarly, in 1334, reciting that "it was ordained

---

[42] 1 *Calendar Of The Close Rolls, Edward III, 1327–1330*, at 420 (Nov. 10 and 11, 1328) (H.C. Maxwell-Lyte ed., 1896).

[43] 2 *Calendar Of The Close Rolls, Edward III, 1330-1333*, at 131 (April 3, 1330, Woodstock) (H.C. Maxwell-Lyte ed., 1898). See also 1 *Calendar of Plea & Memoranda Rolls of the City of London, 1323-1364*, at 156 (Dec. 19, 1343) (A.H. Thomas ed., 1898) (On Friday before the Feast of St. Thomas, "All suspicious characters arriving in hostelries were to be reported to the officers of the City. All guests in hostelries were to be warned against going armed in the City.").

[44] Letter to Keeper and Justices of Northumberland (Oct. 28, 1332), in 2 H. Maxwell-Lyte ed., *Calendar of the Close Rolls, Edward III, 1330–1333*, at 610 (London: Her Majesty's Stationery Office, 1898).

that no one except a minister of the king should use armed force or go armed in fairs, markets, etc.," the mayor and bailiffs of York were told that "the king has learned that several malefactors and disturbers of the peace, not respecting these statutes, making assemblies and illicit gatherings both by day and night in York, its suburbs and neighbourhood, go about armed and lie in wait for those coming and going to and from that city, and staying there, both the king's ministers and other lieges, and beat, wound and rob them...."[45]

A further law under Edward III, passed in 1350, provided: "And if percase any Man of this Realm ride armed [covertly] or secretly with Men of Arms against any other, to slay him, or rob him, or take him, or retain him till he hath made Fine or Ransom for to have his Deliverance...it shall be judged...Felony or Trespass, according to the Laws of the Land of old Times used...."[46] The offense thus consisted of gangs riding with concealed arms to murder, rob, or kidnap.

Fast forward to the year 2021, when the U.S. Court of Appeals for the Ninth Circuit cited this statute for the proposition: "In 1350, Parliament specifically banned the carrying of concealed arms." It quoted the part about riding armed secretly but deleted the part beginning with "to slay him."[47] The law was cited as an example of the lack of historical support for the right of individuals peaceably to carry arms.

In 1377, when only ten years old, Richard II assumed the crown after his grandfather Edward III died. That same year, the actual council

---

[45] Letter to Mayor and Bailiffs of York (Jan. 30, 1334), in 3 H. Maxwell-Lyte ed., *Calendar of the Close Rolls, Edward III, 1333–1337*, at 294 (London: Her Majesty's Stationery Office, 1898).
[46] 25 Edw. 3, 320, st. 5, c. 2 (1350).
[47] *Young v. State of Hawaii*, 2021 WL 1114180, *15 (9th Cir. 2021) (en banc).

that governed for Richard ordered the mayor and bailiffs of Newcastle to arrest persons "making confederacies, congregations, unlawful assemblies or other mischief in that town, going armed, bearing arms or leading an armed power to the disturbance of the peace...." Such persons, "fearing not" the Statute of Northampton and other laws, "have gone and go armed and bearing arms wander hither and thither, laying snares for men coming to or from the town and those dwelling therein, beating, wounding and evil treating them, robbing some of their property and goods...in breach of the peace and to the terror of the people in those parts."[48]

The above recitation explains the enforcement of the Statute of Northampton as a tool to clamp down on gangs who assaulted and robbed others and created terror. That context demonstrates that the actual purpose of the Statute was to subdue armed criminals, not to suppress harmless nobles, burghers, and peasants who might carry weapons to defend themselves from such criminals. Indeed, many of these potential victims of attack and robbery likely armed themselves for self-defense.

Having suppressed the Peasants' Revolt in 1381, Richard II enacted a law two years later that "no Man shall ride in Harness within the Realm, contrary to the Form of the Statute of Northampton thereupon made, neither with Launcegay...."[49] That referred to a knight on horseback with a lance. Chaucer depicted such a knight in *The Tale of Sir Thopas* thus:

Dressed in armor and with my lance [launcegay],

---

[48] 1 *Calendar Of The Close Rolls, Richard II, 1377–1381*, at 34 (Dec. 1, 1377, Westminster) (H.C. Maxwell-Lyte ed., 1914).
[49] 7 Rich. 2, c. 13 (1383).

I'll slay you through your underpants,

And end your sorrow,

With your guts bestrewn.[50]

In 1388, citing the Statute of Northampton, Richard II ordered the bailiffs of Scardburgh to arrest subjects "going armed within the town, leading an armed power, making unlawful assemblies, or doing aught else whereby the peace may be broken and the people put in fear...."[51] A half century later, Henry VI issued an order with similar language.[52] These orders reflect the turbulent times in which kings sought to retain power against competing armed factions.

A guide to legal restrictions in London published in 1419 provided, "That no one, of whatever condition he be, go armed in the said city or in the suburbs, or carry arms, by day or by night, except the vadlets of the great lords of the land, carrying the swords of their masters in their presence," and various royal and city officials. So carrying arms was reserved for the privileged classes. But traveling with arms was not banned, as every innkeeper was required to "cause warning to be given unto his guests that they leave their arms in their hostels where they shall be harboured...."[53]

---

[50] Chaucer, *The Canterbury Tales* (modernized version), https://www.sparknotes.com/nofear/lit/the-canterbury-tales/sir-thopas-tale/page_5/.

[51] 3 *Calendar Of The Close Rolls, Richard II, 1385–1389*, at 399–400 (May 16, 1388, Westminster) (H.C. Maxwell-Lyte ed., 1914).

[52] 4 *Calendar Of The Close Rolls, Henry VI, 1441–1447*, at 224 (May 12, 1444, Westminster) (A.E. Stamp ed., 1937).

[53] John Carpenter, *Liber Albus: The White Book of the City of London* 335 (London: Richard Giffen, 1840). In an earlier edict, The First Proclamation after the Beheading of the Bishop of Exeter (1326), Edward II decreed "that no man go armed by night or day ...." 1 *Calendar of Plea & Memoranda Rolls of the City of London, 1323-1364*, at 15 (Nov. 1326) (A.H. Thomas ed., 1926); *id.* (Jan. 2, 1327) ("The bearing of arms is forbidden").

Henry VIII, who had a bad habit of beheading his wives and religious dissidents, passed several acts restricting crossbows and handguns, which were quite large at the time. His act of 1533 provided that no person "shall shote in any handgonne or crosse bowe, or use or kepe in hys or theire houses or els where any crose bowe or handgonne," except persons with the yearly value of one hundred pounds. It made an exception for persons "to whome it may please the Kynge our Soverainge Lorde…to geve lycence by hys letters patentes under hys greate seale" to shoot and to have and keep crossbows and handgonnes in his house for its defense.[54] This was the epitome of a discretionary gun licensing scheme.

Henry's repression of the Catholic Church and other grievances led to a revolt in northern England in 1536-37 called the Pilgrimage of Grace. Among the demands for reform in religion and government was a call to repeal the statutes restricting handguns and crossbows to the wealthy. The rebellion was brutally repressed and, as usual in those days, the leaders lost their heads.[55]

Henry VIII's further act of 1541 found that "persons have used and yet do daily use to ride and go in the King's highways and elsewhere, having with them Crossbows and little handguns," and it prohibited handguns of less than one yard in length and hagbutts (an arquebus) of less than three-quarters of a yard. Persons not meeting the property qualification of one hundred pounds per annum in land, annuities, or offices could not "carry or have, in his or their journey going or riding in the King's highway or elsewhere, any Crossbow or

---

[54] An Acte for Shotyng in crosbowes and handgonnes, 25 Hen. 8, c. 17 (1533).
[55] Lois G. Schwoerer, *Gun Culture in Early Modern England* 53 (Charlottesville: University of Virginia Press, 2016).

Gun charged or furnished with powder, fire or touche for the same...."[56]

Yet anyone could shoot a handgun, demyhake, or hagbutt in town "at a butt or bank of earth in place convenient, or for the defense of his person or house...." Gentlemen, yeomen, servingmen, and all inhabitants of cities and towns could "have and keep in every of their houses," and shoot at butts with handguns, hagbutts, and demyhakes of the minimum length. The maximum punishment for possession of a short handgun by a person worth less than one hundred pounds was a fine of ten pounds.[57]

Further, the act did not apply to areas within five miles from the coast, twelve miles from Scotland, and other places that were more subject to attack. Firearms of any length could be possessed and used there except for hunting certain fowl.[58]

In 1544, just three years after its passage, Henry revoked the above act, wanting "his loving subjects practiced and exercised in the feat of shooting handguns and hackbuts [arquebuses]...for the annoyance of his majesty's enemies in time of war and hostility." Any subject aged sixteen and up could have a gun[59] The reason for the revocation was war with France and Scotland, but when peace came, Henry revoked the revocation in 1546.[60] When war with France erupted anew in 1557, the law was repealed again, this time by Mary I.[61]

---

[56] An Acte Concerninge Crosbowes and Handguns, 33 Hen. VIII ch. 6 (1541).
[57] *Id.*
[58] *Id.*
[59] Noel Perrin, *Giving Up the Gun* 59 (Boston: David R. Godine, 1979); Schwoerer, *Gun Culture* 60.
[60] Schwoerer, *Gun Culture* 60.
[61] Perrin, *Giving Up the Gun* 62.

Edward VI inherited the throne at age nine from his father Henry VIII, but he never reached maturity, and a regency council governed the realm. During his reign, a law was enacted restricting the firing of multiple pellets at once, the predecessor of today's shotgun balls. Decrying the destruction of game and damage to buildings from shot, it provided that no person under the degree of a Lord of Parliament may shoot a gun in a city or town at fowl or at a mark (target), nor may anyone shoot multiple balls of shot at one time. Qualified persons based on worth of at least one hundred pounds per year were exempted.[62]

Edward VI named Lady Jane Grey as his heir, but the Privy Council disagreed and named Edward's half-sister Mary as queen. "Bloody Mary" had the 16-year-old Jane beheaded and distinguished herself by having almost 300 religious dissenters burned at the stake. When Mary died, her half-sister Elizabeth ascended to the throne.

While Parliament did not enact further restrictions in this period, royal proclamations were issued. Elizabeth I, daughter of Henry and Anne Boleyn (whom Henry had beheaded when Elizabeth was two-and-a-half years old), issued several decrees on point. Her decree of 1600 ordered justices of the peace to enforce laws against "car[r]ying and use of Gunnes…and especially of Pistols, Birding pieces, and other short pieces and small shot…."[63] That was during the Nine Years' War,

---

[62] An Acte againste the shootinge of Hayle shott, 2 & 3 Ed. 6, c.14 (1548).

[63] By the Quenne Elizabeth I: A Proclamation Prohibiting the Use and Cariage of Dagges, Birding Pieces, and other Gunnes, Contrary to Law 1 (London: Christopher Barker, 1600). See also By the Quenne Elizabeth I: A Proclamation Against the Carriage of Dags, and for Reformation of Some Other Great Disorders (London, Christopher Barker, 1594) ("there have been great disorders lately … by common carrying of Dags, otherwise called Pistols, to the terrour of all people professing to travel and live peaceably").

in which Spain backed an Irish revolt against England; Elizabeth relied on spies and took severe repressive measures against Catholics.

Similarly, James I, successor to Elizabeth and the first of the Stuart monarchs, issued a proclamation in 1613 forbidding "the bearing of Weapons *covertly*, and specially of short Dagges, and Pistols...."[64] (A Dagge or Dag was a type of heavy pistol.) In another proclamation three years later, James declared that "the use of Steelets, pocket Daggers, and pocket Dags and Pistols, which are weapons utterly unserviceable for defence, Militarie practise, or other lawfull use, but odious, and noted Instruments of murther, and mischiefe...." Disregarding that such use depended on the intent of the user, he commanded all persons not "to weare or carie about them any such arms, upon paine of Our Princely Indignation and displeasure, Imprisonment and Censure in the Starre-Chamber."[65] Again, this was a royal decree, not a common law offense, and its reference to the Star Chamber – the court that became an insidious tool of monarchial abuse – should give caution to any implication that such decrees somehow found their way into the American Bill of Rights.

A warrant issued under the Statute of Northampton in 1608 was described as follows: "Forasmuch as the Court is informed of the outragious misdemeanours etc. of James Harwood of Danby, who goes armed and weaponed with a lance-staff plated with iron, pistolls, and other offensive weapons, to the great terrour...a warrant be made to attach the said Harwood and him &c to be bound &c."[66] Under that

---

[64] By The King James I: A Proclamation Against The Use Of Pocket–Dags 1 (London, Robert Barker, 1613).
[65] By the King: A Proclamation against Steelets, Pocket Daggers, Pocket Dagges and Pistols (London: Robert Barker, 1616).
[66] Quarter Sessions at Malton (Oct. 4-5, 1608), in 1 *Quarter Session Records* 132 (London: North Riding Record Society, 1884).

description, Harwood went armed with "offensive weapons" and he did so "to the great terror" of others. The warrant directed that he be summoned and bound to keep the peace.

The Statute of Northampton's first mention in a known judicial decision was in a 1615 case before the King's Bench styled *Chune v. Piott*, which involved a plaintiff suing the sheriff for an unlawful arrest. The court found that the plaintiff had assisted a prisoner to escape and interfered with the sheriff in attempting to apprehend him.[67] The Statute of Northampton was not involved.

However, Justice Croke, one of four judges who opined in the case, mentioned that "the sheriffe hath power to commit...if contrary to the Statute of Northampton, he sees any one to carry weapons in the high-way, *in terrorem populi Regis*; he ought to take him, and arrest him, notwithstanding he doth not break the peace in his presence."[68] Thus, the carrying of the weapon must be *in terrorem populi Regis* (to the terror of the King's subjects), and the arrest could be made even if the suspect did not break the peace in the sheriff's presence.

In 1618, Cambridge justice of the peace Michael Dalton published *The Countrey Justice*, a simple guide for other justices of the peace who had no formal legal training. He wrote the following:

> If any person shall ride or goe armed offensively, before the Justices, or any other the Kings officers; Or in Faires, Markets, or elsewhere (by night, or by day) in affray of the Kings people (the Sheriffe, and other the Kings Officers, and) every Justice of the peace...may cause them

---

[67] *Chune v. Piott*, 80 Eng. Rep. 1161 (K.B. 1615).
[68] *Id.* at 1162.

to be stayed and arrested, & may binde all such to the peace, or good behaviour....

So of such as shall carry any Daggs or Pistols that be charged: or that shall goe appareled with privie Coats or Doublets....[69]

As stated, riding or going armed had to be done "offensively" and "in affray," meaning aggressively and not peaceably. The additional phrase "[s]o of such" as carry a charged (loaded) dagg or pistol might be read to incorporate the contents of the prior paragraph, i.e., those who did so offensively in the circumstances described may be bound to keep the peace. Or it might be read to state, based on an enactment such as the prior one by Henry VIII, that a person who carried a charged dagg or pistol, even without creating terror, may be bound to keep the peace.

Dalton added the following clarification to the above: "And yet the Kings servants in his presence; and Sheriffes and their officers, in executing the Kings processe, and all others in pursuing the Hue and Crie, where any felony, or other offences be done, may lawfully beare Armour or weapons."[70] That would leave no doubt that such persons could go armed offensively and aggressively without fear of offending the law.

The Statute of Northampton sought to consolidate the monarch's power against roving bands of knights. Sir Edward Coke, whose *Institutes of the Laws of England* first appeared in 1628, explained about the Statute's origins: "For in those days this deed of Chivalry was

---

[69] Michael Dalton, *The Countrey Justice, Conteyning the Practice of the Justices of the Peace out of Their Sessions* 30 (London, 1618).
[70] *Id.*

37

at random, whereupon great peril ensued...."[71] However, Coke added that the Statute did not preclude armed self-defense against those using unlawful force:

> And yet in some cases a man may not only use force and arms, but assemble company also. As any may assemble his friends and neighbors, to keep his house against those that come to rob, or kill him, or to offer him violence in it, and is by construction excepted out of this Act;...for a man's house is his Castle, and *domus sua cuique est tutissimum refugium* [a person's own house is his ultimate refuge]; for where shall a man be safe, if it be not in his house. And in this sense it is truly said, *Armaque in Armatos sumere jura sinunt* [and the laws permit the taking up of arms against armed persons].[72]

Arms could thus be carried in public to go to the houses of friends and neighbors for the defense thereof. Where multiple houses were being attacked, such as in a riot, armed patrols could assemble to be a ready source of protection.

Coke noted that a charge under the Statute of Northampton must allege the element of *In quorandam de populo terror* – to the terror of the people.[73] He referenced the following offense: "Nor to goe armed, by night or by day, &c. before the Kings Justices in any place whatsoever."[74] To illustrate, he summarized the case of Sir Thomas Figett, a knight who "went armed under his garments, as well in the

---

[71] Coke, *Third Institute* 160.

[72] *Id.* at 161–2.

[73] *Id.* at 159.

[74] This passage was quoted in a recent American federal court decision with "before the Kings Justices" deleted, thus changing its meaning. *Peruta v. County of San Diego*, 824 F.3d 919, 931 (9th Cir. 2016) (*en banc*).

Palace, as before the Justices of the Kings Bench," for which he was arrested.[75]

Figett's offense was thus not simply going armed, but doing so before high officials. A 1585 treatise explained that, having been attacked by another knight, he wore armor under his clothing in the king's palace and in Westminster Hall. However, "a man will not go armed overtly, even though it be for his defense, but it seems that a man can go armed under his private coat of plate, underneath his coat etc., because this cannot cause any fear among people."[76]

By the first half of the seventeenth century, it was thus established that a subject may not carry arms in a manner to terrorize other subjects or in a place like a palace where the Justices of the King's Bench were assembled. Peaceably carrying arms in public was not proscribed.

The Restoration of the Stuarts in 1660 entailed measures to disarm the political enemies of the monarchy. King Charles II was a Catholic who ruled predominately Protestant England, and he aimed to create Catholic ascendancy. In 1662, Charles II passed the Militia Act, which empowered the Lords Lieutenants – agents of the Crown in each county who had military and enforcement powers – "to search for and seize all arms in the custody or possession of any person or persons whom the said lieutenant or any two or more of their deputies shall judge dangerous to the peace of the kingdom...."[77] This allowed officials to

---

[75] Coke, *Third Institute* 162.

[76] Richard Crompton, *L'office et Aucthoritie de Justices de Peace* 58 (1584) (translated from Law French by David B. Kopel), quoted in Nicholas J. Johnson et al., *Firearms Law and the Second Amendment* 94 (New York: Wolters Kluwer, 2nd ed. 2018). Note that Crompton spelled his name "Figet."

[77] Militia Act, 13 and 14 Car. II c.3 (1662).

search for and confiscate arms from persons who might threaten the absolute rule of the King.

The minions of Charles dusted off the obsolete law of Henry VIII requiring a property qualification to keep and bear arms. A conviction was upheld in 1669 of a certain William Sanders who "had and kept a certain hand-gun...and then and there with the said hand-gun, charged with gunpowder and hail-shot, unlawfully and unjustly did shoot, against the form of the statute," while not having "lands, tenements, fees, annuities or offices to the yearly value of 100*l* [pounds]."[78]

However, the courts insisted on scrupulous adherence to the strict rules of pleading. A court in 1685, the last year of Charles' reign, quashed the conviction of a defendant who apparently did not meet the property qualification based on the following: "Conviction for a gun contrary to 33 Hen. 8, c.6. The conviction was for having a gun in his house: the statute is, use to keep in his or her house, and perhaps it might be lent him, the words of the statute ought to be pursued."[79]

In 1670, King Charles took further measures to consolidate and protect his power by enacting more laws to oppress his subjects. As part of this effort, for the first time in English history, Charles sought to deprive all commoners of guns through the Game Act of 1670:

> That all and every Person and Persons not having Lands and Tenements...of the clear yearly Value of one hundred Pounds *per annum*...or having Lease or Leases...of the clear yearly Value of one hundred and fifty Pounds, other than the Son and Heir Degree...are

---

[78] *Sanders's Case*, 85 E.R. 311, 1 WMS. Saunders 262 (1669). "[T]he statute 33 H. 8, c. 6, is now obsolete, (a) as the object of it is a matter no longer in any use.... It was repealed by stat. 1 & 2 Will. 4, c. 22." *Id.* n.1 & 1a (editor's note).
[79] *The King v. Lewellin*, 89 E.R. 440, 1 Shower. K.B. 48 (1685).

hereby declared to be persons by the Laws of this Realm not allowed to keep…any Guns, Bows…or other Engines aforesaid; but shall be and are hereby prohibited to have, keep or use the same.[80]

Most persons did not qualify to have guns under this law, which authorized searches of houses for firearms. While calling it a game law suggested that its purpose was about protecting game animals or hunting grounds in England, the reality was far more sinister. As Sir William Blackstone observed, "prevention of popular insurrections and resistance to the government, by disarming the bulk of the people…is a reason oftener meant, than avowed, by the makers of the forest and game laws."[81]

Edward Christian, editor of the 1794 edition of Blackstone, disagreed with that statement on the basis that those who framed the game laws said in several ancient statutes that "the avowed object is to encourage the use of the long-bow, the most effective armour then in use; and even since the modern practice of killing game with a gun has prevailed, everyone is at liberty to keep or carry a gun, if he does not use it for the destruction of game."[82] That statement was often true, but not always, as the above act of Charles II shows.

Blackstone added that the rulers wanted to keep the subjects "in as low a condition as possible, and especially to prohibit them the use of arms. Nothing could do this more effectually than a prohibition of hunting and sporting…."[83]

---

[80] An Act for the Better Preservation of the Game, 22 Car. II c.25, § 3 (1670).
[81] 2 Blackstone, *Commentaries* *412.
[82] 2 Blackstone, *Commentaries* *412 n.2 (E. Christian ed. 1794).
[83] *Id.* at *413.

James II assumed the Crown in 1685 and escalated the repressive policies as Charles II, who was his older brother. As before, ensuring Catholic ascendancy over the Protestant majority required the disarming of political enemies. The Statute of Northampton would be used as another tool to do just that in what became a high profile case.

B) *Rex v. Knight*: "The Crime Shall Appear to Be Malo Animo"

The leading and only significant precedent on the Statute of Northampton arose out of the prosecution of Sir John Knight in 1686. A version of the decision, known as *Sir John Knight's Case*, reported an information against Knight as prosecuted by the Attorney General based on the Statute, which it characterized as having prohibited "all persons from coming with force and arms before the King's Justices, &c., and from going or riding armed in affray of peace...." It was alleged that Knight "did walk about the streets armed with guns, and that he went into the church of St. Michael, in Bristol, in the time of divine service, with a gun, to terrify the King's subjects, *contra formam statuti*."[84]

As further reported, the case was tried before a jury and "the defendant was acquitted." The Chief Justice said that the meaning of the Statute "was to punish people who go armed to terrify the King's subjects. It is likewise a great offence at the *common law*, as if the King were not able or willing to protect his subjects...."[85]

Another version of the decision, styled *Rex v. Knight*, recited counsel for defendant's argument: "This statute was made to prevent the people's being oppressed by great men; but this is a private matter,

---

[84] *Sir John Knight's Case*, 3 Mod. 117, 87 Eng. Rep. 75, 76 (K.B. 1686).
[85] *Id.*

and not within the statute."[86] The Chief Justice held: "But tho' this statute be almost gone in desuetudinem [disuse], yet where the crime shall appear to be *malo animo* [with evil intent], it will come within the Act (tho' now there be a general connivance to gentlemen to ride armed for their security)...."[87] Knight was "acquitted, yet bound to good behaviour."[88]

As the above ruling reveals, the Statute of Northampton was all but forgotten, going armed was a crime only if done so with evil intent, and gentlemen were allowed to ride armed.

Why was Knight acquitted? The facts were undisputed that he had walked in the streets and went into a church with a gun. But the crime was not simply going or riding armed. A further element of the crime was that one must do so "to terrify the King's subjects," with "*malo animo*," and "in affray of peace." Nothing in the evidence suggests that he threatened anyone, brandished a weapon, or started a fight. He had

---

[86] *Rex v. Knight*, Comb. 38, 90 Eng. Rep. 330 (K.B. 1686).

[87] *Id.*, Comb. 38-39, 90 Eng. Rep. 330. The issue of whether a statute had fallen into desuetude appears in numerous cases in the seventeenth century and thereafter. As one court explained, some statutes "however useful when made, have lost all their utility by change of manners and circumstances, and would be considered at present as so many idle restraints upon the liberty of the subject; and desuetude will be presumed from the nature of the thing without necessity of any direct evidence." *Anderson v. Magistrates*, Mor. 1842, 1845 (Ct. Sess. 1749). It added:

> There are but two ways by which a statute can be abrogated; one is by a posterior statute, the other by a contrary custom, inconsistent with the statute, consented to by the whole people; for, if custom have the same force with a statute to make law, custom must have the same force with a statute to unmake law, or to unmake a statute. When we say, therefore, that a statute is in desuetude, the meaning is, that a contrary universal custom has prevailed over the statute; and so much is implied in the very term desuetude.

[88] *Rex v. Knight*, Comb. 38, 90 Eng. Rep. 330 (K.B. 1686) ("Moved per Attorney-General, that the defendant, tho' found not guilty, may be bound to the good behavior").

gone armed, but that did not suffice to be convicted under the Statute of Northampton.

Nothing in the decision suggested that Knight was acquitted for any other reason. Some contemporary commentators have speculated that Knight acted as a government agent, which gave him legal immunity under the Statute of Northampton, but nothing in either reported decision even hints that. As Knight's counsel stated, it was "a private matter," refuting any historical revisionist argument that Knight had been vested with some governmental or official authority.

It is worth noting that three years before the Knight case was decided, a man named Joseph Keble wrote a guide advising magistrates to arrest any person who "shall be so bold as to go or ride Armed, by night or by day, in Fairs, Markets, or any other places," including those "as they shall find to carry Dags [handguns] or Pistols...." Another edition was published three years after the *Knight* decision, which was not acknowledged, and no correction was made to reflect the requirement of evil intent.[89] Lord John Campbell, an expert on the common law who would become Chief Justice of the Queen's Bench, referred to Keble as "[a] drowsy Serjeant of the name of Keble, known only for some bad Law Reports...."[90]

Keble devoted far more attention than the above on how to detect a witch based on marks left by the Devil suckling her teats.[91] The

---

[89] Joseph Keble, *As Assistance to the Justices of the Peace, for the Easier Performance of Their Duty* 224 (London: W. Rawlins et al., 1683, 1689).
[90] 3 John Campbell, *The lives of the Lord Chancellors and Keepers of the Great Seal of England* 43 (London: John Murray, 1846).
[91] Keble, *As Assistance* 217–19.

magistrates would rely on Keble's work in the Salem Witchcraft Trials of 1692.[92]

English legal commentators were typically private individuals who wrote their own opinions of what they believed to be the law. They were not giving official interpretations approved by the judiciary. Some were a condensed, "CliffsNotes" style summary of statutes without any pretense of explaining the common law as set forth in judicial decisions. On the issue at hand here, commentators typically recited the elements of the offense as going or riding armed to the terror of the subjects. Some were written before, or simply disregarded, the judicial decision in *Sir John Knight's Case*, and instructed justices of the peace to arrest persons who went armed, without referring to the required element of doing so in a manner to terrorize others. To the extent that arrests were made on that basis, it would have been the duty of the magistrates trying the cases to be aware of the relevant judicial opinions and to require that all elements of the offense be proven.

A decision was rendered after the *Knight* case that discussed armed assemblies rather than just an individual going armed. In *Queen v. Soley* (1707), indictments for rioting were dismissed for failure to allege necessary elements of the offense. While arms were not involved in the case, the court noted:

> If a number of men assemble with arms, *in terrorem populi*, though no act is done, it is a riot. If *three* come out of an ale-house and go armed, it is a riot. Though a man may ride with arms, yet he cannot take two

---

[92] Devon McMahon, *Suckling Familiars and Unnatural Protrusions: The Witch's Mark in the Salem Witchcraft Trials of 1692*, at 4, 10.
http://citeseerx.ist.psu.edu/viewdoc/download?doi=10.1.1.950.980&rep=rep1&type=pdf.

with him to defend himself, even though his life is threatened; for he is in the protection of the law, which is sufficient for his defence.[93]

Once again, the element of terror to the subjects – *in terrorem populi* – was required. One could ride with arms but could not "take two [men] with him," as three or more armed men were considered a riot. But the bad-acts element was still present, as the court further referred to "riots without any act done, as going armed, &c. it must be said *in terrorem populi*...."[94]

The proscription on three or more persons going armed was based on a law passed in the reign of Henry VII. That law would be cited in *Semayne's Case*, decided in 1603, for the rule that "every one may assemble his friends and neighbours to defend his house against violence: but he cannot assemble them to go with him to the market, or elsewhere for his safeguard against violence . . . ."[95] Based on the same medieval law, Matthew Hale wrote that "a man may assemble people together for the safeguard of his house, which he could not do in relation to travel, or a journey."[96] These rules did not question individuals peaceably going armed in public.

William Hawkins, in his influential *Treatise of the Pleas of the Crown* (first published in 1716), cited *Sir John Knight's Case* for the following:

> [N]o wearing of arms is within the meaning of the statute unless it be accompanied with such circumstances as are apt to terrify the people; from when it seems clearly to follow, that persons of quality are in no

---

[93] *Queen v. Soley*, 88 Eng. Rep. 935, 936-37 (1707).

[94] *Id.*

[95] *Semayne's Case*, 77 Eng. Rep. 194, 195 (K.B. 1603) (citing 21 H. 7. 39).

[96] 1 Matthew Hale, *History of the Pleas of the Crown* 547 (London: E. & R. Nutt, 1776) (citing 21 H. 7. 39).

danger of offending against this statute by wearing common weapons, or having their usual number of attendants with them for their ornament or defence, in such places, and upon such occasions, in which it is the common fashion to make use of them, without causing the least suspicion of an intention to commit any act of violence or disturbance of the peace. And from the same ground it also follows, that persons armed with privy coats of mail, to the intent to defend themselves against their adversaries, are not within the meaning of the statute, because they do nothing *in terrorem populi.*[97]

Despite the reference to "persons of quality," the same rules applied to the poor and uninfluential. To repeat, Hawkins said that the wearing of arms was not a crime, whether by "persons of quality" or by commoners, unless "accompanied with such circumstances as are apt to terrify the people...."[98]

As noted, Hawkins also wrote that "persons armed with privy coats of mail" for self-defense do not violate the Statute "because they do nothing *in terrorem populi.*"[99] The *Dictionarium Anglo-Britannicum* of 1708 included the following definitions: "Privy, secret, private...." "Coat of Mail, a piece of Armour, made in the form of a Shirt, and wrought over with many Iron-rings."[100] A privy coat has been otherwise defined as "An armoured coat (usually of chain mail) worn concealed under ordinary clothing."[101] Wearing a privy coat of mail could not be seen and would thus not alarm anyone.

---

[97] 2 William Hawkins, *A Treatise of the Pleas of the Crown* 21–22 (London 7th ed., 1795), citing 3 Mod. 117 (*Sir John Knight's Case*).
[98] 2 Hawkins, *Pleas*, at 21–22.
[99] *Id.*
[100] John Kersey, *Dictionarium Anglo-Britannicum or a General English Dictionary* (1708).
[101] "Privy coat," *UK Dictionary*, https://www.lexico.com/definition/privy_coat.

Wearing heavy armor in public was another matter. Hawkins wrote, "That a man cannot excuse the wearing such armour in publick, by alleging that such a one threatened him, and that he wears it for the safety of his person from his assault."[102] Per the definitions in the *Dictionarium*, "*Armour*, Warlike Harness, defensive Arms that cover the body." "*Harness*, all the Accoutrements of an Armed Horse-Man...."[103] Such "armour" included solid plate armor, a helmet, and perhaps a shield such as would be worn for battle that was "designed to both protect and intimidate."[104] Wearing such armor, which could not be concealed from public viewing, could create terror to the public.

Elsewhere, Hawkins wrote that "persons riding together on the road with unusual weapons, or otherwise assembling together in such a manner as is apt to raise a terror in the people," might constitute an unlawful assembly.[105] Again, riding armed with common weapons in a peaceable manner was not an offense under the Statute of Northampton or otherwise.

Rightly having and using arms for the defense of oneself or of others found further exposition in the law of justifiable homicide. Hawkins wrote:

> If those who are engaged in a riot or a forcible entry, or detainer, stand
> in their defense, and continue the force in opposition to the command
> of justice of peace, & c. or resist such justice endeavouring to arrest
> them the killing may be justified; and so perhaps may the killing of
> dangerous rioters by any private persons, who cannot otherwise

---

[102] 2 Hawkins, *Pleas*, at 21.
[103] Kersey, *Dictionarium*.
[104] "The Armour of an English Medieval Knight,"
https://www.ancient.eu/article/1244/the-armour-of-an-english-medieval-knight/.
[105] 2 Hawkins, *Pleas*, at 54.

suppress them or defend themselves from them, inasmuch as *every private person seems to be authorized by law to arm himself* for the purposes aforesaid.[106]

Hawkins analyzed certain statutes that punished use of weapons offensively in crimes. One such law applied to persons who blackened their faces and used "swords, fire arms, or other offensive weapons" in illegal hunting, who would be subject to the death penalty.[107] Another applied to three or more persons "armed with fire-arms or other offensive weapons" involved in smuggling.[108] He did not suggest that firearms or other weapons used for lawful, defensive purposes were "offensive weapons," a term of art that implied to the offensive use of weapons in crime.

However, objects that were used as weapons, such as a hatchet or horsewhip, were not necessarily "offensive weapons" under such statutes. "It is therefore a question of fact for the jury, Whether the instrument was carried for the purposes of offence or not?"[109] These precepts would be applied in a rather humorous decision in 1784 that held: "A set of drunken fellows come from an ale-house, and hastily set themselves to carry away the geneva, but whether with arms or without is not proved."[110]

Hawkins' definitive work demonstrates that some lesser-known manuals failed to give a correct statement of the law. John Bond's guide for justices of the peace, published in 1707, advised: "May punish such as secretly wear Coats of Mail, carry Daggers and Pistols, and such as

---

[106] 1 Hawkins, *Pleas*, at 171.
[107] *Id.* at 187.
[108] *Id.* at 227.
[109] *Id.* at 227 n.1.
[110] *King v. Hutchinson*, 168 Eng. Rep. 273, 274 (1784).

ride armed...."[111] That turned the rule upside down. Persons who secretly wore coats of mail, or "privy coats of mail" in Hawkins' words, did "nothing *in terrorem populi*," and "no wearing of arms" was unlawful unless done in "circumstances as are apt to terrify the people."[112] For that proposition, Hawkins cited *Sir John Knight's Case*, which Bond ignored.

On the same page where Bond stated the above, he listed other powers of justices of the peace, such as: "If any suspected to be a Jesuit or Priest shall refuse to give a direct answer...[he] shall be committed without Bail till he doth."[113] This again illustrates that summaries of old English statutes found in justice of the peace manuals were hardly incorporated into the American common law, much less did they override the Bill of Rights.

Elsewhere, Bond wrote: "Persons with offensive Weapons in Fairs, Markets or elsewhere in Affray of the King's People, may be arrested by the Sheriff, or other [of] the King's Officers...so of those that carry Guns charged...." For that he cited the Statute of Northampton and subsequent statutes, but made no reference to *Sir John Knight's Case*. He added that "all...persons in pursuing Huy and Cry may lawfully bear Arms" and that "Every Subject may arm himself to suppress Riots, Routs, Rebellions, or resist Enemies...."[114]

Other manuals for justices of the peace got it right. Theodore Barlow's 1745 treatise stated: "Wearing Arms, if not accompanied with

---

[111] John Bond, *A Compleat Guide for Justices of the Peace* 14 (London: Atkins, 1707).

[112] 2 Hawkins, *Pleas*, at 21-22.

[113] Bond, *A Compleat Guide* 14.

[114] *Id.* at 42-43. See also *id.* at 181 ("A person going or riding with offensive Arms may be arrested by a Constable, and by him be brought before a Justice," who may require sureties of him.).

Circumstances of Terror, is not within this Statute; therefore People of Rank and Distinction do not offend by wearing common Weapons."[115]

In sum, the two reported decisions in Sir John Knight's case and the detailed exposition by Hawkins clarified that, whether under the Statute of Northampton or the common law, going armed in a peaceable manner was not an offense, but doing so in a manner to terrorize others was a crime. These sources informed legal minds on both sides of the Atlantic, whether in England or America. More details about the Knight case would be revealed in later centuries, and they confirmed the same understanding, i.e., carrying arms for peaceable purposes was lawful.

C) The Hidden History of the Knight Case

More is now known about the Knight case, but not from sources to which English or American jurists or lawmakers had access. In addition to internal government records and historical accounts, Narcissus Luttrell, a historian and member of Parliament, kept a journal that was published in 1857. Also, Roger Morrice, a Puritan minister, kept a diary that first became public in 2007. These contemporaneous sources provide substantially more detail about the Knight case and the court's ruling on the meaning of the Statute of Northampton.

Sir John Knight was a politician from the seaport town of Bristol who, at one time or another, held the offices of councilman, sheriff, mayor, and member of Parliament. A staunch Protestant of the

---

[115] Theodore Barlow, *The Justice of Peace: A Treatise Containing the Power and Duty of That Magistrate* 12 (London: Lintot, 1745).

predominant Anglican variety, he was caught up in the conflict with Catholics that so defined his times.[116]

In April 1686, Knight learned that a small Catholic congregation was assembling to hear Mass, which at that time was a capital offense. The mayor, sheriffs and officers raided the service and arrested the priest, who was imprisoned. Word reached James II, who was Catholic, at the Palace of Whitehall, where Mass was being celebrated daily.[117] The King was greatly displeased, as was set forth in a letter dated May 1 from Robert Spencer, the Earl of Sunderland, to Bristol Mayor Henry Somerset, the Duke of Beaufort:

> The King, being informed that the Mayor and some other magistrates of Bristol lately seized upon a priest, who was going to officiate privately in a house there, committing him and those present, who exceeded not seven or eight persons, to prison; and having received an account that Sir John Knight was not only the informer but a busy actor in the matter by going himself to search, would have you let the Mayor and magistrates know that he is displeased at this proceeding and that, having reason to be much dissatisfied with Sir John Knight's late carriage upon several occasions, they will do well to have a care not to be drawn into inconveniences by the pretended zeal of Sir John Knight. He leaves it to you to notify this to the magistrates in such matter as you shall think convenient.[118]

---

[116] "Knight, Sir John," excerpts from B. D. Henning ed. *The History of Parliament: the House of Commons 1660–1690* (Woodbridge, England: Boydell & Brewer, 1983). https://www.historyofparliamentonline.org/volume/1660-1690/member/knight-sir-john-1718.

[117] John Latimer, *Annals of Bristol in the Seventeenth Century* 438–39 (Bristol: William George's Sons, 1900).

[118] 2 *Calendar of State Papers Domestic: James II, 1686–7*, at 118 (London: Her Majesty's Stationery Office, 1964).

The King ordered the release of the priest. Diarist Morrice wrote that on May 17, the "priest (Mac Don, I thinke)…was brought up hither on Habeas Corpus and was discharged" after the Attorney General told the court, "I have nothing against him." He added that Sir John Knight "has already been once kickt or beaten in the streets since then," and that two men continued to pursue him.[119] The attack prompted Knight to begin going armed.

Dr. Owen Wynne wrote to Sir William Trumbull, a devout Anglican and member of Parliament: "Sir John Knight the younger of Bristol having been lately affronted by some Irish gentlemen and priests passing that way, is so flown out into some extravagancies as to go armed with blunderbusses, like an Armadillo, and to expose the Popish religion with odious figures and representations, etc., which makes great noise here at present."[120] Disturbances between Protestants and Catholics had broken out in Bristol that soldiers were called out to repress.[121]

The blunderbuss, if that is what Knight actually carried, is a firearm having a barrel with a wide muzzle that fired multiple projectiles, typically pistol balls. The designs included both shoulder arms and pistols, which would be carried in pairs.[122] A blunderbuss with a shoulder stock would be similar to a shotgun today. Blunderbusses were carried by travelers on coaches, farmers going to

---

[119] 3 Roger Morrice, *The Entring Book of Roger Morrice 1677–1691*, at 126 (Woodbridge, England: Boydell Press, 2007).

[120] Historical Manuscripts Commission, *Report on the Manuscripts of the Marquess of Downshire*, vol. 1, part 1, at 172–73 (London 1924) (letter dated May 24, 1686).

[121] John Latimer, *Annals of Bristol in the Seventeenth Century* 439 (Bristol 1900).

[122] On seventeenth century blunderbusses, see D. R. Baxter, *Blunderbusses* 12–26 (Harrisburg, Pa.: Stackpole, 1970).

market, and itinerant journeymen, and most large houses had at least one.[123]

Knight's arrest was ordered by King James. On May 22 a warrant was issued "to apprehend Sir John Knight for several seditious practices and to bring him before the Privy Council to be examined and further dealt with according to law."[124] On June 1, the agent who arrested him "returned from Bristol whither he was sent to fetch up Sir John Knight, information being against him for words which might tend to the disturbance of the government. The Mayor and several Aldermen of Bristol are ordered to attend his Majesty in Council."[125]

Knight, the Mayor, and five of the Aldermen appeared before the Privy Council on June 5. The King blamed the Mayor and Aldermen for the recent disturbances. The Ministry ordered Knight to be prosecuted, and he was charged with brandishing a sword "to the terror of the public" in the streets of Bristol.[126] Nothing about the above information against him for "words" creating a disturbance would be reflected in the two reported judicial decisions.[127]

Knight would be prosecuted based on an information rather than an indictment. While an indictment would have been found by a grand jury, the information brought here was the type Blackstone explained as being "in the name of the king alone...filed ex officio by his own immediate officer, the attorney-general...." Such cases were perceived

---

[123] *Id.* at 34.
[124] 2 *Calendar of State Papers Domestic: James II, 1686–7*, at 136.
[125] *Id.* at 152.
[126] Latimer, *Annals* at 439.
[127] In those days, judges would render decisions orally from the bench, and one or more private scriveners would record what they heard (or thought they heard). That contrasts with later practices such as in use today, in which judges would write their own opinions.

to be "such enormous misdemeanors, as peculiarly tend to disturb or endanger his government, or to molest or affront him in the regular discharge of his royal functions."[128]

Thus reappeared the Statute of Northampton, which had fallen into disuse, but was now revived by Catholic monarch James II as a political weapon to disarm Protestant opponents such as Knight.[129]

On June 7, from London, Sir John Knight wrote to the aforementioned Earl of Sunderland that he hoped "to discover the cause of the misinformations brought from Bristoll" and to "know the particulars of my charge, that I may apply myself to laying my case nakedly before his Majesty." Regarding the statement in the Duke of Beaufort's letter to the Bristol Mayor "that the King was displeased with the seizing the priest," Knight responded: "The present Bishop [Trelawny]...particularly pressed the Mayor to be careful to prevent mass in the city, and the Mayor gave his orders to the officers to that intent." Further, just before the priest was seized, the Bishop "gave the same charge to the Grand Jury," and months earlier challenged a Captain Rooke to a duel for charging him "with Popish inclinations." Town Clerk Romsey, Knight's accuser, had "no small hand in the disorders in Bristoll" because of Knight's "zeal against Popery." Knight was "desirous fully to inform his Majesty of these particulars that it may appear what reason there is for such a prosecution."[130]

---

[128] 4 Blackstone, *Commentaries* *304.

[129] Joyce Lee Malcolm, *To Keep and Bear Arms: The Origins of an Anglo-American Right* 104–05 (Cambridge: Harvard University Press, 1994).

[130] 2 *Calendar of State Papers Domestic: James II, 1686–7*, at 159. See also Latimer, Annals, 439–40.

On June 12, as reflected in Morrice's journal, the Mayor and Aldermen requested forgiveness based on their "ignorante [ignorance] of the Lawes in that Case," and were discharged. However, a high bail was set for Knight.[131] The information alleged that Knight "had caused Musketts or Armes to be carried before him in the Streets, and into the Church to publick service to the terrour of his Majesties Liege people." Pleading not guilty, Knight claimed to have been assaulted by Mac-Don, against whom the Attorney General refused to file charges. Knight cited the assault "as his reason for having some Company with him and Muskets carried before him for his Safety."[132]

Luttrell recorded that on November 12, 1686, "sir John Knight pleaded not guilty to an information exhibited against him for goeing with a blunderbus in the streets, to the terrifyeing his majesties subjects."[133] Days later, he added:

> The 23rd, Sir John Knight, the loyall, was tried at the court of kings bench for a high misdemeanour, in goeing armed up and down with a gun att Bristoll; who being tried by a jury of his own citty, that knew him well, he was acquitted, not thinking he did it with any ill design, to the great disappointment of some persons who appeared very fierce against him; 'tis thought his being concerned in taking up a popish priest at Bristoll occasioned this prosecution.[134]

The above reinforces the decision of the King's Bench that going armed was a crime only if done in a manner to terrify the subjects.

---

[131] 3 Morrice, *Entring Book*, at 136.

[132] *Id.* at 141–43.

[133] 1 Narcissus Luttrell, *A Brief Historical Relation of State Affairs from September 1678 to April 1714*, at 380 (Oxford: Oxford University Press, 1857).

[134] *Id.* at 389. Being considered "loyall" was important in that age, as illustrated in two other entries in Luttrell's diary on that date; "the lord Altham…convicted of speaking words against the king when he was drunk, was sentenc'd to pay 100 marks," and "Dr. Edes…being convicted of commending a seditious book, was adjudg'd to pay 100*l.*" *Id.*

Knight was acquitted not because of doubt of whether he carried a gun, but because he did so without "any ill design." That some were disappointed with the verdict suggests the political motivation behind the prosecution.

Morrice recorded a more detailed account of the trial. After release of the priest, two Irishmen pursued Knight and "did fall upon" him near the town hall. Aid rendered by bystanders kept Knight from being killed. The attackers beat a woman when she refused to disclose Knight's whereabouts. Knight took refuge in the countryside, and rode armed when he came to town. He "did one Lords day go to a Church in Bristol with his Sword and Gun when the two Irishmen were thought to looke for him, and left his gun in the Church Porch with his man, to stand upon the Watch &c."[135]

Given the above testimony, "It seemed to be doubted by the Court whether this came within the equity and true meaning of the Statute of Northampton...." The Lord Chief Justice Herbert "seemed not be seveare upon Sir John," Morrice guessed, "because the matter would not beare it, Or for any reason of State or Composition...." The Chief Justice criticized the Attorney General, Sir Robert Sawyer, noting that "if there be any blinde side of the Kings business you will always lay your finger upon it, and shew it to the Defendants...." The jury found Knight not guilty.[136]

Three days after his acquittal, on November 21, as Luttrell recorded, the court denied Knight's motion "to discharge his recognizance, since his aquittall, but t'was refused, and he ordered to

---

[135] 3 Morrice, *Entring Book*, at 307-08.
[136] *Id.* at 308.

give sureties for his good behavior."[137] While this did nothing to negate the jury's finding of not guilty to the charge, the judge apparently wanted no future trouble from Knight. That the judge required sureties is inconsistent with the theory that he was somehow acting as a government agent, as such official status would not have required sureties.

Finally, on January 24, 1687, Morrice recorded that Knight appeared in court again. His counsel moved "that the Bonds might be given up in which he was bound when he was under that Information of which he was found not gilty upon Tryall the last Term. The Court said those Bonds fell in Course and so they were Nulled &c."[138]

Knight's acquittal proved that James II could not rely on the Statute of Northampton to disarm Protestant opponents who carried arms in public. That had required firearm seizures and prosecutions of individuals on a piecemeal basis. The test case against Knight proved that judges would recognize that going armed must be to the terror of the subjects, and that juries could not be trusted to convict.

D) Revisionist Claims About the Knight Case

Contemporary American opponents of the right of commoners to bear arms have sought to spin a revisionist history of Sir John Knight's case. They argue that the legal heritage of going armed peaceably was a crime per se, without the additional element of the offense that one must do so in a manner to terrify one's fellow citizens. Their goal is to convince American courts that the English background supersedes and legally cancels the literal text in the Second Amendment that "the

---

[137] 1 Luttrell, *A Brief Historical Relation of State Affairs*, 380.
[138] 3 Morrice, *Entring Book*, at 349.

people" have a right to bear arms. Actual English history supports no such claims.

Author Patrick Charles argues that going armed per se was a crime and that doing so as to terrify the subjects was not an essential element of the crime. Further, supposedly Knight was acquitted on the basis of being "cloaked with governmental authority because he committed the act in accordance with the Mayor and Aldermen of Bristol," and that "when Knight was armed to apprehend the priest he was under the license of the king's service."[139] Charles appears to be conflating and confusing two entirely different events. In April 1686, Knight and these other officials apprehended the Catholic priest, and they were arrested "for several seditious practices" arising out of that incident.[140] But Knight was not prosecuted for that. It was after that event that Knight was assaulted and later began going armed. Knight was prosecuted for going armed in the streets and into the church of St. Michael, in Bristol, "in the time of divine service, with a gun, to terrify the King's subjects...."[141] St. Michael was an Anglican (Protestant) church where Knight went to worship on a certain Lord's day, leaving his arms on the porch with an assistant to stand watch.[142]

Mr. Charles further claims that "the jury acquitted Knight because he was a government official that was well-affected to the crown," and that "[t]he jury agreed with this defense, finding Knight to be 'loyall.'"[143] But it was Luttrell's diary, not the jury, who called Knight

---

[139] Patrick J. Charles, "The Faces of the Second Amendment Outside the Home," 60 *Clev. St. L. Rev.* 1, 28, 30 (2012).

[140] 2 *Calendar of State Papers Domestic: James II, 1686–7*, at 136.

[141] *Sir John Knight's Case*, 3 Mod. 117, 87 Eng. Rep. 75, 76 (K.B. 1686).

[142] "Church of St Michael," https://historicengland.org.uk/listing/the-list/list-entry/1129078; 3 Morrice, *Entring Book*, at 307-08.

[143] Charles, "Faces," 29-30 & n.145, citing Luttrell, 389.

"loyall," and Luttrell said that the jury acquitted Knight because he had no "ill design," just as the court said he had no "*malo animo*" or evil intent.[144]

Nothing in the two judicial opinions on the same Knight case suggest that he pled that he could go armed based on governmental immunity. None of the details mentioned by Charles imply that going armed per se was banned. Nor do any details suggest that going armed in a manner to terrify the subjects was not an element of the offense.[145]

Charles misinterprets the above history as part of an attempt to show that the American Founders meant to override the Second Amendment right to "bear arms" with a version of the Statute of Northampton that peaceably going armed was and should remain a crime. But the Founders were hardly fans of English King James II, and they did not seek to incorporate his royalist vision into the Bill of Rights. The Founders had access to the King's Bench decision in the Knight case and to Hawkins' treatise, which characterized the crime as going armed in a manner to terrorize others.

Professor Saul Cornell argues that the decision in the Knight case is not precedent for any right peaceably to bear arms. Although neglecting the required element of carrying arms to terrify the subjects, Cornell criticizes the jury's decision to acquit. Knight was "a militant Protestant, who opposed tolerance for Catholics," and "[t]he jury, composed of other militant Protestants drawn from Knight's community, was sympathetic to his anti-Catholicism and acquitted

---

[144] Luttrell, *A Brief Historical Relation of State Affairs*, at 389; *Rex v. Knight*, Comb. 38-39, 90 Eng. Rep. 330 (K.B. 1686).
[145] Charles, "Faces," 28-30.

him."[146] This claim is speculative and is not borne out by the historical record. While Luttrell is cited for that proposition, he said no such thing, and instead wrote that the jury acquitted Knight "not thinking he did it [went armed] with any ill design...."[147] Indeed, as discussed above, the jury heard evidence that Knight had been assaulted and carried arms for self-defense.

Cornell adds that "Knight escaped punishment thanks to a sympathetic jury...."[148] But he cites no evidence for such conjecture. Could it be that Knight was acquitted because he was not guilty of the charge of "going or riding armed in affray of peace" with "malo animo," or "to terrify the King's subjects"? That is all that was reflected in the opinion of the King's Bench as well as in the diaries of Luttrell and Morrice.

Cornell also asserts that "Knight was still punished for his actions" because "the government still imposed a peace bond on him as a surety of good behavior in the future."[149] But as Blackstone explained, and as discussed at greater length below, requiring a bond or surety, then as today, was "not meant as any degree of punishment...."[150] Cornell's revisionist interpretation of Knight's case is utterly unsupported by any genuine historical evidence—and is in fact affirmatively contradicted by Luttrell's diary, the only primary source he cites.

---

[146] Saul Cornell, "The Right to Keep and Carry Arms in Anglo-American Law: Preserving Liberty and Keeping the Peace," 80 *Law & Contemp. Probs.* 11, 27 (2017), citing Luttrell, 389.

[147] 1 Luttrell, *A Brief Historical Relation of State Affairs*, 389.

[148] *Id.*

[149] Cornell, "The Right to Keep and Carry Arms," at 27.

[150] 4 Blackstone, *Commentaries* *249.

Hawkins wrote that "no wearing of arms is within the meaning of the statute unless it be accompanied with such circumstances as are apt to terrify the people," and gave as an example "persons of quality…wearing common weapons…."[151] Cornell ignores that "*no wearing of arms*" is within the Statute without the terror element by asserting, "Hawkins expressly noted that 'persons of quality,' a term that signified elite status and class rank, were not subject to arms restrictions in public."[152] But Hawkins did not limit the rule to such persons; since "no wearing of arms" peaceably was within the Statute, it would include the wearing of arms by commoners.

Professor Tim Harris argues that merely going armed per se constituted a crime, and proof was not required that it be done so in a manner to terrify.[153] But going armed in a manner to terrify were two separate elements of the offense that had to be alleged in the indictment and proven.[154] A sheriff could not even arrest the person unless, "if contrary to the Statute of Northampton, he sees any one to carry weapons in the high-way, *in terrorem populi Regis*…."[155]

Harris adds that "all elements of an indictment" did not need to be proven.[156] That muddles the fact that crimes have elements, while

---

[151] 2 Hawkins, *Pleas*, at 21-22.

[152] Saul Cornell, "The Right to Carry Firearms Outside of the Home: Separating Historical Myths from Historical Realities," 39 *Fordham Urb. L.J.* 1695, 1713 n.101 (2012). See also Charles, "The Faces of the Second Amendment," 25-26.

[153] Tim Harris, "The Right to Bear Arms in English & Irish Historical Context," in Jennifer Tucker et al. eds, *A Right to Bear Arms?* 23, 24 (Washington, D.C.: Smithsonian, 2019).

[154] *Rex v. Smith*, 2 Ir. R. 190, 204 (K.B. 1914). Similarly, to be convicted of a riot, the indictment must allege the element of terror. *Rex v. Hughes*, 172 E.R. 746, 4 Carrington & Payne 372 (1830) ("these defendants cannot be convicted of the riot, as the indictment does not conclude *in terrorem populi*").

[155] *Chune v. Piott*, 80 Eng. Rep. 1161, 1162 (K.B. 1615).

[156] Harris, "The Right to Bear Arms," 23, 24.

indictments have allegations. An indictment must allege each and every element of an offense, and each and every element of the offense must be proven. This is true today in the United States. And, as Blackstone wrote, it was true in the English tradition.

"An indictment is a written accusation...of a crime or misdemeanor," explained Blackstone, adding: "The offence itself must also be set forth with clearness and certainty; and in some crimes, particular words of art must be used...to express the precise idea which it entertains of the offence...."[157] A demurrer to the indictment is allowed "when the fact as alleged is allowed to be true, but...the fact, as stated, is no felony...or whatever the crime is alleged to be."[158] In short, all elements of a crime must both be alleged in the indictment and then proven at trial.

Harris further suggests that, based on diaries not known until centuries later, "it is not clear what issue *Rex v. Knight* resolved," since "gentlemen were certainly in the habit of wearing swords and even carrying firearms," and thus the case does not establish that a subject could carry a gun "so long as his doing so did not terrify people."[159] Yet that is exactly what the Knight decision resolved. The lawfulness of peaceably carrying arms is the only reading that is consistent with the two reported judicial decisions on the Knight case, not to mention Hawkins' treatise. And as discussed below, British courts through the twentieth century would hold that going armed and doing so to terrify were separate elements of the offense.

---

[157] 4 Blackstone, *Commentaries* *299, 302.
[158] *Id.* at *327–28.
[159] Harris, "The Right to Bear Arms," 27.

Finally, in a 2021 decision, the U.S. Court of Appeals for the Ninth Circuit found it "curious" that Knight was "acquitted, yet bound to good behaviour," thus "making Knight's 'acquittal' more of a conditional pardon."[160] It added that "[t]he surety for good behavior essentially allowed those accused of crimes—who could afford it—to avoid punishment...."[161] This insinuation that Knight was somehow guilty after all of going armed, and that the crime did not involve a terror element, misunderstands the effects of Knight's acquittal and recognizance.

"If the jury therefore find the prisoner not guilty, he is then for ever quit and discharged of the accusation," according to Blackstone.[162] Blackstone devoted a chapter to measures "intended merely for prevention, without any crime actually committed by the party, but arising only from a probable suspicion, that some crime is intended or likely to happen; and consequently it is not meant as any degree of punishment...."[163] There were two types of sureties—to keep the peace and for good behavior. A recognizance to keep the peace applied "either generally, towards the king, and all his liege people; or particularly also, with regard to the person who craves the security."[164] "Or, if it be for the good behaviour, then on condition that he shall demean and behave himself well, (or be of good behaviour) either generally or specially, for the time therein limited, as for one or more

---

[160] *Young v. State of Hawaii*, 2021 WL 1114180, *17 (9th Cir. 2021), citing *Knight's Case*, 90 Eng. Rep. at 331.

[161] *Id.* at *17 n.12, citing David Feldman, "The King's Peace," 47 *Cambridge L.J.* 101, 121 (1988). However, Feldman was discussing persons accused of crime to be pardoned if they would be useful to the king in military service, not those who were tried and acquitted of crimes. See *id.*

[162] 4 Blackstone, *Commentaries* *335.

[163] *Id.* at *249.

[164] *Id.* at *249-50.

years, or for life." Finally, "if the condition of such recognizance be broken, by any breach of the peace in the one case, or any misbehaviour in the other, the recognizance becomes forfeited...."[165]

In sum, Knight's acquittal foreclosed any insinuation that he was actually guilty. His being "bound to good behaviour" did not mean that going armed per se was a crime and that the court let him off the hook, and instead it meant only that the court wanted to ensure nothing more than good behavior.

* * *

English James II, as a Catholic monarch, failed in his attempt to set a legal precedent for disarming political enemies by prosecuting them under the obsolete and inapplicable Statute of Northampton of 1328. James II would next turn to direct confiscation of firearms from his opponents, which would lead to his overthrow in the relatively bloodless Glorious Revolution and to the adoption of the guarantee of having arms in the Declaration of Rights of 1689.

---

[165] *Id.* at *250.

Chapter Two

"THAT THE SUBJECTS WHICH ARE PROTESTANTS, MAY HAVE ARMS FOR THEIR DEFENCE"

A) THE DECLARATION OF RIGHTS OF 1689 RECOGNIZES "THE TRUE, ANCIENT, AND INDUBITABLE RIGHT" TO HAVE ARMS FOR SELF-DEFENSE

King James II failed in his attempt to disarm political opponents like Sir John Knight by having them prosecuted under the Statute of Northampton. Yet a weapon remained in the King's armory that would allow the confiscation of firearms not only from those bearing them, but also from subjects merely keeping them at home.

On December 6, 1686, just two weeks after Knight's acquittal, the Earl of Sunderland – the same mouthpiece of the King against Knight discussed above—issued a directive to Richard Boyle, the Earl of Burlington, the Lord Lieutenant of the West Riding of Yorkshire. It read: "The King having received information that a great many persons not qualified by law under pretence of shooting matches keep muskets or other guns in their houses, it is his pleasure that you should send orders to your Deputy Lieutenants to cause strict search to be made for such muskets or guns and to seize and safely keep them till further order."[166]

---

[166] 2 *Calendar of State Papers (Domestic), James II*, no. 1212, at 316 (London: Her Majesty's Stationery Office, 1964) (Dec. 6, 1686).

Similar letters were sent to the Earl of Derby, Viscount Fauconberg, the Duke of Somerset, the Earl of Thanet and the Bishop of Durham.[167] These lords-lieutenants represented the King in each county and organized the county militias.

Most persons were not "qualified by law" under England's 1670 Game Act, which authorized searches of houses for firearms.[168] As the above reflects, gun owners not only kept firearms in their homes, but carried them to shooting matches. In an effort to maintain a tight grip on power, James II meant to put an end to both.

Unfortunately for King James II, his efforts backfired. Through these gun control measures and other repressive policies, James II sparked the Glorious Revolution of 1688. James II's opponents saw James' daughter Mary as a legitimate successor to the English throne. Mary was the wife of William of Orange, who was a stadholder (provincial executive officer) of the Dutch Republic. A coalition of English leaders invited William and Mary to assume the English throne, and at the end of 1688, William landed in England with an army. James' royal army quickly fell apart and James fled into exile. The subsequent reign of William and Mary was Protestant.

A paramount aim of the Glorious Revolution was to abolish James' standing army and to reinstate the fundamental right to keep and carry arms. Parliament would accomplish that in part through enactment of the Declaration of Rights of 1689, which the new monarchs William and Mary fully recognized as a condition of rule.

---

[167] *Id.*
[168] 22 & 23 Charles II, ch. 25 (1671).

On January 28, 1689, a debate ensued in the House of Commons concerning the proposed abdication of James II. Lord John Somers, who would play a leading role in drafting the Declaration of Rights, kept notes of the debate. His notes demonstrate the perceived abuses under the Militia Act of 1662, which had allowed arbitrary searches and seizures of the arms of private citizens. Sergeant Maynard complained: "An Act of Parliament was made to disarm all Englishmen, whom the Lieutenant should suspect, by day or by night, by force or otherwise."[169] Mr. Finch thought that no man would be safe under the King, adding, "The constitution being limited, there is a good foundation for defensive arms."[170]

"Militia bill. – Power to disarm all England. – Now done in Ireland," lamented Sir Richard Temple, according to Somers' notes.[171] Mr. Boscawen's attack on the ministry's arbitrary power indicates that the members of Parliament themselves had no immunity: "Imprisoning without reason; disarming. – Himself disarmed."[172] "An abominable thing to disarm the nation, to set up a standing army," Sergeant Maynard agreed.[173] And Mr. Sacheverel brooded: "Disarmed and imprisoned without cause."[174]

---

[169] 2 *Miscellaneous State Papers from 1501–1726*, Phillip, Earl of Hardwicke compl., 407 (London: W. Strahan, 1778).
[170] *Id.* at 410.
[171] *Id.* at 416.
[172] *Id.* at 416.
[173] *Id.* at 417.
[174] *Id.* at 418.

All of the above members of Commons, each of whom complained about the people being disarmed, were appointed to committees to draft the Declaration of Rights.[175]

The disarming in Ireland described in Somers' notes began in 1685, when James II directed Richard Talbot, the earl of Tyrconnel, to execute his policy of disarming the "disaffected," which meant the Irish Protestants, and of arming the Irish Catholics. This entailed an investigation of the firearms held by private persons and ordering the surrender of the arms of the Protestant militia. As related by historian John Miller, the lord justices complained that the "disarming had left many loyal (Church of Ireland) Protestants at the mercy of robbers and tories"; further, "not only the militia weapons but also many belonging to private individuals had been brought in by the end of 1685...." Tyrconnel armed what was then a mostly Catholic militia, but the disarming was not complete, as many Protestants still had weapons.[176]

The Declaration of Rights of 1689, coming just three years after Sir John Knight's case, further clarified that simply going armed peaceably was a right, not a crime. It listed among the ways that James II attempted to subvert "the Laws and Liberties of this Kingdom," "By causing several good Subjects, being Protestants, to be disarmed, at the same Time when Papists were both armed and employed, contrary to law."[177] The act accordingly declared thirteen "true, ancient and indubitable rights," including the following: "That the Subjects which

---

[175] *Journals of the House of Commons from Dec. the 26th 1688, to Oct. the 26th 1693*, at 15, 22 (London: His Majesty's Stationery Office, 1802).

[176] John Miller, "The Earl of Tyrconnel and James II's Irish Policy, 1685–1688," 20 *Historical Journal*, No. 4, at 803, 817–18 (1977).

[177] An Act Declaring the Rights and Liberties of the Subject, 1 W. & M., Sess. 2, c.2, (1689).

are Protestants, may have Arms for their Defence suitable to their Condition, and as are allowed by Law."[178]

That guarantee was, in the words of Sir William Holdsworth, a reaction to the King's "refusal to allow Protestants the right to carry arms for self-defense...."[179] The general terms that the Protestant subjects "may have Arms for their Defence" was not limited to keeping arms in one's house, but extended to carrying arms in public as well.

The terms "suitable to their Condition" referred to statutes dating back as far as the Assize of Arms of 1181 requiring persons to arm themselves for militia duty based on what they could afford under their economic status. Under that act, a knight had to have a hauberk, a helmet, a shield, and a lance; burgesses and freemen had to have quilted doublets, a headpiece of iron, and a lance.[180]

The phrase "as are allowed by Law" is subject to varying interpretations.[181] It definitely precluded royal decrees to disarm subjects. To the extent it referred to acts of Parliament, limitations must have existed on that power, as the Declaration refers to "true, ancient and indubitable rights." As discussed below, Blackstone read it as reflecting the natural right of self-preservation. "As are allowed by

---

[178] *Id.*

[179] 6 William Holdsworth, *A History of English Law* (7th ed.) 241 (London: Methuen, 1956).

[180] *English Historical Documents, 1042–1189*, at 416 (N.Y.: Oxford University Pres, 1968). See Stephen P. Halbrook, *That Every Man Be Armed* 36–38 (Albuquerque: University of New Mexico Press, 2013).

[181] See Joyce Lee Malcolm, *To Keep and Bear Arms: The Origins of an Anglo-American Right* 120–21 (Cambridge: Harvard University Press, 1994).

law" could also be read to have reference to the common law, which incorporated such longstanding rights.[182]

Two acts of Parliament that had generally fallen into disuse and which seem to have been inconsistent with the Declaration nonetheless made brief reappearances. In *Rex v. Silcot* (1690), a conviction "upon the statute of 33 Hen. 8, c. 6, for *keeping* of a gun" was quashed for failure to allege that "the offender had not 100*l*. a-year when the offence was committed."[183] A conviction under the same law of Henry VIII of a defendant who, "not having the hundred pounds a-year did shoot in a gun," was overturned in *Rex & Regina v. Bullock* (1692), because the delay between the violation and the trial left the justice of the peace with no authority to try him.[184]

No further judicial decisions regarding prosecutions under 33 Hen. 8, c. 6 after the above 1692 case could be located. The prior decisions that could be located all concerned the property qualification; none concerned the act's restrictions on handguns under a certain size. Evidently the arms guarantee in the Declaration of Rights was being taken seriously, and the word filtered down to the justices of the peace who had enforced Henry VIII's statute. It would be formally repealed

---

[182] A game act restriction on hunting did "not extend to prohibit a man from keeping a gun for his necessary defense, but only from making that forbidden use of it." *Rex v. Gardner*, 7 Mod. 279, 280, 87 Eng. Rep. 1240, 1241 (K. B. 1739). "[As] these acts restrain the liberty which was allowed by the common law, and are also penal, they ought not to be extended further than they must necessarily be." *King v. Gardiner*, Andrews 255, 256–57, 95 Eng. Rep. at 386, 387 (1739).

[183] *Rex v. Silcot*, 87 E.R. 186, 3 Modern 280 (1690).

[184] *Rex & Regina v. Bullock*, 87 E.R. 315, 4 Modern 147 (1692). That appeared to be the reason for reversing another conviction "for going with an hand-gun, not being qualified." *The King v. Litten*, 89 E.R. 644, 1 Shower. K.B. 367 (1689).

with a host of other game laws by William IV, who was, ironically, the son of George III.[185]

And in *King & Queen v. Alsop* (1691), the conviction under Edward VI's law of a defendant who shot conies (rabbits) but did not meet the property qualification was reversed because a justice of the peace only had authority to punish offenses under statutes concerning the peace of the nation; but under this law, "the peace is no wise concerned, because the offence thereby created is for want of due qualification of the person to shoot, which is not an offence against the peace."[186]

Based on complaints of abusive prosecutions, Parliament repealed the act of Edward VI in 1694 with the following explanation: "Which said Act however useful in those days hath not for many yeares last past been putt in execution but became uselesse and unnecessary yett neverthelesse several malicious persons have of late prosecuted several Gentlemen qualified to keep and use Guns upon the said Act."[187]

Given the demise of the above acts of Henry VIII and Edward VI, it would be difficult to argue that they were consistent with the guarantee of the Declaration of Rights that "the Subjects which are Protestants, may have Arms for their Defence…as are allowed by Law." The property qualifications of the old laws were inconsistent with the general right accorded to Protestant subjects. Henry's ban on handguns under a yard in length had long receded into history with the development and general distribution of pistols both large and small,

---

[185] An Act to amend the Laws in England relative to Game, 1 & 2 Will. 4, c.22 (1831).
[186] *King & Queen v. Alsop*, 87 E.R. 256, 4 Modern 49 (1691).
[187] 6 & 7 Will. 3, c. 13, § 3 (1694).

which gave practical meaning to what were considered "Arms for their Defence."

In 1692, Robert Gardiner published *The Compleat Constable*, which stated that "if any Person shall Ride or go Armed offensively . . . in affray of their Majesties Subjects, and breach of the Peace; or wear or carry any Daggers, Guns, or Pistols Charged," a constable could "carry the Persons wearing them before a Justice to give Surety to keep the Peace."[188] For the first part of that he cited the Statute of Northampton, which he read consistent with *Sir John Knight's Case*, but for the second part – referring to the mere wearing or carrying of arms – he cited laws of Richard II, which had fallen into disuse. He did not realize the sea change of the Glorious Revolution, as he also wrote that the lieutenants of the militia could "search for, and seize Arms" kept by any person they judged "dangerous," citing Charles II's Militia Act of 1662 – an abuse the Declaration of Rights was intended to prevent.[189]

Blackstone discussed the Declaration of Rights in the broader context of "the principal absolute rights which appertain to every Englishman" of "personal security, personal liberty, and private property," which would be a "dead letter" without "certain other auxiliary subordinate rights of the subject...."[190] In addition to the right to petition the government, those auxiliary rights included "that of having arms for their defence suitable to their condition and degree, and such as are allowed by law." Which is also declared by the same

---

[188] Robert Gardiner, *The Compleat Constable* 18 (London: Richard & Edward Atkins, 1692) (citing 2 Ed. 3. ca. 3. 7 R. 2. 13. 20. R. 2. c. 1.).
[189] *Id.* at 68.
[190] 1 Blackstone, *Commentaries* *136.

statute 1 W. & M. st.2 c.2 [the English Bill of Rights], and it is indeed, a public allowance under due restrictions, of the natural right of resistance and self-preservation, when the sanctions of society and laws are found insufficient to restrain the violence of oppression."[191]

To protect the rights and liberties of the Englishmen, Blackstone continued, the subjects were entitled to justice in the courts, to the right of petitioning for redress of grievances, and "to the right of having and using arms for self-preservation and defense."[192] Obviously, the rights to petition and to have arms were not limited to one's house.

But the right to have and use arms for self-preservation and defense did not give license to persons to go armed in a manner to terrorize the subjects. Blackstone explained:

> The offence of riding or going armed, with dangerous or unusual weapons, is a crime against the public peace, by terrifying the good people of the land; and is particularly prohibited by the Statute of Northampton, upon pain of forfeiture of the arms, and imprisonment during the king's pleasure: in like manner as, by the laws of Solon, every Athenian was finable who walked about the city in armour.[193]

That did not include peaceably carrying weapons not considered dangerous and unusual. Regarding Blackstone's comment about Athenians who walked about the city in armour, recall Hawkins' more detailed explanation that neither "wearing of arms" unless done in a

---

[191] *Id.* at *139.

[192] *Id.* at *140.

[193] 4 Blackstone, *Commentaries* *148–49. Less than two decades before publication of the *Commentaries*, a defendant was convicted "for going Armed with a Cutlass Contrary to the Statute" and "for making an Assault upon one John Jew," indicating that he was carrying with malo animo. *Rex v. Edward Mullins* (K.B. 1751), Middlesex Sessions: Justices Working Documents, available at http://bit.ly/1U8OhO7.

way to terrify others, nor wearing "privy coats of mail" because (being under garments) they did not terrify others, were within the Statute, but that "wearing such armour in publick" did offend the Statute.[194]

Blackstone described the nature of the offense of going armed to terrorize the subjects more fully in the power of a justice of the peace to "bind all those to keep the peace who in his presence make any affray, or threaten to kill or beat another, or contend together with hot and angry words, or go about with unusual weapons or attendance, to the terror of the people...by causing the person to post a surety as security for the peace."[195] Requiring sureties was "intended merely for prevention" where there was "a probable suspicion, that some crime is intended or likely to happen; and consequently it is not meant as any degree of punishment...."[196] That was a far cry from having, carrying, and using arms lawfully in exercise of one's natural right of resistance and self-preservation.

At this point in English history, the tyranny of James II had been deposed. The Declaration of Rights, affirming "true, ancient and indubitable rights," included confirmation "[t]hat the Subjects which are Protestants, may have Arms for their Defence," [197] thus guaranteeing, in Blackstone's words, "the right of having and using arms for self-preservation and defense." That did not include the carrying of dangerous and unusual weapons in a manner to terrorize one's follow subjects.

---

[194] Hawkins, *Pleas* 21–22.
[195] 4 Blackstone, *Commentaries* *254–55.
[196] *Id.* at *249.
[197] An Act Declaring the Rights and Liberties of the Subject, 1 W. & M., Sess. 2, c.2, (1689).

But if the right of English Protestants to bear arms was safely formalized in a solemn charter, England's Catholic minority was excluded from that declaration. And in Ireland, with its Catholic majority, the rule was turned upside down such that no right to bear arms was recognized.

B) A Right to Bear Arms for Protestants, But Not Irish Catholics

Unlike Protestants, Catholics were not recognized by the Declaration of Rights as having the right to keep or bear arms. That would have long-term impact in Ireland, since it was predominately Catholic. The passage of Irish arms acts and debates thereon demonstrate the basic rule that Englishmen had a right to carry arms and, as its mirror image, that Irishmen did not. In these legislative processes, it never occurred to anyone that Irish Catholics, like everyone else, had no right to bear arms based on the unmentioned Statute of Northampton, enacted over 350 years earlier.

In 1689, Parliament sought to restrict the use of arms by die-hard supporters of the Catholic James II in England by enacting, "That no Papist or reputed Papist, so refusing [to take a loyalty oath] or making Default, as aforesaid, shall or may have or keep in his House, or elsewhere...any Arms, Weapons, Gunpowder, or Ammunition (other than such necessary Weapons, as shall be allowed to him by Order of the Justices of the Peace...for the Defense of his House or Person)...."[198] Catholics who took the loyalty oath to William and Mary were not so restricted.

---

[198] An Act for the Better Securing the Government by Disarming Papists and Reputed Papists, 1 W.&M., Sess. 1, c. 15 §4 (1689).

The Jacobite forces of James II fought on in Ireland until they capitulated to William III's English army in 1691, resulting in the Treaty of Limerick. Referring to upper class Irish who took the oath of allegiance to the King, it provided: "Every nobleman and gentleman...shall have liberty to ride with a sword and case of pistols, if they think fit, and keep a gun in their houses for the defence of the same, or for fowling."[199] The treaty did not require that Irish Catholics in general disarm.

But in 1692, the Protestant-dominated Irish House of Commons resolved that "the great number of Papists, and reputed Papists, who go and are armed in this kingdom...is of very dangerous consequence," and thus the Lord Lieutenant must have such arms seized and recall "such licenses granted to any Papists in this kingdom for carrying or bearing arms...."[200] (This is just one of many instances when "carrying" and "bearing" were used synonymously.) Irish Protestants did not need a license to bear arms.

A bill to disarm Papists was proposed with the explanation by the Irish Lord Deputy Henry Capell, that a similar bill had already passed "in England where the Papists are less numerous and formidable than they are in this country," and thus the bill was necessary "for the security of his Majesty's authority and the safety of the whole Protestant interest in this Kingdom."[201]

---

[199] Treaty of Limerick, Civil Articles, ¶ 7 (1691).
[200] Arthur Browne, *A Brief Review of the Question: Whether the Articles of Limerick Have Been Violated* 92 (Dublin: William McKenzie, 1788).
[201] Capell and council, to English lords justices, June 17, 1695, quoted in Charles I. McGrath, "Securing the Protestant Interest," 30 *Irish Historical Studies* 25, 37 (May 1996).

Passed in 1695 as an Act for the better securing the government, by disarming papists, it required all Catholics to surrender "all their arms and ammunition, notwithstanding any licence for keeping the same heretofore granted...."[202] There were two exceptions. First, "Papist gentlemen who can prove themselves comprized under the Articles of Limerick may have a sword, a case of pistols, and a gun for defence of their house or for fowling."[203] Second "the chief governors may by order of the privy council licence any person to keep such arms as shall be particularly expressed in such licence."[204] Whether a license would be granted to a Catholic was subject to the discretion of the issuing authority.

In 1704, the Council-Chamber in Dublin issued a proclamation declaring that "several Persons not qualified by the Laws of this Realm to carry Arms, have nevertheless in Contempt and Violation of the Laws, taken on them to ride and go Armed" under licenses that had been recalled, counterfeited, or forged.[205] Catholics who were qualified by law to have arms could apply for new licenses, which would entitle them to "bear and keep such Arms" as were listed on the licenses.[206] (Not surprisingly, "bear" was defined at the time, as now, as "carry";[207] to bear arms simply meant to carry arms.) A listing was made of the Catholics licensed to carry arms, which typically included a sword, a brace of pistols, and a gun.[208]

---

[202] An Act for the Better Security of the Government, by Disarming the Papists, § 1, 7 W & M., c. 5 (Ireland 1695).

[203] *Id.* § 4–5.

[204] *Id.* § 7.

[205] "Irish Catholics Licensed to Keep Arms (1704)," 4 *Archivium Hibernicum* 59, 64 (1915).

[206] *Id.* at 64–65.

[207] John Kersey, *Dictionarium Anglo-Britannicum or a General English Dictionary* (1708).

[208] "Irish Catholics Licensed to Keep Arms," 59–64.

Three quarters of a century later, at a time when the American Revolution was erupting, the Crown saw fit to take precautions in Ireland. George III's 1776 Act to prevent tumultuous Risings of Persons, applicable in Ireland, provided that any person "being armed with any fire arms, flintlock, pistol, or any offensive weapon" who "shall rise, assemble, or appear...to the terror of his Majesty's subjects" would be guilty of a high misdemeanor. Penalties included fine and imprisonment, or the pillory, whipping, or other corporal punishment.[209] This part of the Act was not limited to papists.

The Act further provided that several persons had arms and ammunition despite the laws disarming papists, and thus justices of the peace and other officials may, by day or night, search for and seize all arms possessed by a papist "not duly licensed to keep and carry the same," and to enter into any house or other place where reasonable cause existed to suspect such arms to be secreted. Persons suspected of secreting such items could be required to be examined under oath.[210] Persons who refused to deliver up their arms or to declare what arms they had were subject to fines or imprisonment, or to the pillory or whipping.[211]

As noted, this statute was enacted in 1776, at a time when British policy in America had gone beyond disarming and other repressive policies to full-fledged war against the American patriots. In America, of course, the carrying of arms never had to be licensed in the first place.

---

[209] 15 & 16 Geo. III, c.21, § 2 (Ireland 1776).
[210] *Id.* § 15.
[211] *Id.* § 17.

In 1793, numerous grievances were presented in a Petition to the King on behalf of the Catholic Subjects of Ireland. One provision stated:

We are totally prohibited from keeping or using weapons, for the defence of our houses, families, or persons, whereby we are exposed to the violence of burglary, robbery, and assassination; and to enforce this prohibition, contravening that great original law of nature, which enjoins us to self-defence, a variety of statutes exist, not less grievous and oppressive in their provisions, than unjust in their object; by one of which, enacted so lately as within these sixteen years, every one of your Majesty's Catholic subjects, of whatever rank or degree, peer or peasant, is compellable by any magistrate to come forward and convict himself of what may be though a singular offence in a country professing to be free – keeping arms for his defence; or, if he shall refuse so to do, may incur not only fine and imprisonment, but the vile and ignominious punishments of the pillory and whipping, penalties appropriate to the most infamous malefactors, and more terrible to a liberal mind than death itself.[212]

The above law referenced as having been passed sixteen years previously was the Act to Prevent Tumultuous Risings of Persons of 1776. As discussed above, it banned firearm possession by papists, compelled Catholic gun owners to incriminate themselves, and was enforced by the pillory and whipping.

The petition was taken up in the Irish Parliament in Dublin along with a bill to grant limited relief to Catholics. The bill was reluctantly managed by Robert Hobart, with an eye to maintaining the Protestant ascendancy. Summarizing various aims of the legislation, Hobart

---

[212] Henry Parnell, M.P, *A History of the Penal Law Against the Irish Catholics* 158–59 (Dublin: H. Fitzpatrick, 1808).

explained that "the laws which prevent them [Catholics] from carrying arms, should be so far repealed as to persons possessing a certain degree of property; but by no means so as to put arms into the hands of the lower order of people."[213]

Dr. Patrick Duigenan, a virulent anti-Catholic, launched into a lengthy tirade against any reforms. Attacking the Catholic petition line by line, he came to the part relating, in his words, "to the laws, which restrain papists from carrying arms; laws certainly very necessary when they were enacted, and, from recent experience, very proper to be now rigorously enforced."[214] The petition was false when it alleged, first, that Catholics were prohibited from keeping and using arms for defense, because "all the statutes enacted to prevent Catholics from keeping arms in this kingdom, give a power to the Lord Lieutenant and Privy Council to licence any Catholic they may think fit, to keep and carry arms; and that no Catholic nobleman, gentleman, or even farmers of respectable characters, have ever been refused such licences, when they have properly applied for them...."[215]

Second, regarding the claim that the 1776 law compels Catholics of either convicting themselves of keeping arms or risking imprisonment, the pillory, and whipping, Duigenan responded that "all Catholics are not subject to the provisions of this act, but such only as are not duly licenced by the Lord Lieutenant and Privy Council, to keep or carry arms...." Further, the law only applied if the person was convicted, and "the punishment of pillory or whipping was never

---

[213] 13 *The Parliamentary register: or, History of the proceedings and debates of the House of Commons of Ireland* 88 (Dublin: P. Byrne, 1793) (Feb. 4, 1793).
[214] *Id.* at 104.
[215] *Id.* at 105.

inflicted on any malefactors, but on those of the lowest and meanest degree...."[216]

Third, Duigenan maintained that "these laws have been seldom put in execution, and then never generally, but in small districts of the country, which have been infested by dangerous commotions, and insurrections of Catholics!"[217] However, "the better sort of Catholics never imagined" that such laws would be applied to them, as illustrated by the peaceable marching in Dublin of armed Protestant corps and armed Catholic corps, the latter "without a man of them having a license to carry arms, or having ever applied for one...."[218]

An underlying cause of disorder and discontent in Ireland was economic deprivation. Duigenan himself noted its historical root: "As all the Catholics of Ireland, who were of age able to take arms, had engaged in the rebellion, in the years 1689, 1690, and 1691, the estates of almost all the Catholics of Ireland, except the few who qualified themselves to take the benefit of the capitulation of Limerick, became forfeited by that rebellion, and were granted to Protestants...."[219] As that comment reflected, instead of seeking reconciliation and mutual prosperity, English policy was to keep Irish Catholics poor, disarmed, and without political power.

Finally, Duigenan contrasted Irish Catholics from the English as follows: "Catholics in Ireland are prohibited from keeping arms; no such prohibition is in England; but every Irish Catholic of any rank above the mere working artizan or peasant may obtain a licence to keep

---

[216] *Id.* at 105–06.
[217] *Id.* at 106.
[218] *Id.* at 107.
[219] *Id.* at 122.

and carry arms, at the expense of one shilling, if he thinks fit to apply for it...." Besides being excluded from grand juries and the right to vote for representatives in Parliament, he continued, "[t]he only difference then in the situation of Catholics in England and in Ireland, is that Catholics in Ireland may be deprived of arms, unless they obtain licences for using them...."[220]

Those comments once again verify that the long forgotten Statute of Northampton had no application to the right peaceably "to keep and carry arms." The English, even Catholics, could bear arms without a license; only the Irish Catholics required a license, and only the wealthy could get one.

In the midst of consideration of the bill to accord Catholics more limited rights, Attorney General Arthur Wolfe, the 1st Viscount Kilwarden, alerted the House that "considerable quantities of gunpowder and fire-arms had been clandestinely imported, and seized as they were secretly [being] convey[ed] to the interior parts of the kingdom...." Trouble was brewing. He thus proposed a bill "to prevent the exportation of gun-powder and fire-arms, without a licence from the chief governor, and also to prevent the keeping of gun-powder, above a certain quantity, without licence."[221]

Lord Edward Fitzgerald objected "that the clause imposing penalties on the removal of arms from one place to another, was an infringement on the liberty of the subject." He depicted that provision

---

[220] *Id.* at 123.
[221] *Id.* at 149 (Feb. 5, 1793).

in a larger context, asking: "In case of an attack upon his House, would he not be allowed arms, without license, for its defence?"[222]

Robert Graydon defended the Catholic petition, which "is substantially true; it complains that the Catholic, by law, cannot carry arms – the law is so; it complains that the Catholics, on refusing to discover their arms, are liable to be whipped. That law is yet in force...." Nor could it be denied "that the Catholics are excluded from the franchise of the constitution...."[223]

Regarding the prohibition on Catholics carrying arms, Graydon asked about Protestants, if "we are afraid we have injured you too much, to suffer you to carry arms even for your own defence? It is a prohibition of conscious severity...." But it was "constantly broken, and meritoriously departed from by yourselves, who arm Catholic servants against your own laws; as you arm Catholic soldiers against your enemies, and against your law...." He continued:

> [A] Catholic farmer wants to preserve his life and property, that is no reason for arming him according to law; you use, in this particular, the laws as your sport, and the Papists as your property; they may arm as your servants and as your mercenaries, but not as citizens; thus, by our connivance as individuals, and severity as legislators, they are encouraged to despise the laws, and to hate them.[224]

Finally, Graydon observed that, as long as the Catholics feared criminals more than the legal punishment, "this law, prohibitory on carrying arms, is not observed, and cannot be observed; what more can

---

[222] *Id.* at 153 (Feb. 7, 1793).
[223] *Id.* at 280 (Feb. 22, 1793).
[224] *Id.* at 290.

the state take away than the robber? Unless the penalty is made something more, than the loss of property and life, men will carry arms to defend both."[225]

Fear was expressed about the spread of radical ideas and even armies from Revolutionary France, which had just declared war on Great Britain. Moderate voices argued that according all of the rights of Englishmen to the Irish Catholics would remove the supposed need for the historical repression. Henry Grattan, who championed a liberalized policy toward Ireland, observed that "the most effectual way of combating French principles in this country, was not by arms, but by giving to Ireland all the advantages of a British constitution...."[226] That was not to be.

The Irish Parliament went forward and enacted An Act for the Relief of His Majesty's Popish, or Roman Catholick Subjects of Ireland (1793). Its preamble noted that "various acts of Parliament have been passed, imposing on his Majesty's subjects professing the Popish or Roman Catholic religion, many restraints and disabilities to which other subjects of this realm are not liable; and, from the peaceable and loyal demeanour of his Majesty's Popish or Roman Catholic subjects, it is fit that such restraints and disabilities shall be discontinued...."[227]

While removing various legal disabilities imposed on Catholics, the law also contained limits, one of which applied to arms:

> That nothing herein contained shall extend to authorize any Papist or person professing the Popish or Roman Catholic religion, to have or

---

[225] *Id.*
[226] *Id.* at 151 (Feb. 6, 1793).
[227] An Act for the Relief of His Majesty's Popish, or Roman Catholick Subjects of Ireland, § 1, 33 Geo. 3, c.21 (1793).

keep in his hands or possession any arms, armour, ammunition, or any warlike stores, sword blades, barrels, locks, or stocks of guns or fire arms, or to exempt such person from any forfeiture or penalty inflicted by any act respecting arms, armour or ammunition, in the hands or possession of any Papist, or respecting Papists having or keeping such warlike stories....[228]

This provision applied to commoners, not to persons of sufficient wealth. The ban exempted "Papists or persons of the Popish or Roman Catholic religion, seized of a freehold estate of one hundred pounds a-year, or possessed of a personal estate of one thousand pounds or upwards, who are hereby authorized to keep arms and ammunition as Protestants now by law may...." Nor did it apply to Catholics "possessing a freehold estate of ten pounds yearly value, and less than one hundred pounds, or a personal estate of three hundred pounds, and less than one thousand pounds," who took the oath of allegiance to the King; such persons "may keep and use arms and ammunition as Protestants may...."[229] No license was required.

For the majority of Irish Catholics who had limited means, it was enforcement as usual. A 1795 enactment applicable to Dublin authorized magistrates to search places "for concealed arms" and to seize firearms possessed by any person "not qualified by law to bear or carry arms...."[230] Even so, a separate law restricting the importation of arms allowed a person "to land such arms as he shall have actually carried for the defence of his person, and as are usually carried for personal defence," on registering them with the port authority.[231]

---

[228] *Id.* § 6.
[229] *Id.*
[230] An Act for more effectually preserving the Peace within the City of Dublin, 35 Geo. 3, c.36, § 37 (1795).
[231] An Act to Prevent the Importation of Arms, 35 Geo. 3, c.42, § 2 (1796).

In short, unlike Englishmen, Irish Catholics were not recognized as having a right to bear arms. In the context of the pertinent laws and debates thereon, to "bear arms" simply referred to an individual carrying arms, not to service in a militia. Significantly, this history took place beginning a century before, and ending just after, America's adoption of the Second Amendment, which guaranteed the right to bear arms to the people at large without any distinction between Protestants and Catholics.

Chapter Three

A RIGHT FOR ALL SEASONS

The right of an Englishman to bear arms, even in tumultuous times, would be reaffirmed in legal opinions and in debates in Parliament during the eighteenth and nineteenth centuries. The Declaration of Rights of 1689 was read to protect the right to carry arms, without any hint that such right was prohibited by the Statute of Northampton or otherwise. What was seen as a universal right in England was reversed in Ireland, due to the anti-Catholic prejudice felt by the English people and their Protestant rulers.

It was not until 1870 that a license to carry a gun was required in England, but anyone could buy the license at a post office. And it was not until after World War I, in 1920, that an Englishman had to show a "need" to the authorities for a license to carry, representing the loss of the right to bear arms. The medieval Statute of Northampton made rare, inconsequential guest appearances, only to flicker out in the early twentieth century.

A) The Right "To Keep and Bear Arms": The Gordon Riots

During June 2–9, 1780, London was racked with unprecedented rioting and destruction that began with an anti-Catholic protest led by

Lord George Gordon[232] and was fueled by grievances of the working class. Army and militia units suppressed the riots at the cost of hundreds of lives. The Gordon riots raised issues about use of the standing army in civil disorders and the extent to which law-abiding citizens could associate and go armed to protect themselves and their communities.

In debate in the House of Lords on June 19, 1780, the Duke of Richmond, Charles Lennox, regretted the failure of the magistrates, who were in charge of law enforcement, to suppress the riots and the use of the military in their place. He denounced the letters from Lord Jeffrey Amherst, commander-in-chief of the British army, ordering his forces "to disarm the citizens, who had taken up arms, and formed themselves into associations, for the defense of themselves and their properties. The letters he considered as a violation of the constitutional right of Protestant subjects to keep and bear arms for their own defense."[233] Except for the reference to Protestants, that was the same terminology used in the American state arms guarantees and that would reappear in the Second Amendment, and it clearly referred to the right of individuals to carry arms. It is noteworthy that the Duke was a reformer who supported the American colonists and, in 1778, initiated the debate proposing the removal of the British troops from America.[234]

Lord Amherst replied that a mob had gotten possession of firelocks and other arms and were doing great mischief. The letters ordered that the arms be seized from the rioters, but they could not be

---

[232] One grievance was an act repealing some of the discriminatory provisions against Catholics, the Papists Act 1778, 18 George III c.60.

[233] 49 *The London Magazine or Gentleman's Monthly Intelligencer* 467 (1780).

[234] 19 *Parliamentary History of England* 842 (London: T. C. Hansard, 1814) (Mar. 5, 1778).

construed to mean "that the arms could be taken away from the associated citizens, who had very properly armed themselves for the defence of their lives and property."[235]

Earl Henry Bathurst, President of the Privy Council, "stated the difference between the right of bearing arms for personal defense, and that of bodies of the subjects arraying themselves, without a commission from the king; the latter he declared to be unlawful."[236] So for the Earl, individuals, but not large groups, had a right to carry arms for self-defense. Interestingly, he was an author of the Intolerable Acts of 1774 that so enraged the Americans.

Debate ensued in the English Parliament about whether the military should be used in civil disorders.[237] No one questioned the right of individuals to bear arms for self-defense against the rioters.

In his tract *The Ancient Common-Law Right of Associating with the Vicinage*, Granville Sharp advocated the right of forming armed associations for mutual protection against rioters and favored a popular militia over a standing army. He argued that "the law not only *permits*, but absolutely *requires*, EVERY PERSON to *have arms*, and be EXERCISED in the use of them."[238] Specifically, while the law previously required every man to be exercised in the long bow, "the reason of the law holds equally good, to *require the exercise* of ALL MEN in the use of the present fashionable weapons, the *musket* and *bayonet*."[239]

---

[235] 49 *The London Magazine* 467–68.

[236] *Id.* at 468.

[237] *Id.* at 468–69.

[238] Granville Sharp, *Tracts, Concerning the Ancient and Only True Legal Means of National Defence, by a Free Militia* (3rd ed.), 14 (London: Dilly, 1782).

[239] *Id.* at 14–15.

However, without citing any authority, Sharp claimed that "as allowed by law" in the Declaration of Rights of 1689 "respects the limitations" of 33 Hen. VIII c.6 restricting "such arms as were liable to be concealed," including "cross-bows, little short hand-guns, and little hagbuts [arquebuses]...."[240] That referred to An Acte Concerninge Crosbowes and Handguns (1541), which prohibited persons not having property of the yearly value of one hundred pounds to "shote in...or use to kepe in his or their houses or elsewhere" the listed weapons.[241]

That 1541 act of Henry VIII had fallen into disuse before the seventeenth century.[242] Decades before the Glorious Revolution of 1688, gunsmiths had designed, among other handguns, the English screw-barrel flintlock pistol, and they were being made in ever-greater quantities, in pocket and medium sizes, by the end of the century.[243] During and after the reign of Queen Anne, who succeeded William III, these pistols were widely carried, such as by travelers for defense against highwaymen.[244]

In a 2016 opinion, an American court implied that Henry VIII's gun law, and Granville Sharp's claim that such law provided context to the Declaration's reference to "as are allowed by law," somehow supported a ban on carrying firearms under America's Second Amendment.[245] America's Founders would have considered Henry VIII's law to be the very type of infringement the Second Amendment was adopted to prevent. And if the Declaration of Rights was read to

---

[240] *Id.* at 17–18.
[241] 33 Hen. VIII c.6.
[242] Robert Held, *The Age of Firearms* 66–67 (New York: Bonanza Books, 1957).
[243] *Id.* at 90; John Nigel George, *English Pistols & Revolvers* 37 (New York: Arco Publishing, 1962).
[244] George, *English Pistols & Revolvers*, 46-47.
[245] *Peruta v. County of San Diego*, 824 F.3d 919, 932 (9th Cir. 2016) (en banc).

mean that handguns could be banned because Henry VIII passed such a law, that would be no more acceptable than limiting the right to have arms—as the Declaration explicitly did—to Protestants. As Judge Diarmuid O'Scannlain of the U.S. Court of Appeals for the Ninth Circuit wrote, "instead of stitching into the Second Amendment every odd law that hemmed in the rights of fourteenth century Englishmen, we are to consider those English laws only to the extent they inform the original public understanding of the Second Amendment."[246]

Henry VIII, who had two of his wives beheaded, also got Parliament to pass the Treasons Act of 1534, which imposed the death penalty on anyone who disavowed the prior Act of Supremacy making the King the head of the Church of England.[247] Sir Thomas More was beheaded for doing just that. Imagine an American court citing that law to justify restrictions on the free exercise of religion and freedom of speech under America's First Amendment.

While Granville Sharp's reference to the obsolete act of Henry VIII seems odd, he went on to say that *proper arms for defence...*are clearly authorized," and that English law had "always required the people to be armed, and not only to be *armed*, but to be *expert in arms*...."[248] In short, "the people are required to have *'arms of defence and peace,'* for mutual as well as private defence...."[249]

The Recorder of London, the city's top legal advisor, agreed, weighing in with his opinion of July 1780 as follows:

---

[246] *Young v. Hawaii*, 2021 WL 1114180, *148 (9th Cir. 2021) (en banc) (O'Scannlain, J. dissenting).
[247] 26 Hen. 8. c.13.
[248] Sharp, *Tracts*, 18.
[249] *Id.* at 27.

The right of his majesty's Protestant subjects, to have arms for their own defense, and to use them for lawful purposes, is most clear and undeniable. It seems, indeed, to be considered, by the ancient laws of this kingdom, not only as a *right,* but as a *duty*; for all the subjects of the realm, who are able to bear arms, are bound to be ready, at all times, to assist the sheriff, and other civil magistrates, in the execution of the laws and the preservation of the public peace. And that right, which every Protestant most unquestionably possesses, *individually,* may, and in many cases *must,* be exercised collectively, is likewise a point which I conceive to be most clearly established by the authority of judicial decisions and ancient acts of parliament, as well as by reason and common sense.[250]

Nothing in the broadly worded right of subjects "to have arms for their own defense" limited its exercise to one's home. It was an individual right that may be exercised individually and collectively, meaning that people in a community could arm, associate, and defend themselves and their neighborhoods. That had occurred during the Gordon riots, and it was vindicated in the above debate in the House of Lords and the opinion of the Recorder of London.

B) The Seizure of Arms Act

In 1819, some sixty thousand unarmed demonstrators assembled in St. Peter's Field, Manchester, England, to protest high bread prices and demand parliamentary reform. Cavalry units, including the Manchester Yeomanry, were called out to disperse the crowd, and they did so with gun and saber, killing a dozen or so and injuring hundreds. It was called

---

[250] William Blizard, *Desultory Reflections on Police: With an Essay on the Means of Preventing Crime and Amending Criminals* 59-60 (London: Baker & Galabin, 1785) (emphasis in original).

the Peterloo Massacre, a caustic reference to the recent battle of Waterloo.

Americans across the Atlantic viewed the Peterloo Massacre as an example of the potential abuse of a select militia that could be ordered to attack fellow citizens, in contrast with a general militia composed of the body of the people, which would not do so. Former President John Adams wrote: "The American states have owed their existence to the militia for more than two hundred years....Impose its constitution by every prudent means, but never destroy its universality. A select militia will soon become a standing army, or a corps of Manchester yeomanry."[251]

In a demonstration shortly after the Peterloo Massacre, some protestors carried sticks, pikeheads, and pistols, but the crowd dispersed without violence. Parliament would react with legislation against potential social upheaval, placing restrictions on assembly, the press, and arms. The protest leaders would be charged with instigating an unlawful, armed assembly.[252]

The disorders prompted passage of the Seizure of Arms Act (1819), which provided that in certain designated counties, on credible evidence that a person possessed a pike or spear, or possessed a dagger, pistol, or other weapon "for any purpose dangerous to the Public Peace," a justice of the peace could obtain a warrant to search a house for the arms, which could be seized unless the owner prove that the arms were not possessed for such purpose. Also, a person could be

---

[251] William H. Sumner, *An Inquiry into the Importance of the Militia to a Free Commonwealth in a Letter...To John Adams...With His Answer* 70 (Boston: Cummings & Hilliard, 1823).
[252] Malcolm, *To Keep and Bear Arms*, 166–68.

arrested if "found carrying Arms in such manner and at such times…for purposes dangerous to the Public Peace…."[253] Merely carrying arms by itself remained lawful.

In debates in the House of Commons, T. W. Anson opposed the bill because he found it "so much at variance with the free spirit of their venerated constitution, and so contrary to that undoubted right which the subjects of this country had ever possessed – the right of retaining arms for the defence of themselves, their families, and property…."[254] Lord Castlereagh saw precedents for the bill in the acts to disarm the Scottish Highlands of 1715 and 1745.[255]

Mr. Brougham averred that "an Englishman's house [is] his castle against the unwarranted intrusion of the police, or against the attack of thieves," and that "he had a right to arms for his defence…to remind those rulers that the weapons of defence might be turned against them if they broke the laws, or violated the constitution."[256] But Mr. Canning reminded his colleagues why the Declaration of Rights of 1689 "recognized the general right of the subject to have arms," yet excluded Papists, who "were armed against the existing government," just as the

---

[253] An Act to Authorise Justices of the Peace, in Certain Disturbed Counties, to seize and detain Arms collected or kept for purposes dangerous to the Public Peace, 60 Geo. III & 1 Geo. IV c.2, §§ 1 & 3 (1819). This temporary law with limited scope required evil intent to make carrying firearms unlawful. It leads one to question why an 1806 manual for justices of the peace would state that a constable may arrest a person "wearing [h]augbuts, or guns, or pistols, of any sort," and require them to obtain a surety, "unless they be licensed from the Council or the Commander in chief" – apparent references to the Council of State in the Interregnum and to the Lord Protector Oliver Cromwell. 1 Gilbert Hutcheson, *Treatise on the Offices of Justice of Peace* app. I at xlviii (Edinburgh: William Creech, 1806) (citing Cromwell, *Instructions Concerning Constables* (1665)).

[254] 41 *Hansard's Parliamentary Debates* 1128 (London: T. C. Hansard, 1840) (March 14, 1819).

[255] *Id.* at 1134–35.

[256] *Id.* at 1140–41.

pending bill "excepted the disaffected in the disturbed districts who were in arms against the law and authorities of the land."[257]

Further discussion clarified that possession of pikes was considered prima facie evidence of intent to use them unlawfully, but that did not "apply to common arms, such as guns, pistols, &c.," which "might be kept merely for purposes of defence...."[258] Earl Gray objected to the bill on the basis that, under the Bill of Rights, "every man was entitled to the possession of his arms, not only for defence against the assassin or the midnight robber, but to enforce his constitutional right of resistance to oppression, if deprived of the benefit of the laws."[259] The Seizure of Arms Act nonetheless would pass in 1819 as a temporary measure to prevent insurrection.

But the right of individuals peaceably to carry arms continued to be recognized. In the criminal case of *Rex v. Dewhurst*, which arose out of the demonstration following the Peterloo massacre, the judge gave the following jury instruction based on the Declaration of Rights:

"The subjects which are Protestants may have arms for their defence suitable to their condition, and as allowed by law."

But are arms suitable to the condition of people in the ordinary class of life, and are they allowed by law? A man has a clear right to protect himself when he is going singly or in a small party upon the road where he is traveling or going for the ordinary purposes of business. But I have no difficulty in saying you have no right to carry arms to a public

---

[257] *Id.* at 1143.
[258] *Id.* at 695 (Dec. 3, 1819) (exchange between the Earl of Rosslyn and Lord Sidmouth).
[259] *Id.* at 749 (Dec. 6, 1819).

meeting, if the number of arms which are so carried are calculated to produce terror and alarm....[260]

In sum, debate on the Seizure of Arms Act in 1819 revealed the continued vitality of the Englishman's right to keep and bear arms. In supposedly disaffected districts, pikes were suspect, but guns and pistols could be seized only if evidence existed of the intent to use them unlawfully. Individuals and small groups could peaceably carry arms, but armed crowds that produced alarm were not protected by the Declaration of Rights.

C) The "Universal Right" to Bear Arms in England "Is Reversed in Ireland"

In England, it was lawful for the subjects to carry arms peaceably without a license or authorization. That was the legacy of the Declaration of Rights, and the obsolete Statute of Northampton from 1328 did not apply. In largely oppressed Ireland, it was the opposite— an Irish subject could not carry arms without a license, and most Catholics were ineligible for one because they lacked the wealth to satisfy the property qualification. That status was based on the anti-Irish Catholic discriminatory statutes, and not based on the again irrelevant Statute of Northampton. The following analyzes how these two opposite traditions played out in the enactment of Irish arms acts in 1807 and 1843.

The United Kingdom of Great Britain and Ireland was established by the Acts of Union of 1800. The Irish Parliament was merged into

---

[260] *Rex v. Dewhurst*, 1 State Trials, New Series 529, 601-02 (1820).

the English Parliament. Legislation for both England and Ireland was thereafter passed by the U.K. Parliament.

The 1807 Arms Act required every Irish person who "by Law is entitled to keep Arms" to register them and imposed other restrictions.[261] In debate, Lord Milton objected that the bill "would not be borne with in England, but in cases of the most imperious necessity...."[262] Recalling the prelude to the American Revolution, Milton "had hoped the attempt to disarm New England, as we had done, would not so soon have been forgotten, but would have operated to restrain ministers from thus attempting to disarm Ireland. He had hoped, instead of this, that the Irish would be restored to their rights, and henceforward be allowed the rights of Englishmen."[263]

"Ministers were well aware that by the Bill of Rights every British subject had a right to bear arms," Mr. Dillon noted, cautioning against "unnecessary infractions of the best articles of the constitution...."[264] Proponents did not deny these principles as to the English, but Ireland had to be kept under the heel, and so the bill was passed into law.

An even stricter law for Ireland would be enacted in 1843 requiring everyone in possession of a firearm to apply for a license to keep arms, which would also authorize the arms to be carried outside the home. For the first time, firearms would require a serial number corresponding to the registration of the firearm to a specific person.

---

[261] An Act to prevent improper Persons from having Arms in Ireland, 47 Geo. 3 Sess. 2, c.54, §§ 1 & 2 (1807).
[262] 9 *Hansard's Parliamentary Debates* 1086 (Aug. 7, 1807).
[263] *Id.* at 1087.
[264] *Id.* at 1092.

Lord Edward Eliot, a Tory who was the chief spokesman for the bill, explained that Ireland had long been subject to special restrictions on the possession of arms.[265] Mr. Grattan conceded that the proposal was "a restriction on the liberty of the subject," but that from the time of William III to 1783, "no man professing the Roman Catholic religion was entitled to carry arms"; that was relaxed in 1783 so that "men possessed of a certain amount of property were allowed to bear arms. Thus the common-law right of carrying arms, which every subject possessed, has long been limited in a very great degree in Ireland...."[266]

Lord Clements detailed how applications to possess arms were arbitrarily denied based on the applicant's appearance or the fact that he lived in a thatch house.[267] Mr. Ross opposed the bill as "a restriction on the common-law right to bear arms" and "an invasion of a constitutional right," the same right "that enabled the people of the United States to oppose to our tyranny."[268] W. S. O'Brien "claimed for Ireland the same rights with respect to bearing arms as those enjoyed by Englishmen...."[269] Mr. Watson saw the bill as "contrary to the constitution of the country. It was acknowledged by the Bill of Rights, which being declaratory was part of the common law, that every citizen had a right to possess himself with arms for any lawful purposes, and that bill was as applicable to Ireland as to England."[270]

M. J. O'Connell held that "the common law in the two countries was identical, and by the bill of rights, the right to carry arms for self-

---

[265] 69 *Hansard's Parliamentary Debates* 996–97 (May 29, 1843).
[266] *Id.* at 999.
[267] *Id.* at 1020.
[268] *Id.* at 1098–99.
[269] *Id.* at 1118.
[270] *Id.* at 1123.

defence was not created, but declared as of old existence."[271] Mr. Wyse saw no "violent or revolutionary outbreak" that would justify curtailing "the right to bear arms for self-protection."[272] "He considered the people of Ireland to possess every constitutional right equally with the people of England," and thought it improper "to restrict the Irish people from the free exercise of their admitted constitutional right to bear arms."[273]

Proponents of the 1843 bill conceded the right of Englishmen to carry arms, but they still thought restrictions were necessary in Ireland. Sir James Graham admitted "that the carrying of arms is a noble and distinguishing mark of freedom, and a constitutional right of great value. I would not infringe that right without the most grave consideration...." But he agreed with Lord Eliot that serious crimes abounded in Ireland.[274]

Lord John Russell, the Whig and Liberal politician who would in later years serve as Prime Minister, explained succinctly:

> the right to bear arms, which is the universal right in England, and qualified only by individual circumstances, is reversed in Ireland; the right to bear arms here being the rule, the right to bear arms in Ireland being the exception. The noble Lord admits that it has been the principle of all Governments that you should require in Ireland a licence to bear arms, and that the right to bear arms should he held an exception to the general rule, although it be the general rule in England

---

[271] *Id.* at 1151.

[272] *Id.* at 1153 (May 31, 1843).

[273] *Id.* at 1578, 1581 (June 15, 1843).

[274] *Id.* at 1175–76 (May 31, 1843).

without any licence that every individual should be entitled to bear arms.[275]

Proponents of the bill did not dispute that, and instead argued that Ireland was a special case in need of special limitations. "Lord Eliot had always thought that the restriction on the common law right of the subject to carry arms was only to be justified by necessity...."[276]

William Sharman Crawford, who advocated equal rights for the Irish across the board, proposed a motion that read:

> That the unrestricted power of having, carrying, and using arms, for all legal purposes, is a right enjoyed by Englishmen and Scotchmen, and is one of the essential safeguards of freedom. That to limit or withhold this privilege, as regards Irishmen, creates an unjust, impolitic, and insulting distinction, and is a violation of that equality of rights which can be the only safe and just basis of imperial legislation....[277]

That motion failed, and the Parliament proceeded to pass An Act to Amend and Continue the Laws in Ireland Relative to the Registering of Arms (1843). To have arms, a person was required to submit an application, and an official would decide whether the applicant was "a fit and proper Person."[278] The law provided that "when any Person shall be found carrying Arms," a justice of the peace would examine the markings on the firearm and require the person to identify himself to ensure that it was registered.[279] If the firearm was registered to the

---

[275] 70 *Hansard's Parliamentary Debates* 66 (June 16, 1843).

[276] *Id.* at 456 (June 29, 1843).

[277] *Id.* at 1359–60.

[278] An Act to Amend and Continue...the Laws in Ireland Relative to the Registering of Arms, and the Importation, Manufacture, and Sale of Arms, Gunpowder, and Ammunition, 6 & 7 Vict. c. 74, §§ 1 & 3, (1843).

[279] *Id.* § 15.

bearer, he could go on his way, as no separate license to carry a firearm was required.

The debates on these Acts of 1807 and 1843 show that to "bear arms" was consistently used to refer to an individual carrying arms, which was described as an ancient liberty and a common law, constitutional right that was recognized in the Declaration of Rights. Englishmen were entitled to exercise that right without a license. But as Lord Russell put it so well above, "the right to bear arms, which is the universal right in England…is reversed in Ireland; the right to bear arms here being the rule, the right to bear arms in Ireland being the exception."

Those debates add insights into the understanding in America of the meaning of the Second Amendment as well. Americans also spoke English, and their British cousins meant the term "bear arms" to include the carrying of arms by an individual. So did the Americans in referring to the right to bear arms. The English understood their common law and Declaration of Rights to guarantee a universal right for the people at large to bear arms, and, as documented in the next unit of this book, the Americans had exactly the same understanding.

D) Mandatory Issuance of a License to Carry, 1870–1920

An Englishman could lawfully carry a firearm without any license requirement until 1870. In 1870, the Parliament enacted a law requiring a license to carry a firearm. Anyone could obtain the license by paying a small fee at a post office, and could then carry a firearm on the streets of London or just about anywhere else. Carrying a firearm without a license subjected the bearer to a fine, but not jail time.

No one suggested that the long-forgotten Statute of Northampton, even though it had not been repealed, had any applicability. This is yet another nail in the coffin of the claim by advocates in the United States today that the Statute prohibited the peaceable bearing of arms.

The Gun Licenses Act of 1870 provided for a "licence to be taken out yearly by every person who shall use or carry a gun in the United Kingdom [in] the sum of ten shillings." A gun included a firearm or an air gun. The license was an excise tax, and included the person's name, address, and date of purchase. Its issuance was mandatory to any individual who paid the tax; no official had discretion to decide whether the person had a "need" to carry a firearm. Any person who would "use or carry a gun elsewhere than in a dwelling-house or the curtilage thereof" without the license was subject to a penalty of ten pounds.[280]

In debate in the House of Commons, in response to the concern that the term "carrying" might apply to a seller carrying a gun to the buyer, the Chancellor of the Exchequer explained that "the clause was only intended to prevent arms being carried with the intention of using then."[281] One member unsuccessfully proposed setting the tax at five shillings for each chamber or barrel of a gun, "to put an end to the practice of carrying revolvers, which was growing among the working population in the Northern counties."[282] Another "thought the Bill a most arbitrary police measure for interfering with the freedom of Englishmen without excuse."[283] It would pass with little fanfare.

---

[280] Gun License Act, Act 33 & 34 Vict. c. 57 (1870).
[281] 202 *Hansard's Parliamentary Debates* 853 (June 23, 1870).
[282] *Id.* at 854 (Sir Henry Selwin-Ibbetson).
[283] *Id.* at 856 (Mr. Newdegate).

A poster announcing the Gun Licenses Act summarized its provisions and ended: "Licenses ten shillings each may be obtained at any post office...."[284] Anyone who paid the small tax could lawfully carry a firearm. As a member of Parliament would remark in debate on what became the Firearms Act of 1965: "The Gun Licence Act, 1870, is a revenue measure for county councils to obtain money for gun licences, in much the same way as county councils collect money for dog licences."[285] It remained on the books until 1967.[286]

The Pistols Act of 1903 restricted the sale of pistols to, and the carrying of pistols by, persons under 18 years old, as well as the sale of pistols to persons who were intoxicated or of unsound mind. "Pistol" was defined to include a firearm with a barrel under 230 mm (9 inches).[287] No further gun legislation would pass until 1920.

E) The Firearms Act of 1920: The "Good Reason" Requirement

If anyone thought that the moribund Statute of Northampton prohibited the peaceable carrying of firearms, the highest U.K. officials didn't know about it. The status of the law on carrying firearms was summarized in the Report of the Committee on the Control of Firearms of 1918 by Sir Ernley Blackwell of the Home Office as follows:

> In Great Britain prior to the Pistols Act of 1903 any person could purchase or keep in his possession a gun, pistol or other firearm or any number of such weapons without any restriction. The Gun License Act of 1870 only makes it necessary for him to obtain an Excise License before he can legally use or carry a gun outside the curtilage of his

---

[284] See photograph of poster at
https://en.wikipedia.org/wiki/Firearms_regulation_in_the_United_Kingdom.
[285] 707 *Hansard's Parliamentary Debates* 1165 (March 2, 1965) (Gordon Oakes).
[286] See Colin Greenwood, *Firearms Control: A Study of Armed Crime and Firearms Control in England and Whales* 17–18 (London: Routledge & Kegan Paul, 1972).
[287] Pistols Act of 1903, 3 Edward VII, c. 18.

dwelling-house, but a license can be obtained by the simple formality of buying one at a Post Office for the sum of 10s [shillings]. The Pistols Act of 1903 puts certain difficulties in the way of purchasing a pistol, i.e. a firearm with a barrel not exceeding nine inches in length, but even under that Act a person over 18 years of age has only to obtain a gun license from a Post Office, and on producing it to a dealer he can purchase a pistol or any number of pistols. If in succeeding years he wishes to use or carry a pistol, he must, of course, comply with the Act of 1870, and take out a gun license under that Act, but otherwise neither the Act of 1870 nor the Act of 1903 places any restriction upon the mere possession of guns, rifles, pistols or other firearms, or of any quantity of ammunition for them. Experience has shown that the Pistols Act is ineffective even for its limited purpose, as it is constantly evaded by making and selling pistols with barrels just over nine inches in length.[288]

Issued just four days after Armistice Day that ended the Great War, the Blackwell Report worried that "large numbers of pistols, and possibly other weapons, will have come into the possession of private persons, notably discharged soldiers and their relatives, and that the number of men skilled in the use of firearms will have greatly increased." Danger was expected from "(1) the savage or semi-civilised tribesmen in outlying parts of the British Empire, whose main demand is for rifles and ammunition, and (2) the anarchist or 'intellectual' malcontent of the great cities, whose weapons are the bomb and the automatic pistol."[289]

The concern abroad was the threat to the colonial Empire posed by movements for national self-determination, and domestically the menace was from radical elements that threatened the ruling class. The

---

[288] Report of the Committee on the Control of Firearms (unpublished, Home Office Nov. 15, 1918). http://dvc.org.uk/dunblane/blackwell.html.
[289] *Id.*

year before, the Russian Czar had been deposed and the Bolsheviks, a far left Communist party led by Vladimir Lenin, seized power. The Bolsheviks executed Czar Nicholas II and his family and sought to instigate world revolution. These events terrified the ruling elites throughout Europe and in the United Kingdom. In light of these fears and perceived threats, these same elites believed that far more stringent controls were needed than the meager requirement of paying the annual tax under the Gun Licenses Act to use and carry a firearm.

The result was enactment of the Firearms Act of 1920, which required a firearm certificate to purchase, possess, use, or carry a firearm, and gave discretion to the chief of police to decide if an applicant had "good reason for requiring such a certificate."[290] The Act was prompted more by fear of revolution than of crime. After a secret meeting of the Cabinet during its drafting, a skeptical secretary recorded: "I felt I had been to Bedlam. Red revolution and blood and war at home and abroad."[291]

In debate in the House of Commons, Lieutenant Commander Joseph Kenworthy opposed the bill on the basis that "one of the most jealously guarded rights of the English was that of carrying arms," which "is our last line of defence against tyranny...."[292] Earl Winterton found it "intolerable that...such a doctrine should be preached in this House as that it is desirable that people should arm themselves against the State," noting that "it is because of the existence of people of that type that the Government has introduced this Bill...."[293] Specifically,

---

[290] An Act to amend the Law relating to Firearms, 10 & 11 Geo. V, c.43, § 1 (1920).

[291] 1 Thomas Jones, *Whitehall Diary*, ed. Keith Middlemas 97 (Oxford 1969), quoted in Malcolm, *To Keep and Bear Arms*, 171.

[292] 130 *Hansard's Parliamentary Debates* 658 (June 10, 1920).

[293] *Id.* at 663–64.

"since the War, there are far more people...who not only know how to use firearms, but who...are prepared to use those firearms against the State and its officers" for "political reasons."[294]

So it was not until 1920 that a citizen of the United Kingdom needed a certificate from the police to authorize carrying a firearm. No one even remotely hinted that the Statute of Northampton already prohibited the peaceable bearing of arms. The reality was that such peaceable carry was lawful and that the ancient Statute was inapplicable and forgotten.

F) Final Flicker of the Statute of Northampton

No mention of the Statute of Northampton seems to appear in any English judicial decision in the eighteenth and nineteenth centuries. There were actually two prosecutions under the Statute in the early twentieth century that generated judicial decisions. In the second half of the twentieth century, three decisions on the subject of affrays discuss not only the Statute, but also Sir John Knight's case and Hawkins' commentaries thereon.

These five judicial decisions drive the final nails in the coffin of the argument that going armed peaceably was considered a crime under English law, and confirming that doing so in a manner to terrorize others was an essential element of the offense.

Rex v. Meade (1903) involved a chimney sweep from Bangor who drank heavily. One day, after quarreling with his brother, witnesses saw him fire a shot into the bedroom of his brother's house. At trial, he said he couldn't remember anything about the incident. The judge instructed

---

[294] *Id.* at 664–65.

the jury that "not only was the offense charged against the prisoner one under the Statute of Edward III, but also under the common law, by which he was liable to punishment for making himself a public nuisance by firing a revolver in a public place, with the result that the public were frightened or terrorized."[295] The magistrates were right to send this case for trial, the judge added, "in order that the public might know that people could not fire revolvers in the public streets with impunity."[296]

Meade was not liable under the Statute merely for carrying the revolver—he was liable for shooting it in public, thereby terrorizing people. More details of the case, and why the prosecution dug up the Statute of Northampton, was revealed over sixty years later.

Although the Statute had already fallen into desuetude by the time of Sir John Knight's Case in 1686, Parliament did not get around to repealing it formally, along with many other obsolete laws, until the Criminal Law Act of 1967.[297] In discussion in the House of Lords, Viscount Colville of Culross noted about the "incredibly ancient" Statute:

> [I]t was used in 1903 to effect the conviction of a gentleman who had had rather too much to drink in Bangor and went around the streets letting off a revolver to the peril of the populace. It appears that there was nothing else with which they could charge him, so they went back to the Statute of Northampton of 1328 and convicted him of riding in the street armed to the peril of the population.[298]

---

[295] *Rex v. Meade*, 19 L. Times Repts. 540, 541 (1903).
[296] *Id.*
[297] Criminal Law Act 1967, Schedule 3, Part I—Repeals of Obsolete or Unnecessary Enactments ("2 Edw. 3. c.3. The Statute of Northampton. The whole Chapter.").
[298] 278 *Hansard's Parliamentary Debates* 459 (Nov. 24, 1966).

That case, of course, was *Rex v. Meade,* discussed above. Lord Stonham, a junior minister at the Home Office, added that "though the case he mentioned was not quite that of a man riding about on the cobbles in armour, this Act makes it an offence punishable with life imprisonment to wear armour or display force except in the areas and at the times appointed for holding tournaments – that is, the medieval equivalent of military manæuvres." He added that "firing a revolver in the street" was also "an offence at Common Law," and that the Statute "can only be used for any modern purpose by stretching its terms...."[299]

Lord Stonham's comment that the Statute was about "a man riding about on the cobbles in armour" recalls Sir Edward Coke's explanation that the Statute originated in the days when "this deed of Chivalry was at random, whereupon great peril ensued,"[300] and the argument by Sir John Knight's counsel that the Statute "was made to prevent the people's being oppressed by great men."[301]

The Crown made one more attempt to revive the Statute, in the case of *Rex v. Smith,* decided in 1914 by the King's Bench in Ireland. The defendant fired a shot at the victim and challenged him to fight. He was indicted for firing at a person with felonious intent, but that was dropped in favor of a prosecution under the Statute of Northampton.[302] His conviction was reversed on appeal because the indictment failed to allege each element of the offense:

> Without referring to old principles, which are admitted by all, we think
> that the statutable misdemeanour is to ride or go armed without lawful
> occasion in terrorem populi.... The words "in affray of the peace" in

---

[299] *Id.* at 460.
[300] Coke, *Third Institute* 160.
[301] *Rex v. Knight,* Comb. 38, 90 Eng. Rep. 330 (K.B. 1686).
[302] *Rex v. Smith,* 2 Ir. R. 190, 202 (K.B. 1914).

the statute, being read forward into the "going armed," render the former words part of the description of the statutable offence. The indictment, therefore, omits two essential elements of the offence – (1) That the going armed was without lawful occasion; and (2) that the act was *in terrorem populi*.[303]

Recall that the Statute provided, in the language of 1328, that a person may "bring no force in affray of the peace, nor to go nor ride armed...."[304] As the *Smith* court held, the latter is read forward of the former, so that it means to go or ride armed in affray of the peace, which included the element of terror.

The *Meade* and *Smith* decisions should finalize any debate about the elements of the offense under the Statute of Northampton as including both going armed *and* doing so to the terror of the people. No small wonder that no mention is made of these decisions by adherents of the view that the Statute banned peaceable bearing of arms and overrides the right of the people to "bear arms" in the Second Amendment.[305]

G) English Courts Interpret the Crime of "Affray"

Other than *Meade* and *Smith*, there were three cases in the U.K.—decided in 1957, 1973, and 2001—in which courts had occasion to discuss the Statute of Northampton in the context of prosecutions for affray. As defined by Blackstone, "AFFRAYS (from *affraier*, to

---

[303] *Id.* at 204.

[304] 2 Edw. III c.3 (1328).

[305] "What does the Statute of Northampton provide us in terms of evaluating the protective scope of the Second Amendment outside the home? The answer is armed individual self-defense outside the home deserves only minimalist protection or categorical exclusion." Patrick J. Charles, "The Faces of the Second Amendment Outside the Home," 60 *Clev. St. L. Rev.* 1, 43 (2012).

terrify) are the fighting of two or more persons in some public place, to the terror of his majesty's subjects...."[306] As noted, the Statute itself would be formally repealed in 1967, along with a slew of other obsolete laws. The three decisions provide insightful analyses on the Statute by judges with no stake in any American controversy about the right to bear arms.

The first case was *Regina v. Sharp*, decided in 1957 by the Court of Criminal Appeal, which consisted of three judges.[307] The Lord Chief Justice Raynor Goddard wrote the opinion.

The issue was "whether, in the absence of any direct evidence that anyone was put in terror, it is sufficient if there is proof that the fight was between two persons in a public place and of such a nature as might well intimidate or frighten reasonable people."[308] A police constable came upon a crowd watching a fight between the two defendants, who were covered with blood from severe cuts and wounds, and one of whom had a razor.[309] The court found it remarkable that no reported case dealt with the issue, although Coke and Blackstone implied that combat in public necessarily implied terror to the subjects.[310] However, one commentator stood out:

> The author who devotes most attention to the matter is Hawkins, Volume 1, Chapter 28. He lays down that there may be an affray when there is no actual violence, as when a man arms himself with *dangerous and unusual weapons in such a manner as will naturally cause a terror* to the people. This, he says, was always an offence at common law and

---

[306] 4 Blackstone, *Commentaries* *145.
[307] *R. v. Sharp*, 41 Cr. App. R. 86 (1957).
[308] *Id.* at 89–90.
[309] *Id.* at 90.
[310] *Id.* at 90–91.

dealt with by many statutes. He then quotes in particular the Statute of Northampton, 1330 (2 Edw. 3, Chap. 8). Dealing with that statute, he says that *no wearing of arms is within the meaning of this statute unless it be accompanied with such circumstances as are apt to terrify the people.*[311]

This of course is Hawkins' classic statement that peaceably carrying arms was lawful, but carrying dangerous and unusual weapons in a manner that caused terror violated the Statute. While "wearing of unusual or dangerous weapons in public is only one species of affray," the court continued, it was up to the jury to find whether an affray was proven if no one testifies that he was put in terror.[312] The court then commented on the nature of dangerous and unusual weapons as follows:

> Just as the mere wearing of a sword in the days when this was a common accoutrement of the nobility and gentry would be no evidence of an affray, while the carrying in public of a studded mace or battle axe might be, so, if two lads indulge in a fight with fists, no one would dignify that as an affray, whereas, if they used broken bottles or knuckle dusters and drew blood, a jury might well find it was, as a passer-by might be upset and frightened by such conduct.[313]

The above examples are revealing. A sword was a common arm that was useful both for personal defense and for military purposes. By contrast, the mace and battle axe were military weapons that would be brought out only for combat. The impact from a mace could dent armor and thereby break bones and cause internal injury to organs.[314] Swung

---

[311] *Id.* at 91 (emphasis added).
[312] *Id.*
[313] *Id.* at 91–92 (emphasis added).
[314] "The Mace," https://renaissanceweapons.weebly.com/the-mace.html.

with two hands, a long-handed battle-axe could behead a man or a horse.[315] It would have been unusual for civilians to carry these offensive weapons, which would be apt to terrify others.

As the court went on to say, a traditional indictment for affray would have alleged an act to the terror of the subjects, which would have included acts such as "endeavouring by a display of force, though without necessarily using actual violence, to overawe the public, which was what was aimed at by the Statute of Northampton."[316] While evidence of the element of terror is required, it need not necessarily entail a person saying "I was terrified."[317]

While there was evidence in this case of an affray, the trial judge incorrectly instructed the jury that it did not matter who started the fight and that self-defense was immaterial. As the court held as to a person who is attacked: "If he was only defending himself and not attacking, that is not a fight and, consequently, not an affray."[318] The court thus quashed the convictions and ordered the defendants to enter into a recognizance and give a surety fifty pounds to keep the peace.[319]

Repeal of the Statute of Northampton was commented on in *Taylor v. Director of Public Prosecutions*, decided in 1973 by five members of the House of Lords,[320] which at the time was the court of

---

[315] The Battle Axe," https://www.english-heritage.org.uk/learn/teaching-resources/story-of-1066/collectible-9/.

[316] *R. v. Sharp*, 41 Cr. App. R. at 92.

[317] *Id.*

[318] *Id.* at 93.

[319] *Id.* at 94.

[320] *Taylor v. Director of Public Prosecutions*, 57 Cr. App. R. 915 (Lords 1973).

last resort in the U.K. (That function was replaced by the Supreme Court of the United Kingdom in 2007.)

The *Taylor* case involved a melee in which two police officers fought three brothers at a social club, tables were overturned, beer thrown all over, and frightened people screamed.[321] In pertinent part, counsel for the defendant contended that "brandishing a threatening weapon" was one type of affray provided by the Statute of Northampton, and counsel for the Crown submitted that the court should resolve "whether there was a common law offence of affray consisting in the brandishing of unusual weapons to the terror of the public and, if there was, whether this had survived the repeal of the Statute of Northampton 1328 (2 Edw. 3, c.3) by the Criminal Law Act 1967."[322]

While weapons were not involved in the fight, the above issue was relevant to the question of whether a single person could be guilty of an affray. Two of the brothers had been acquitted, so could the conviction of the third stand? The court ruled that one person in a fight could commit an affray where the fight terrorized others.[323]

The Lord Chancellor (Lord Hailsham of St. Marylebone) opined for the court that the offence of affray, "a very ancient common law misdemeanour," had been "brought into extensive use, after a long period of relative desuetude, only since the end of the last war," and particularly since a 1966 decision that an affray could occur in a private place, not just a public place.[324] That an affray could be committed by

---

[321] *Id.* at 916.
[322] *Id.* at 917–18.
[323] *Id.* at 922–23.
[324] *Id.* at 919.

one person was clear under the Statute of Northampton, which "forbids amongst other things the carrying or brandishing in public of unusual or terrifying weapons. The Statute of Northampton was relied on to sustain an indictment as recently as 1903."[325] That was the case of *Rex v. Meade*, which involved firing a revolver in a public place.[326] That wasn't very recent, and indicated that the Statute was a dead letter in the intervening years. It was now "repealed as obsolete or unnecessary by the Criminal Law Act 1967...."[327]

In considering whether the "display of force...without actual violence" but where terror is present can be an affray, the court noted that "the brandishing of a fearful weapon does constitute the offence, and has always done so.... From the older authorities it seems plain enough that mere words, unaccompanied by the brandishing of a weapon or actual violence, are not enough."[328] Stressing the necessity of "the element of terror," the court continued: "From the very earliest days the offence of affray has required this element, and all the early textbooks stress the derivation of the word from the French 'effrayer,' to put in terror."[329]

The offense of carrying a dangerous and unusual weapon includes the element of terror, which is not present in the peaceable carrying of a weapon. The court's reasoning makes that very clear:

> To my mind, it is essential to stress that the degree of violence required to constitute the offence of affray must be such as to be calculated to terrify a person of reasonably firm character. This should not be

---

[325] *Id.*
[326] *Rex v. Meade*, 19 L. Times Repts. 540, 541, 19 T.L.R. 540 (1903).
[327] *Taylor*, 57 Cr. App. R. at 919.
[328] *Id.* at 923–24.
[329] *Id.* at 924.

watered down. Thus, it is arguable that the phrase "*might* be frightened or intimidated" may be too weak. The violence must be such as to be *calculated* to terrify (that is, might reasonably be expected to terrify), not simply such as *might* terrify, a person of the requisite degree of firmness.[330]

That sinks the argument of the American advocates that going armed in and of itself would necessarily terrify others, without any evidence of such terror. [331] As stated above, the threat must be "calculated to terrify a person of reasonably firm character."

Lord James Reid added a concurring opinion noting that the offense (under the then-repealed Statute of Northampton) of "brandishing offensive weapons to the terror of the King's subjects," terror is "an essential element in the offence."[332] While it may not be necessary for persons present at an affray to testify that they were terrified, the circumstances must be such that "ordinary people like them would have been terrified. I say 'would,' not 'might,' have been."[333]

The nature of an affray arose again before the House of Lords in the 2001 case of *I v. Director of Public Prosecutions*.[334] ("*I*" was used instead of a name as the defendant was a juvenile.) When police approached a large gang of youths, they ran away, including eight who threw away petrol bombs they were carrying. None of the bombs were

---

[330] *Id.*

[331] E.g., Patrick J. Charles, "The Faces of the Second Amendment Outside the Home," 60 *Clev. St. L. Rev.* 1, 6 (2012) ("the Statute did not solely seek to regulate a particular conduct with the intent to terrify, but the activity of carrying arms among the public concourse. It was the act of carrying arms itself that was deemed to terrify the people").

[332] *Id.* at 926–27.

[333] *Id.* at 927.

[334] *I v. Director Of Public Prosecutions*, 2 Cr. App. R. 14, 216 (Lords 2001).

lit or brandished, and there was no fighting or disturbance.[335] The case posed two issues. First, "Whether the overt possession of a weapon may constitute a threat of violence for the purpose of affray when it is not used or brandished in a violent manner."[336] The second issue was, "In order to constitute the statutory offence of affray does the threat of unlawful violence have to be towards a person or persons present at the scene?"[337]

The opinion by Lord Brian Hutton, joined by the two other judges, held that "the carrying of dangerous weapons, such as petrol bombs by a group of persons can, in some circumstances, constitute the threat of violence, without those weapons being waved or brandished."[338] The court quoted from the *Sharp* decision Hawkins' words that an affray may exist where "a man arms himself with dangerous and unusual weapons in such a manner as will naturally cause a terror to the people," but that "no wearing of arms is within the meaning of this statute unless it be accompanied with such circumstances as are apt to terrify the people."[339]

The court reiterated the comment in *Sharp* that "the mere wearing of a sword in the days when this was a common accoutrement of the nobility and gentry would be no evidence of an affray," but that "the carrying in public of a studded mace or battle axe might be...."[340] It further noted that "endeavouring by a display of force, though without necessarily using actual violence, to overawe the public...was what

---

[335] *Id.*
[336] *Id.* at 218.
[337] *Id.* at 220.
[338] *Id.* at 223.
[339] *Id.* at 223–24.
[340] *Id.* at 224 (citation omitted).

was aimed at by the Statute of Northampton."[341] However, "mere words, unaccompanied by the brandishing of a weapon or actual violence, are not enough."[342]

Accordingly, the court held that "the carrying of dangerous weapons such as petrol bombs by a group of persons can constitute a threat of violence" under the law, or in the words of the lower court in this case, "the visible carrying in public of primed petrol bombs by a large number of what was obviously an East London gang out for no good was clearly capable of constituting a threat of unlawful violence."[343] (The lower court was the Queen's Bench, which was an intermediate appellate court consisting of two judges.)

The above was further qualified by the words of the Queen's Bench, fully endorsed here by Lord Hutton, as follows: "I stress, however, that mere possession of a weapon, without threatening circumstances of the sort that I have mentioned, is not enough to constitute a threat of unlawful violence. So, for example, the mere carrying of a concealed weapon could not itself be such a threat."[344] Agreeing, another Queen's Bench judge in the same case had added:

1. Mere possession of an offensive weapon does not amount automatically to a threat of unlawful violence;

---

[341] *Id.*

[342] *Id.* (citation omitted).

[343] *Id.* at 225.

[344] *Id.* at 226, quoting *I v. Director of Public Prosecutions*, 1 Cr. App. R. 251, 257 (Queen's Bench 1999) (opinion by Auld L.J.).

2. It may, however, do so if the weapon is visible and held in circumstances amounting to a threat to another of unlawful violence. Whether it does or not is a question of fact;

3. A group of 40 or 50 young men, of whom eight or nine are openly carrying petrol bombs, in a normally populous place, on the concourse outside of a block of flats, and in an area with a history of gang warfare, is capable of amounting to a threat of unlawful violence.[345]

The above comments about visibility stemmed directly from the principle that, to be an offense, the carrying of dangerous weapons must be done in a manner to create terror to the subjects, which would not exist if the arms were carried concealed. While the opinions of the Lords agreed with points one and two above, those opinions disagreed with the third point because no one was actually present who would have been terrorized.

Thus, even when the weapons are carried openly, no affray exists if no persons are present who would be terrorized.[346] Recall that the persons present where the petrol bombs were carried were all members of the same gang, all of whom fled when police arrived. There was thus no threat of violence to anyone: "Whether there is a threat of violence towards a person present at the scene constituted by the carrying of a weapon or weapons…does not arise in the present case because, apart from the police officers towards whom there was no threat, no one was present at the scene."[347]

While not guilty of an affray, the court concluded, the defendants could have been charged with carrying an offensive weapon or

---

[345] *Id.*, 1 Cr. App. R. at 259–60 (opinion by Hughes J.).
[346] *Id.*, 2 Cr. App. R. at 229.
[347] *Id.* at 231.

possession of explosives.[348] The court added: "The present case demonstrates that a person should not be charged with the offence [of affray] unless he uses or threatens unlawful violence towards another person actually present at the scene and his conduct is such as would cause fear to a notional bystander of reasonable firmness."[349]

It is noteworthy that the United Kingdom's highest court, with no stake in American gun control controversies, read the Statute of Northampton not to ban the wearing of arms unless done in a manner to terrify others. That speaks volumes about current efforts to distort its meaning with the aim of reaching desired results in litigation in the United States.

In sum, the above English courts agreed with Hawkins that an affray may take place when dangerous and unusual weapons are carried "in such a manner as will naturally cause a terror to the people," but that "no wearing of arms" is within the Statute unless done so in a manner "apt to terrify the people." Thus, the brandishing of a fearful weapon calculated to terrify could be an affray. But the mere carrying of a concealed weapon could not be so, as no one would be terrorized.

From *Sir John Knight's Case* in 1686 to *I v. Director of Public Prosecutions* in 2001, the English courts read the Statute of Northampton to prohibit going armed in a manner to terrorize the subjects, but not to ban the peaceable carrying of arms, whether openly or concealed. Such courts may never have occasion to mention the Statute again, but one thing is clear—this medieval relic of English

---

[348] *Id.* at 231–32.
[349] *Id.* at 232.

history does nothing to diminish the American right to bear arms.

A final comment is in order about the historical context of the Statute of Northampton. Aside from its murky fourteenth century language, it appears to have been largely enforced against armed criminals who preyed on peaceable subjects. While the Statute fell into desuetude (disuse) by the seventeenth century, when attempted to be revived to prosecute Knight, it was read to apply only to going armed to the terror of the subjects. And as well be seen, as understood by the Americans in the eighteenth century and thereafter, the crime of going armed in a manner to terrorize others was fully consistent with the right peaceably to bear arms for self-defense.

Part Two

THE FUNDAMENTAL RIGHT TO BEAR ARMS AT THE AMERICAN FOUNDING

Chapter Four

FROM COLONIES TO INDEPENDENT STATES

From Jamestown to Plymouth Rock, the American settlers brought with them their rights as Englishmen and their arms to protect their lives, liberties, and property. When the British Crown sought to deprive them of their rights, the Americans resorted to their arms and created an independent America. This chapter traces the status and perception of the right to bear arms from colonial times through the American Revolution.

A) The Right to Bear Arms in the Colonies

The settlers had the liberty to carry their privately-owned arms openly or concealed in a peaceable manner. Most of the colonies required able-bodied males to provide their own arms and participate in the militia, and at times required persons to carry arms to church and other places. The main exception was that slaves were prohibited from having firearms in the same manner that the slaves were also denied their freedom.

Apart from restrictions on slaves, only four of the thirteen colonies appear to have imposed any limitations on carrying firearms outside the home during the fourth quarter of the seventeenth century: Virginia, New Jersey, Massachusetts, and New Hampshire. As discussed below, Virginia restricted armed assemblies, while part of New Jersey had an odd restriction on carriage. The only restrictions in Massachusetts and New Hampshire were laws prohibiting going armed "offensively." The other colonies appear to have left public carriage more or less unregulated.

This part examines laws in the colonies of Virginia and New Jersey during the seventeenth century, as well as typical colonial-era arms-bearing requirements and restrictions on slaves. These narrow and limited laws—viewed against the backdrop of the absence of any regulation in nine of the thirteen colonies—leave no doubt that the American colonies recognized and accepted a practically unlimited right to carry firearms outside the home.

Virginia

Carrying arms for defense was seen as both a right and a duty for English settlers in the New World. Under the First Charter of Virginia (1606), subjects were to have "Furniture of Armour, Weapons, Ordinance, Powder, Victual, and all other things, necessary for the said Plantations, and for their Use and Defence there...."[350] There were no restrictions on carrying arms from the time Jamestown was actually settled in 1607 until 1838, when the habitual carrying of a concealed weapon was made subject to a fine.

The recent immigrants learned quickly that having arms at the ready was necessary for mere survival. In 1619, the Virginia House of

---

[350] 7 *Federal and State Constitutions, Colonial Charters, and Other Organic Laws*, ed. Francis Newton Thorpe, at 3783, 3786 (Washington, D.C.: Government Printing Office, 1909). Similarly, the 1620 Charter of New England authorized the subjects "to take, load, carry, and transport in...Shipping, Armour, Weapons, Ordinances, Munition, Powder, Shott...and all other Things necessary for the said Plantation, and for their Use and Defense...." *Id.*, vol. 3, at 1834-35.

Burgesses required that "all suche as beare armes shall bring their pieces, swords, pouder and shotte" to church on the Sabbath day.[351]

In 1622, near the Jamestown settlement, hostile Native Americans initiated a series of surprise attacks: "In plantation after plantation from west to east, north and south of the James, the Indians turned on their unsuspecting hosts, in some places while sharing 'breakfast with people at their tables,' and with axes, hammers, shovels, tools, and knives slaughtered them indiscriminately, 'not sparing eyther age or sexe, man, woman, or childe; so sodaine in their cruell execution that few or none discerned the weapon or blow that brought them to destruction.'"[352]

Following the massacre, it was enacted that "every dwelling house shall be pallizaded for defence against the Indians," "no man go or send abroad without a sufficient partie will armed," "men go not to worke in the ground without their arms," and "the commander of every plantation take care that there be sufficient of powder and amunition within the plantation under his command and their pieces fixt and their arms compleate."[353]

In 1676, Virginia provided "that in going to churches and court in these times of danger, all people be enjoined and required to go armed for their greate[r] security."[354] Such laws were a double-edged sword

---

[351] Lyon Gardiner Tyler, *Narratives of Early Virginia, 1606-1625*, at 273 (New York: Charles Scribner's Sons, 1907).

[352] Bernard Bailyn, *The Barbarous Years: The Peopling of British North America: The Conflict of Civilizations, 1600-1675*, at 101–02 (New York: Random House, 2012).

[353] Laws of Virginia, March, 1623-4, 1 Statutes at Large (Virginia), ed. William W. Hening 127 (New York: R. & W. & G. Bartow, 1823). See also revised law of 1632, *id.* at 198.

[354] An Act for the Safeguard and Defence of the Country Against the Indians, 28 Car. II, 2 *id.* at 333.

for rulers, whose power was threatened by commoners who asserted arms-bearing as a right.

That was exemplified by Bacon's Rebellion in 1676, in which the lower classes seeking land rose against the colonial government, which opposed settlement on Indian lands. Led by Nathaniel Bacon, the revolt would be suppressed and its leaders hanged. Sir William Berkeley, Virginia's royal governor, captured the moment in his complaint: "How miserable that man is who governs a people when six parts of seaven at least are Poore Endebted Discontented and Armed."[355]

As Professor John Shy would note, the "distribution of weaponry" among the poor set the stage for a "politics of consent" in the coming century.[356] Bacon's Rebellion was the first insurrection against British rule, and it would be replicated, this time successfully, a century later.

A series of acts in 1677 sanctioned the execution of rebels and of anyone who spoke or wrote "any matter or thing tending to rebellion," and provided for whipping anyone who said anything disrespectful of those in authority.[357] Yet the right to bear arms was sufficiently off limits such that Berkeley only made it an offense for five or more persons to assemble with arms:

> And whereas by a branch of an act of assembly under Bacon made in March last, liberty is granted to all persons to carry their arms wheresoever they go, which liberty hath been found to be very

---

[355] Hellen H. Miller, *The Case for Liberty* 76 (Chapel Hill: University of North Carolina Press, 1965).

[356] John W. Shy, *A People Numerous and Armed* xii (Oxford: Oxford University Press, 1976).

[357] An Act for the Releife of Such Loyal Persons as have Suffered Losse by the Late Rebells, 29 Car. II, 2 Statutes at Large (Va.) 385 (1676–1677).

prejudicial to the peace and welfare of this colony. Be it therefore enacted…that if any person or persons shall…presume to assemble together in arms to the number of five or upwards without being legally called together in arms the number of five or upwards, they be held deemed and adjudged as riotous and mutinous….[358]

The book of record of Samuel Wiseman, principal clerk to the King's commissioners, contains the following entry regarding the complaints of the people of James City County:

Grievance: They ask that for their own defence they may be free to keep guns, buy ammunition and have their confiscated arms restored.

Answer: The restraint was only during the rebellion. Now every man may bear arms. They think, where possible, confiscated arms should be restored to their former owners. The meaner sort rely on their arms to get part of their livelihood.[359]

Other than the above restriction on armed assemblies, free subjects in Virginia could carry arms peaceably at will. However, a 1680 law provided that "it shall not be lawfull for any negroe or other slave to carry or arme himselfe with any club, staffe, gunn, sword or any other weapon of defence or offence…."[360]

George Webb, a Justice of the Peace of New-Kent County, Virginia, published a manual in 1736 listing among the powers of a constable: "He may take away Arms from such who ride, or go, offensively armed, in Terror of the People, and may apprehend the

---

[358] *Id.* at 386.

[359] *Bacon's Rebellion*, John D. Neville compl., 340 (Jamestown: Jamestown Foundation, 1976). And see *id.* at 360, 363, and 366.

[360] An act for preventing Negroes Insurrections, 32 Car. II, 2 Statutes at Large (Va.) 481 (1680).

Persons, and carry them, and their Arms, before a Justice of the Peace."[361] This clearly excluded persons who went armed peaceably. The title page of the manual averred that its contents were collected from the common law and statutes of England and Virginia's acts of assembly, and adapted to the constitution and practice of Virginia.

From the time the Commonwealth of Virginia was first settled in 1607 through the early nineteenth century, a free person could peaceably carry a firearm openly or concealed. Restrictions on carrying a pistol, dirk, or like edged weapon hidden from common observation would not be enacted until 1838. Today, it remains lawful in Virginia to carry firearms openly, i.e., visible to the public, while a permit to carry a concealed handgun is required but is available to the citizenry at large.

New Jersey

New Jersey had no restrictions on carrying firearms when it became a state in 1776. It did not restrict the carrying of concealed firearms until the early twentieth century, and left open carry untouched until 1966.[362] The following discusses its early colonial laws.

When the Province of New Jersey was claimed by England in 1664, the lords proprietors granted lands to persons who agreed to settle or plant there under certain conditions. Every freeman who arrived the first year "arm'd with a good musket" and ammunition and with six months provisions would be granted 150 acres. In the second year, "every free man and free woman that shall arrive in the said Province,

---

[361]George Webb, *The Office and Authority of a Justice of Peace* 92-93 (Williamsburg: William Parks, 1736).
[362] See sources at end of this discussion on New Jersey.

arm'd and provided as aforesaid," would receive 90 acres for planting.[363] In 1678, the colony would be divided between the provinces of East and West New Jersey.[364]

In 1686—three years before the adoption of the English Declaration of Rights—the province of East New Jersey enacted a law having no parallel in any other colony or even in West New Jersey. It provided that no person "shall presume privately to wear any pocket pistol...or other unusual or unlawful weapons"—which did not affect open carry—and that "no planter shall ride or go armed with sword, pistol, or dagger...excepting...all strangers, traveling upon their lawful occasions thro' this Province, behaving themselves peaceably."[365] The former is the only known restriction in any of the colonies on concealed carry. The latter provision on going armed may have implied an element of doing so offensively, as under a 1682 law East New Jersey constables pledged "to arrest all such persons, as in my presence, shall ride or go arm'd offensively, or shall make or commit any riot, affray, or other breach of the King's peace...."[366]

That element was explicit in the laws of some other colonies. A 1694 Massachusetts law punished "such as shall ride or go armed Offensively before any of their Majesties Justices, or other Their Officers or Ministers doing their Office or elsewhere, by Night or by

---

[363] The Concession & Agreement of the Lords Proprietors of the Province of New Caesarea, or New Jersey, to & with all and every the Adventurers & all such as shall settle or plant there (1664), in *The Grants, Concessions & Original Constitutions of the Province of New Jersey* 21–22 (Philadelphia: W. Bradford, 1881).

[364] "1676 Division of New Jersey – the East West Boundary," http://www.njfounders.org/history/1676-division-new-jersey-east-west-boundary.

[365] The Grants, Concessions & Original Constitutions of the Province of New Jersey at 289–90.

[366] A Bill for the Office of Coroner & Constable, ch. 18 (Mar. 1, 1682), in *The Grants, Concessions & Original Constitutions of the Province of New Jersey* 251.

Day, in Fear or Affray of Their Majesties Liege People...."[367] The crime was to go armed "offensively" in a manner to cause fear, not just to go armed *per se* with weapons that could be used for offense or defense.

Similarly, a 1699 New Hampshire law instructed justices of the peace to arrest "affrayers, rioters, disturbers or breakers of the peace, or any other who shall go armed offensively...."[368] These laws were not limited to specific types of arms such as handguns; the prohibition was on going armed offensively with any type of arms.

Back in England, the Glorious Revolution of 1688 overthrew the Catholic King, James II, who had disarmed Protestants. The Glorious Revolution resulted in the enactment of the Declaration of Rights, with its protection of the individual right to have arms. The significant political and legal changes brought about by the Glorious Revolution, the ousting of James II and the enactment of the Declaration of Rights, all led to the overthrow or reform of the royal governments in some of the American colonies, including Sir Edmund Andros' regime in New England, New York, and New Jersey.[369]

East New Jersey's 1686 law may or may not have survived the Glorious Revolution. A 1694 East New Jersey law made it unlawful for a slave "to carry any gun or pistol" into the woods or plantations unless with the owner or a white man, which implied that the latter persons could carry such arms.[370] The political division between East and West

---

[367] Mass. Acts, no. 6, 11-12 (1694).

[368] N.H. Laws 1 (1699).

[369] David S. Lovejoy, *The Glorious Revolution in America* 235 (N.Y.: Harper & Row, 1972).

[370] An Act concerning Slaves, &c., § 1, East New Jersey Laws, October 1694, ch.II, L&S 340-342. http://njlegallib.rutgers.edu/slavery/acts/A8.html.

New Jersey ended in 1712. A 1722 New Jersey law provided that any "Indian, Negro or Mullato Slave...carrying or Hunting with any Gun, without License from his Master, shall...be Whipt...."[371] Given that a free person had the legal authority to permit a slave to carry a firearm, obviously that same free person could lawfully carry a firearm directly.

New Jersey had no restrictions on the peaceable carrying of arms by free persons in the period 1776–1800, which included the period of the American Revolution and the adoption of the Bill of Rights with its Second Amendment.[372] In fact, New Jersey did not require a permit to carry a concealed firearm until 1905.[373] Open carry of firearms was perfectly legal in New Jersey until 1966, when a permit requirement was imposed.[374] Thus, in its entire history until 1966, the state of New Jersey allowed law-abiding citizens to carry firearms in some manner without first being authorized to do so by the state.[375]

Laws Requiring Citizens to Bear Arms Outside of Their Homes

Far from being prohibited from carrying firearms, colonial Americans were often required by law to carry them. These laws were designed to defend the settlers from attacks by hostile Indians, violence committed by criminals, and raids by pirates on the coast. This history was apparently not lost upon Justice Anthony Kennedy, who referenced the need of the settler to "to defend himself and his family against hostile

---

[371] An Act to prevent the Killing of Deer out of Season, and against Carrying of Guns & Hunting by Persons not qualified, § 6, 2 Bush 293, 295 (May 5, 1722). http://njlegallib.rutgers.edu/slavery/acts/A15.html.
[372] Acts of the General Assembly of the Province of New Jersey 235 (Burlington 1776); *Laws of the State of New Jersey* 19-21 (1800).
[373] 2 Compiled Statutes of New Jersey, 1759 (Soney & Sage 1911).
[374] N.J. Stat. Ann. § 2A:151–41 (1966).
[375] See *Drake v. Filko*, 724 F.3d 426, 447–49 (3rd Cir. 2013) (Hardiman, J., dissenting), *cert. denied*, 572 U.S. 1100 (2014).

Indian tribes and outlaws, wolves and bears and grizzlies and things like that...."[376]

It is difficult for modern Americans to appreciate the acute, consuming fear of "Indian raids" held by early Americans.[377] As American settlers continued to press westward, their expansion sparked increasing hostility from the Native Americans populating the frontier. After clashes in western Virginia in 1774, James Madison wrote that the attacking Indians were "determined in the extirpation of the inhabitants...."[378]

Moreover, the tensions between the settlers and the native peoples were repeatedly inflamed by first one European power and then another seeking to enlist the support of various tribes in their struggle to dominate the New World.[379] During the Revolutionary War, patriot militia captured British General Henry Hamilton, whose reputed nickname was "hair-buyer" for his payment to Indians of twenty dollars per scalp for men, women, and children.[380]

Firearms were also needed outside the home to defend against attack by domestic criminals. There was no professional police force at this time, so law-abiding, private citizens were often the first line of defense against criminal assaults.[381] A leading study of historical crime

---

[376] Transcript of Argument at 8, *District of Columbia v. Heller*, Mar. 18, 2008 (No. 07–290).
[377] D.R. Palmer, *The Way of the Fox: American Strategy in the War for America, 1775–1783*, at 86–92 (Westport, Conn.: Greenwood Press 1975).
[378] Noah Feldman, *The Three Lives Of James Madison* 15 (New York: Picador, 2017).
[379] Maurice Matloff ed., The Revolutionary War: A Concise Military History of America's War for Independence 16–17 (New York: David McKay Co., 1980).
[380] Feldman, *The Three Lives*, 32.
[381] Samuel Walker and Charles Kates, *The Police in America: An Introduction* 29 (New York: McGraw-Hill, 2013).

records found that, throughout most of the seventeenth century, the "peacetime murder rates for adult colonists…ranged from 100 to 500 or more per year per 100,000 adults, ten to fifty times the rate in the United States today."[382]

There was no shortage of criminals in the New World. Georgia was initially conceived of as a penal colony for debtors,[383] and though that plan was ultimately scrapped, in the eighteenth century Britain exported an estimated fifty thousand or more convicted criminals to America.[384]

The constant threat of foreign invasion and war also necessitated the citizen to be armed and ready to defend the country. King William's War (1688-1697) and Queen Anne's War (1702–1713) were just two of the wars between European powers that spilled over into America and kept the colonies in a constant state of violence and hostilities. The French and Indian War, the Revolutionary War, the Quasi-War with France in 1798–1800, and the War of 1812 were just the big events that precluded any pacifist illusions.

As noted above, as early as 1619, Virginia mandated the public carrying of arms when going to and fro in certain circumstances, such as when traveling to church. It was far from the only colony to do so.

---

[382] Randolph Roth, *American Homicide* 27, 39 fig.1.3 (Cambridge: Belknap Press/Harvard University Press, 2009).

[383] "A Brief Account of the Establishment of the Colony of Georgia, under General James Oglethorpe, February 1, 1733," in 1 *Tracts and Other Papers Relating Principally to the Origin, Settlement, and Progress of the Colonies in North America from the Discovery of the Country to the Year 1776*, at 24 (Washington: Peter Force, 1886).

[384] Anthony Vaver, *Bound with an Iron Chain: The Untold Story of How the British Transported 50,000 Convicts to Colonial America* 2 (Westborough: Pickpocket Publishing, 2011); James Davie Butler, "British Convicts Shipped to American Colonies," 2 *Am. Hist. Rev.* 12 (1896).

Plymouth Colony in 1632 "ordered that every freeman or other in habitant of this colony provide for himselfe and each under him able to beare armes a sufficient musket and other serviceable peece with bandeleroes and other apurtenances with what speede may be...."[385] A 1636 Massachusetts law likewise required citizens to "come to the public assemblies with their muskets, or other pieces fit for service," and further provided that "no person shall travel above one mile from his dwelling house, except in places where other houses are near together without some arms."[386] A 1639 Rhode Island act ordered "that no man shall go two miles from the town unarmed, either with gunn or sword; and that no one shall come to any public meeting without his weapon."[387]

A 1642 Maryland law provided that "no man able to bear arms to go to church or chapel or any considerable distance from home without fixed gun and one change at least of powder and shot."[388] And a 1650 Connecticut law ordered "[t]hat all persons that are above the age of sixteene yeares, except Magistrates and Church officers, shall beare arms...and every male person within this jurisdiction, above the said age, shall have in continuall readines, a good muskitt or other gunn, fitt for service...."[389]

---

[385] *The Compact with the Charter and Laws of the Colony of New Plymouth*, William Brigham ed., 31 (Boston: Dutton & Wentworth,1836) (enacted 1632).

[386] 1 Nathaniel B. Shurtleff, *Records of the Governor and Company of the Massachusetts Bay in New England* 190 (Boston: William White, 1853) (law of March 9, 1636).

[387] 1 John R. Bartlett, *Records of the Colony of Rhode Island and Providence Plantations, in New England* 94 (Providence: A. C. Greene, 1856) (law of 1639).

[388] William Hand Browne, *Archives of Maryland: Proceedings of the Council of Maryland 1636–1667*, at 103 (1885) (law of June 23, 1642).

[389] 1 *Public Records of the Colony of Connecticut*, ed. J. H. Trumbull, 542 (Hartford: Brown & Parsons, 1850) (enacted 1650).

In 1740, South Carolina required that "every white male inhabitant of this Province, (except travelers and such persons as shall be above sixty years of age,) who…is…liable to bear arms in the militia of this Province," who shall "go and resort to any church or any other public place of divine worship," must "carry with him a gun or a pair of horse-pistols…with at least six charges of gunpowder and ball."[390] And in 1770, Georgia required that "every male white inhabitant of this province, (the inhabitants of the sea port towns only excepted who shall not be obliged to carry any other than side arms) who is or shall be liable to bear arms in the militia…and resorting…to any church…shall carry with him a gun, or a pair of pistols." Each man was required to "take the said gun or pistols with him to the pew or seat," and these arms were to "be fit for immediate use and service."[391]

These laws indicate that carrying arms for defense of oneself and the community was both a right and a duty. The existence of these laws undercuts any revisionist historical theories, which posit either that (a) carrying private firearms in public was tightly regulated during this period or (b) carrying private firearms in public was banned by colonial versions of the Statute of Northampton. That these laws often required able-bodied men to go armed when traveling alone—not just when attending public community events—shows that their animating purpose was self-defense, not service in the militia.

Restrictions on the Carriage of Arms by Slaves

Unfortunately, not all people residing in the American colonies were entitled and expected to carry firearms. Many colonies forbade or

---

[390] 7 David J. McCord, *Statutes at Large of South Carolina* 417–19 (Columbia, S.C.: A.S. Johnston, 1840) (enacted 1740, re-enacted 1743).
[391] Horatio Marbury and William A. Crawford, *Digest of the Laws of the State of Georgia*, 241–42 (1802) (law of Feb. 27, 1770, § 1).

tightly limited carriage by enslaved and freed African Americans. A 1704 Maryland law provided that "no negro or other slave within this province shall be permitted to carry any Gunn or any other Offensive Weapon from off their master's land without lycense from their said Master."[392] A 1723 Virginia law only allowed an enslaved or "free negro, mulatto, or indian" "to keep and use guns" after "having first obtained a licence for the same, from some justice of the peace."[393] A 1740 South Carolina act made it unlawful "for any slave, unless in the presence of some white person, to carry or make use of firearms or any offensive weapon whatsoever, unless such negro or slave shall have a ticket or license in writing from his master, mistress or overseer, to hunt and kill game, cattle, or mischievous birds or beasts of prey."[394] The next year, North Carolina similarly provided that "no Slave shall go armed with Gun, Sword, Club or other Weapon, or shall keep any such Weapon, or shall Hunt or Range in the Woods, upon any pretence whatsoever" without a "Certificate" from his or her master.[395] And in 1768, Georgia enacted a license requirement substantively identical to South Carolina's 1740 law.[396]

As discussed below, these restrictions continued into the antebellum period—and even after the Civil War. But this unfortunate, racist legacy of carriage restrictions teaches two important modern lessons. First, these bans and licensing requirements were seen as permissible precisely because slaves and free persons of color were not

---

[392] William H. Browne, *Proceedings and Acts of the General Assembly September 5, 1704–April 19, 1706*, at 261 (1906) (law of Sept. 29, 1704).
[393] 4 *Statutes at Large (Va.)*, at 131 (1723) (law of May 1723).
[394] 1740 S.C. Acts 168, § 23.
[395] 1741 N.C. Sess. Laws 201, ch. 24, § 40.
[396] Robert Watkins and George Watkins, *A Digest of the Laws of the State of Georgia* 153 (1800) (law of Dec. 24, 1768).

understood to be entitled to the full rights of citizens. If they had been, as Justice Roger Taney later crystalized the point in his infamous Dred Scott decision, they would have been entitled "to keep and carry arms wherever they went."[397] And second, these racist restrictions only make sense against the background understanding that free, white colonists were entitled to freely carry arms in public. After all, if carrying arms in public had been understood as off-limits for everyone, there would have been no need to impose special, express limits on carriage by enslaved and free African Americans.

B) The Road to the American Revolution

The American colonists freely carried firearms. Historian George Neumann relates: "Among eighteenth-century civilians who traveled or lived in large cities, pistols were common weapons. Usually they were made to fit into pockets...."[398] That was illustrated in a Virginia record from the third quarter of the 1700s stating that "we find it necessary to carry with us some defensive weapons...a pair of pistols....let them be small, for the conveniency of carrying in a side pockett...."[399] As advertised, one could freely buy "a genteel pair of pocket pistols," muskets, blunderbusses, and cutlasses.[400]

But carrying firearms was also normal for other everyday purposes. Founding father and future President John Adams, who was born in 1735, wrote that he spent his childhood "above all in shooting,

---

[397] *Scott v. Sanford*, 60 U.S. (19 How.) 393, 417 (1857).
[398] George Neumann, *History of Weapons of the American Revolution* 151 (New York: Harper & Rowe, 1967).
[399] William Allason Letter Book 1757–1770, f. 134, Virginia State Library.
[400] Advertisements in the *Virginia Gazette* (Williamsburg), May 1, 1778, at 3, col. 1 ("a genteel pair of pocket pistols"); July 10, 1778, at 3, col. 3 ("three pair of four pound guns and carriages, and every other implement complete, 150 pair of pistols" for sale); Feb. 12, 1780, at 3, col. 2 ("Blunderbusses, pistols with swivels, muskets, cutlasses").

to which Diversion I was addicted to a degree of Ardor which I know not that I ever felt for any other Business, Study or Amusement."[401] In 1766, the 11-year-old James Monroe attended Campbell Academy. His routine: "Well before dawn, James left for school, carrying his books under one arm with his powder horn under the other and his musket slung across his back."[402]

The British government's conduct after the French and Indian War ended in 1763 began a cascade of events ultimately leading to the start of the American Revolution. In 1765, the British Parliament enacted two laws that enraged the American colonists: the Stamp Act and the Quartering Act. The Stamp Act required that legal documents, magazines, newspapers, and even playing cards have a tax stamp.[403] The Quartering Act ordered the colonies to pay for and provide barracks and other housing together with food for British soldiers based in America.[404]

These laws prompted the birth of the Committees of Correspondence and the Sons of Liberty, which organized protests, petitions, and a boycott of British goods. With escalating tension with the British Redcoats, the colonists saw an increasing need to obtain and carry pistols and other firearms.

Captain John Montrésor, an engineer with the British forces, was stationed in New York during the Stamp Act disturbances in 1765-66. His diary describes massive protests against the landing of ships with

---

[401] 3 *Autobiography of John Adams* 257-61 (Cambridge, Mass.: Harvard University Press, 1961). https://founders.archives.gov/documents/Adams/01-03-02-0016-0002.
[402] Tim McGrath, *James Monroe: A Life* Kindle loc. 244 (N.Y.: Dutton, 2020).
[403] 5 Geo. III, c.12 (1765).
[404] 5 Geo. III, c.33 (1765).

the stamps, attempts to seize and destroy the stamps, violence between soldiers and citizens, burning officials in effigy, and threats against stamp agents.[405] "The Sons of Liberty as they term themselves," he wrote, "openly defying powers, office and all authority sole rulers."[406]

In one incident, when the militia was called out to guard tax stamps, thirty-five of the forty militiamen voted to burn them.[407] From Connecticut, it was reported that colonists "already provided themselves with a magazine for Arms, Ammunition & c. and 10,000 men at the shortest warning for opposing the Stamp act...."[408]

When the Stamp Act passed, Benjamin Franklin was in London as a representative of the Pennsylvania Assembly. Back home in America, he was accused of supporting the Act. In September 1765, a mob gathered in Philadelphia with the aim of destroying the houses of Franklin and his supporters. Aware of the plot, Franklin's wife Deborah and some friends readied to defend her house. As she later wrote to her husband, she told her cousin "to fetch a gun or two, as we had none. I sent to ask my brother to bring his gun." Supporters confronted the mob, which dispersed with the show of force.[409]

"I honor much the spirit you showed," Benjamin wrote back to Deborah, adding: "The woman deserves a good house that is determined to defend it."[410] As this exemplifies, the Founders not only regarded the right to keep and bear arms as fundamental right, they

---

[405] "The Montresor Journals," G. D. Scull ed., *Collections of the New-York Historical Society for the Year 1881*, Chapter VIII (New York, 1882).
[406] *Id.* at 342 (Dec. 8, 1765).
[407] *Id.* at 343 (Dec. 21, 1765).
[408] *Id.* at 355 (Mar. 24, 1766).
[409] Walter Isaacson, *Benjamin Franklin: An American Life*, 224–25 (New York, N.Y.: Simon & Schuster, 2004).
[410] *Id.*

were also ready to use arms to protect their lives and habitations from mob violence.

The Americans succeeded in nullifying the Stamp Tax. Colonial legislatures denounced it, the Sons of Liberty intimidated tax collectors into resigning, armed men demanded surrender of the stamps, newspapers appeared on unstamped paper, and individuals evaded it.[411]

"This day is the Joyfull Day indeed for all America & all the people are to Rejoice this day for the Joyful News Brou[ght] their vessels from London that the Stamp Act is Repealed," wrote Boston merchant John Rowe in his diary on May 19, 1766.[412] As the *Boston Gazette* reported, "the Bells in the Town were set a ringing, the Ships in the Harbour display'd their Colours, Guns were discharged in different Parts of the Town...."[413]

But tensions ensued over other grievances. Indeed, accompanying the repeal of the Stamp Act, Parliament enacted the Declaratory Act, proclaiming that Parliament "had hath, and of right ought to have, full power and authority to make laws and statutes of sufficient force and validity to bind the colonies and people of America...in all cases whatsoever."[414]

The colonists saw that as an affront, as they had no representation in Parliament. Montrésor described the continuing resistance:

---

[411] Bernhard Knollenberg, *Origin of the American Revolution: 1759–1766*, at 217–27 (New York: Free Press, 1975, reprint, Indianapolis: Liberty Fund, 2002).

[412] John Rowe, *Letters and Diary of John Rowe, Boston Merchant 1759–1762, 1764–1779* at 95 (Boston: W. B. Clarke Co., 1903). See 6 Geo. III, c. 11 (1766).

[413] "Boston, May 26," *Boston-Gazette*, May 26, 1766, at 2.

[414] 6 Geo. III, c.12 (1766).

"Seventeen hundred of The Levelers [Sons of Liberty] with firearms are collected at Poughkeepsie."[415] And there were clashes:

> A considerable mob assembled on the Common consisting of 2 or 3000 chiefly Sons of Liberty, headed by Sears in order to come to an Explanation with the Officers and Soldiers for Cutting down a pine post where they daily exercised, called by them the Tree of Liberty. These Sons of Liberty used the most scurrilous and abusive language against the officers and soldiers present who never seemed to resent it, till a volley of Brick Bats ensued and wounded some, upon which they defended themselves with their Bayonets....[416]

Captain Sherrieffe and some fellow officers sought to intervene, and they were "publickly called Rascals to their Face by one Dawson formerly a provincial officer and Inhabitant here," who "with a stick attempted to knock down Capt Sherrieffe who drew his sword in his defence, when the mob instantly drew out of their pockets a case of pistols each...." It was not clear that the citizens were actually at fault, as a commanding officer arrived and "publickly declared to the mob that if his Soldiers were the aggressors they should be punished...."[417]

New taxes and other restraints on America were imposed by the Townshend Acts in 1767–68. Writs of assistance empowered British officials to conduct warrantless searches for smuggled goods at any places whatever, even houses.

British member of Parliament William Gerard Hamilton, who opposed taxing the American colonies, warned in 1767 about the colonists:

---

[415] "The Montresor Journals," 376 (June 29, 1766).
[416] *Id.* at 382 (Aug. 11, 1766).
[417] *Id.*

> There are, in the different provinces, about a million of people, which we may suppose at least 200,000 men able to bear arms; and not only able to bear arms, but having arms in their possession, unrestrained by any iniquitous Game Act. In the Massachusetts government particularly, there is an express law, by which every man is obliged to have a musket, a pound of powder, and a pound of bullets by him....[418]

In short, the colonists exercised the right to bear arms in a variety of ways, including the carrying of muskets and concealed pistols in public. No record exists that anyone thought this violated any law, much less the ancient Statute of Northampton.

C) "The Inhabitants to Be Disarmed": The Military Occupation of Boston Before the Revolution

In early September 1768, Massachusetts Governor Francis Bernard leaked information that British troops were sailing to Boston.[419] The greater part of Boston's populace turned out for a stormy meeting at Faneuil Hall and its surrounding square on September 12–13.[420] The assembly passed a resolution that began by quoting the English Declaration of Rights of 1689 "that the Subjects being Protestants, may have arms for their Defence...." Tellingly, the Americans snipped off the rest of the sentence "suitable to their Condition, and as are allowed by Law," thus reflecting the view that the right to bear arms in America was considered broader than the right recognized in England. The resolution recalled the law that "every listed Soldier and other

---

[418] William Gerard Hamilton to Gerard Calcraft, February 1767, Chatham Correspondence, in Frank A. Mumby, *George III and The American Revolution* 173 (London: Constable & Co., 1924).

[419] Knollenberg, *Growth of the American Revolution*, 81 & 401 n.3; John R. Alden, *General Gage in America* 160 (N.Y.: Greenwood Press, 1969).

[420] 1 Mercy Otis Warren, *History of the Rise, Progress and Termination of the American Revolution* 37 (Boston: Manning & Loring, 1805; reprint, Indianapolis: Liberty Classics, 1988).

Householder…shall always be provided with a well fix'd Firelock, Musket, Accouterments and Ammunition…." It resolved "that those of the Inhabitants, who may at present be unprovided, be and hereby are requested duly to observe the said Law at this Time."[421]

As British occupation troops were about to land in Boston, an anonymous patriot signing his name as "A.B.C." issued the following dire warning in the *Boston Gazette* which would be repeated throughout the colonies:

> It is reported that the Governor has said, that he has Three Things in Command from the Ministry, more grievous to the People, than any Thing hitherto made known. It is conjectured 1st, that the Inhabitants of this Province are to be disarmed. 2d. The Province to be governed by Martial Law. And 3d, that a Number of Gentlemen who have exerted themselves in the Cause of their Country, are to be seized and sent to Great-Britain.[422]

The troops, some seven hundred infantrymen, landed on October 1, 1768.[423] Following on the heels of the occupation of Boston came the newspaper column "Journal of the Times," which was reprinted in newspapers all over the colonies. Its anonymous authors included patriots like Samuel Adams, John Adams, and Josiah Quincy II.[424]

In one issue, Samuel Adams defended against attacks on the Boston vote calling on citizens to arm: "For it is certainly beyond

---

[421] *Boston Chronicle*, Sept. 19, 1768, at 363, col. 2. A 1645 law required "that all inhabitants…are to have armes in their houses fit for service." 2 *Records of the Governor and Company of the Massachusetts Bay in New England*, Nathaniel B. Shurtleff ed., 119 (Boston: W. White, 1853-54).

[422] *Boston Gazette*, September 26, 1768, at 3, cols. 1-2.

[423] Knollenberg, *Growth of the American Revolution*, 82–83.

[424] *Boston Under Military Rule [1768–1769] as Revealed in a Journal of the Times*, Oliver Morton Dickerson comp., xiii-ix (Westport, Conn.: Greenwood Publishing, 1971).

human art and sophistry, to prove the British subjects, to whom the *privilege* of possessing arms is expressly recognized by the Bill of Rights, and, who live in a province where the law requires them to be equip'd with *arms*, &c. are guilty of an *illegal act*, in calling upon one another to be provided with them, as the *law directs*."[425]

In an article he signed "E.A.," Samuel Adams recalled the Glorious Revolution of 1688 and the rights of Englishmen it recognized as follows:

> At the revolution, the British constitution was again restor'd to its original principles, declared in the bill of rights; which was afterwards pass'd into a law, and stands as a bulwark to the natural rights of subjects. "To vindicate these rights, says Mr. *Blackstone*, when actually violated or attack'd, the subjects of England are entitled first to the regular administration and *free course of justice* in the courts of law – next to the right of *petitioning the King* and parliament for redress of grievances – and lastly, to the right of *having and using arms for self-preservation and defence*." These he calls "auxiliary subordinate rights, which serve principally as *barriers* to protect and maintain inviolate the three great and primary rights of *personal security, personal liberty* and *private property*": And that of *having arms for their defense* he tells us is "a public allowance, under due restrictions, of the *natural right of resistance and self-preservation*, when the sanctions of society and laws are found *insufficient* to restrain the *violence of oppression*." – How little do those persons attend to the rights of the constitution, if they know anything about them, who find fault with a late vote of this town, calling upon the inhabitants to *provide themselves with arms for their defence* at any time; but more

---

[425] *Boston Gazette*, Jan. 30, 1769, at 2, col. 1 (signed "Shippen"); 1 *The Writings of Samuel Adams*, Harry Alonzo Cushing ed., 299 (N.Y.: G.P. Putnam's Sons, 1904).

especially, when they had reason to fear, there would be a necessity of the means of self preservation against the *violence of oppression*.[426]

In yet another installment, the *Journal* authors argued that the "outrageous behavior of the *military* conservators of the peace" demonstrated that Boston's vote "calling upon the inhabitants to provide themselves with arms for their defence, was a measure as prudent as it was *legal*.... It is a natural right which the people have reserved to themselves, confirmed by the Bill of Rights, to keep arms for their own defence; and as Mr. Blackstone observes, it is to be made use of when the sanctions of society and law are found insufficient to restrain the violence of oppression."[427]

The Boston Massacre Trials and the Right to Carry Arms for Self-Defense

In 1770, in a packed courtroom full of tension and drama, the words "Self Defence, the primary Canon of the Law of Nature," could be heard from the floorboards to the rafters. Those words constituted the theme of attorney John Adams, representing eight British soldiers and their officer in charge, Captain Thomas Preston, in their prosecution for unlawful homicide which arose out of the Boston Massacre. That same basic rule of self-defense also meant that "the inhabitants had a right to arm themselves at that time, for their defence, not for offence...."[428]

The Boston Massacre of March 5, 1770, was sparked when a British sentry guarding the Customs House struck a troublesome boy

---

[426] *Boston Gazette*, Feb. 27, 1769, at 3, col. 1; 1 *The Writings of Samuel Adams*, 317–18. Adams is quoting from 1 William Blackstone, *Commentaries*, *140–41, 143–44.
[427] *New York Journal*, Supplement, Apr. 13, 1769, at 1, col. 3.
[428] 3 Adams, *Legal Papers*, 248.

with his musket. A crowd gathered and shouting "kill him" began pelting the sentry with snowballs and other objects. Captain Thomas Preston and seven soldiers from the nearby Main Guard station raced to the Customs House to rescue the lone guard. Crispus Attucks, a sailor who was described as a mulatto, led the growing crowd in an attack on the Redcoats with snowballs, ice, oyster shells, and sticks. Yelling "you lobster scoundrels, fire if you dare," some struck at the soldiers with clubs and a cutlass. The soldiers then fired, killing Attucks and four others and wounding six more.[429]

In his pretrial deposition (the trial transcript did not survive), Captain Preston described the background of tension between the Boston townspeople and the British soldiers. At the trial of a soldier for an unrelated deed, Preston recalled a judge declaring "that the soldiers must now take care of themselves, nor trust too much to their arms, for they were but a handful; that the inhabitants carried weapons concealed under their clothes, and would destroy them in a moment, if they pleased." Recently, "several of the militia came from the country armed to join their friends, menacing to destroy any who should oppose them."[430]

On the evening of the shooting, bells were ringing to summon the townspeople to assemble, and some surrounded the sentry posted at the custom house and "with clubs and other weapons threatened to execute their vengeance on him." Preston mustered up more troops to guard the custom house, while the mob increased, "striking their clubs or bludgeons one against another, and calling out, come on you rascals,

---

[429] Knollenberg, *Growth of the American Revolution*, 86–87.
[430] Deposition of Captain Thomas Preston, March 12, 1770, in "Captain Thomas Preston's account of the Boston Massacre," http://www.bostonmassacre.net/trial/acct-preston1.htm.

you bloody backs, you lobster scoundrels, fire if you dare, G-d damn you...." Preston tried to persuade the mob to break up, and then:

> While I was thus speaking, one of the soldiers having received a severe blow with a stick, stepped a little on one side and instantly fired.... On this a general attack was made on the men by a great number of heavy clubs and snowballs being thrown at them, by which all our lives were in imminent danger.... Instantly three or four of the soldiers fired, one after another, and directly after three more in the same confusion and hurry.[431]

As the soldiers retreated, "there was a constant cry of the inhabitants to arms, to arms, turn out with your guns...." The soldiers then retired to their barracks and the lieutenant-governor persuaded the people to go home. Three justices met and issued warrants to arrest Preston and eight soldiers.[432]

Benjamin Burdick, a witness for the King (the prosecution), was on the scene and testified that during the Boston Massacre: "I had in my hand a highland broad Sword which I brought from home. Upon my coming out I was told it was a wrangle between the Soldiers and people, upon that I went back and got my Sword. I never used to go out with a weapon. I had not my Sword drawn till after the Soldier pushed his Bayonet at me."[433]

In the press, Samuel Adams argued that the slain Mr. Attucks "was leaning upon his stick when he fell, which certainly was not a *threatening* posture: It may be supposed that he had as good right, *by*

---

[431] *Id.*
[432] *Id.*
[433] "The Trial of Captain Preston: Key Evidence,"
http://law2.umkc.edu/faculty/projects/FTrials/bostonmassacre/prestontrialexcerpts.html.

the law of the land, to carry a stick for his own and his neighbor's defence, in a time of danger, as the Soldier who shot him had, to be arm'd with musket and ball, for the defence of himself and his friend the Centinel."[434]

As borne out by the testimony below, both prosecution and defense attorneys stipulated that the citizens had the right to bear arms for purposes of self-defense. Thus, the issue presented at trial was who were the aggressors, i.e., the American inhabitants or the British soldiers.[435] Crown prosecutor Robert Treat Paine argued that due to the long-term abusive conduct of the soldiers, "the most peaceable among us had...found it necessary to arm themselves with heavy Walking Sticks or Weapons of Defense when they went abroad."[436] Similarly, co-prosecutor Samuel Quincy contended that when the soldiers sallied out "with clubs, cutlasses, and other weapons of death; this occasioned a general alarm; every man therefore had a right, and very prudent it was to endeavor to defend himself if attacked; this accounts for the reason of Dr. *Young* or any one inhabitant of the town having a sword that evening...."[437]

Defense counsel John Adams, representing the soldiers, upheld the right of "Self Defence, the primary Canon of the Law of Nature." As to the populace, Adams conceded on the authority of William Hawkins, the great English jurist: "Here every private person is authorized to arm himself, and on the strength of this authority, I do not deny the

---

[434] 2 *The Writings of Samuel Adams*, Harry Alonzo Cushing ed. 119 (N.Y.: G.P. Putnam's Sons, 1904).
[435] 3 John Adams, *Legal Papers* 149 (Cambridge, Mass.: Belknap Press/Harvard University Press, 1965).
[436] *Id.* at 274.
[437] *Id.* at 149.

inhabitants had a right to arm themselves at that time, for their defence, not for offence...."[438]

The court instructed the jury as to the traditional hue and cry: "It is the duty of all persons (except women, decrepit persons, and infants under fifteen) to aid and assist the peace officers to suppress riots & c. when called upon to do it. They may take with them such weapons as are necessary to enable them effectually to do it."[439]

The jury acquitted all of the soldiers, except the one who shot Mr. Attucks who was convicted of manslaughter.[440] While this verdict only fanned the flames among the populace, it demonstrated that a Boston jury could be impartial.

While this was the leading criminal trial of the epoch, the right to have arms for self-defense was also enunciated in other then-contemporary trials. Defending an assault case in 1771, James Otis (co-counsel with Adams and Quincy) relied on "Orat[ion] pro Milone beginning."[441] This referred to the following passage from Cicero's defense of Titus Annius Milo in ancient Rome on murder charges: "When arms speak, the laws are silent; they bid none to await their word.... And yet most wisely, and, in a way, tacitly, the law authorizes self-defense.... The man who had employed a weapon in self-defence was not held to have carried that weapon with a view to homicide."[442]

---

[438] *Id.* at 248.
[439] *Id.* at 285.
[440] Knollenberg, *Growth of the American Revolution*, 87–88.
[441] 1 Adams, *Legal Papers*, 160.
[442] *Id.*, n.16.

Indeed, the right to bear arms for self-defense went unquestioned. James Iredell, a North Carolina lawyer who would become a Justice of the U.S. Supreme Court, wrote to his mother in 1771:

> Be not afraid of the Pistols you have sent me. They may be necessary Implements of self Defense, tho' I dare say I shall never have Occasion to use them.... It is a Satisfaction to have the means of Security at hand if we are in no danger, as I never expect to be. Confide in my prudence and self regard for a proper use of them, and you need have no Apprehension.[443]

D) From the Tea Party to Firearm Confiscations

On December 16, 1773, patriots disguised as Mohawk Indians gathered at Boston harbor, boarded three vessels, broke open 342 chests, and dumped the contents—forty-five tons of tea—into the ocean. The whooping "Indians" were "cloath'd in Blankets with the head muffled, and copper color'd countenances, being each arm'd with a hatchet or axe, and pair pistoles," wrote Boston merchant John Andrews.[444] Andrews had written two weeks before the Tea Party that the inhabitants unanimously opposed the landing of the tea, and "'twould puzzle any person to purchase a pair of p----ls [pistols] in town, as they are all bought up, with a full determination to repell force by force.'"[445]

The raid, thought to have been led by John Hancock, was in protest of the recently-passed Tea Act, which sought to give the British East India Company a monopoly on the tea trade and to suppress importation of the highly taxed Dutch tea which most colonists

---

[443] 1 *The Papers of James Iredell*, Ron Higginbotham ed., 79 (Raleigh: North Carolina Division of Archives and History, 1976).
[444] Letter of Dec. 18, 1773, in John Andrews, *Letters of John Andrews, Esq., of Boston, 1772–1776*, Winthrop Sargent ed., 12 (Cambridge, Mass.: John Wilson & Sons, 1866).
[445] Letter of Dec. 1, 1773, in *id.* at 12.

consumed and which was widely smuggled. The Sons of Liberty depicted the scheme as yet another instance of taxation without representation.

Parliament responded to the Boston Tea Party by enacting the Intolerable Acts. The Boston Port Act closed Boston's port altogether until the colonists paid full reparations for the destroyed tea. Under the new Quartering Act, British troops returned to Boston—they had been removed from the town after the 1770 Massacre—and British ships blockaded the harbor. The Massachusetts Regulating Act gave the colonial governor unprecedented powers, including absolute authority over all judicial and official appointments and removals.[446] General Thomas Gage, the commander in chief of the British Army in North America, was appointed governor and was instructed vigorously to enforce the Boston Port Act.[447]

It was no secret that the people were arming themselves. That could be surmised in newspaper advertisements, such as an early 1774 notice in the *Boston Gazette* that a merchant "has just imported for sale, a neat assortment of guns, complete with bayonets, steel rods and swivels, a few neat fowling pieces, pocket pistols."[448]

British General Gage began to restrict the distribution of gunpowder. Redcoats seized some firearms being carried out of

[446] 1 David Ramsay, *The History of the American Revolution* 99 (Philadelphia: R. Aitken, 1789; reprint, Indianapolis: Liberty Classics, 1990); Knollenberg, *Growth of the American Revolution*, 136–39.

[447] Dartmouth to Gage, April 9, 1774, 2 *The Correspondence of General Thomas Gage with the Secretaries of State, and with the War Office and the Treasury, 1763–1775*, at 158–59 Clarence E. Carter ed. (New Haven: Yale University Press, 1931–33).

[448] *Boston Gazette*, Jan. 24, 1774, at 1, col. 3.

Boston, but the seizure was not considered lawful, and the firearms were returned. Boston merchant John Andrews wrote about:

> [A] waggon's being riffled of four firelocks by the Centinel on guard upon ye. Neck, which I have since been inform'd is a fact, and that the officer of the day return'd them and pleaded much with the party injur'd not to prosecute the matter, as it might be consider'd as a military robbery: which leads me to think that notwithstanding their hostile preparations and formidable appearance, they as yet esteem themselves as liable to the civil law; whether their dispositions when the two infernal acts arrive, with the royall assent, I can't say.[449]

Obviously no law existed to justify seizure of the firelocks that were being transported through Boston Neck. Instead, the seizure may have been considered robbery, which is why they were returned.

Just two days before, Gage had sent two companies of Redcoats to dissolve an illegal town meeting in Salem. The soldiers backed down when swarms of armed patriots began to appear. John Andrews confided about the affair:

> [T]here was upwards of three thousand men assembled there from the adjacent towns, with full determination to rescue the Committee if they should be sent to prison, even if they were oblig'd to repel force by force, being sufficiently provided for such a purpose; as indeed they are all through the country – every male above the age of 16 possessing a firelock with double the quantity of powder and ball enjoin'd by law.[450]

Meanwhile, the Crown-appointed Massachusetts Council had replaced the governing council elected by the legislature. The patriots

---

[449] Andrews, *Letters of John Andrews*, 19–20.
[450] *Id.* at 34.

called it the "Divan," after the despotic Ottoman privy council. It was reported that on August 31, 1774, the Divan deliberated upon "the disarming of the town of Boston, and as much of the province as might be, to which sundry new counsellors advised."[451]

Merchant John Andrews wrote that Gage's gunpowder seizures and the plan to disarm the inhabitants caused the people to be "in arms at all quarters, being determin'd to see us [Bostonians] redress'd." Some three thousand men carried arms from their homes and assembled at Cambridge common.[452] A Connecticut patriot named McNeil reported that "all along were armed men rushing forward," and in "every house, women and children [were] making cartridges...and at the same time animating their husbands and sons to fight for their liberties...."[453]

Lord Hugh Percy, of His Majesty's forces, deplored the fact that the people "have taken up arms in almost every part of this Province," adding that an insurrection would be formidable because of "a law of this Province, wh[ich] obliges every inhabitant to be furnished with a firelock, bayonet, & pretty considerable quantity of ammunition."[454] Percy was peeved that Gage had not clamped down on the citizens, who "have even free access to and from this town, tho' armed with firelocks, provided they only come in small nos."[455]

---

[451] *Boston Gazette*, Sept. 5, 1774, at 3, col. 2.

[452] Andrews, *Letters of John Andrews*, 38.

[453] Diary entry dated Sept. 25, 1774, in 2 Ezra Stiles, *Literary Digest*, F.B. Dexter ed. 479 (New York, 1901), quoted in David Hackett Fischer, *Paul Revere's Ride* 46 (N.Y.: Oxford University Press, 1994).

[454] Percy to the Duke of Northumberland (his father), Sept. 12, 1774, in Hugh Percy, *Letters of Hugh Earl Percy from Boston and New York, 1774-1776*, Charles Knowles Bolton ed., 37–38 (Boston: Charles E. Goodspeed, 1902).

[455] *Id.* at 38.

A committee led by Dr. Joseph Warren, the President of the Massachusetts Provincial Congress, met with Gage to complain about the gunpowder seizures.[456] When going abroad in Boston, British officers would make threatening taunts to Warren, who was a physician. One evening a medical student warned him not to go out to call on a patient, but Warren—"putting pistols in his pocket"—insisted on making the visit.[457] Warren would later help design and implement the famous "one if by land, two if by sea" plan, and sent Paul Revere on his famous ride. Warren's death at the Battle of Bunker Hill was a major blow to the patriots.

Gage ignored their grievances and asked "what occasion there is for such numbers going armed in and out of the Town, and through the country in an hostile manner?"[458] Gage insisted, "it is notorious that...arms are carried out openly by every man that goes out of Boston without molestation."[459]

But Gage had no legal or other authority to seize firearms from persons who carried them. As governor, he was bound by a statute— the English Bill of Rights, which provided: "That the Subjects which are Protestants, may have Arms for their Defence suitable to their Condition, and as are allowed by Law."[460] A 1694 Massachusetts law punished "such as shall ride or go armed Offensively...in Fear or Affray of Their Majesties Liege People...."[461] That descendent of the

---

[456] *Boston Gazette*, Sept. 19, 1774, at 2, col. 1

[457] Richard Frothingham, *Life and Times of Joseph Warren* 452 (Boston: Little, Brown, & Co., 1865).

[458] *Boston Gazette*, Sept. 19, 1774, at 2, col. 1.

[459] Document datelined Boston, Sept. 27, 1774, in 1 *American Archives*, 4th Series, Peter Force ed., 806–07 (Washington, D.C.: M. St. Claire Clarke & Peter Force, 1837).

[460] An Act Declaring the Rights and Liberties of the Subject, 1 W. & M., Sess. 2, c.2, (1689).

[461] Mass. Acts 10, no. 6 (1694).

Statute of Northampton, or such later provision as may have been enacted, was not seen as applicable because the firearms were carried peaceably, not offensively in a manner that caused fear or created an affray.

John Andrews wrote that it was common for men to leave Boston with arms, "for every man in the country not possess'd of a firelock making it a point to procure one, so that I suppose for a month past, or more, not a day has pass'd but a hundred or more are carried out of town by'em."[462]

Sensing that the colonists were becoming too powerful, Gage finally began a policy of seizing arms. Dr. Warren wrote to Samuel Adams that the troops were searching for and seizing arms.[463] As an example, "Mr. Samuel Phillips, jun., of Andover, was this day carrying about a dozen fire-arms over Charleston ferry. The sloop-of-war lying in the river dispatched a boat, and seized them."[464] Phillips appealed to the captain to return his firelocks, but most people hoped for a trial to determine whether the seizure was lawful.[465]

By now searches for and seizures of firearms became more general. Worcester County complained to Gage:

This County are constrained to observe, they apprehend the People justified in providing for their own Defense, while they understood there was no passing the Neck without Examination…& many places searched, where Arms and Ammunition were suspected to be; and if found seized; yet as the People have never acted offensively, nor

---

[462] Andrews, *Letters of John Andrews*, 46-47.
[463] Frothingham, *Life and Times of Joseph Warren*, 381.
[464] *Id.* at 382.
[465] Letter dated Sept. 30, 1774, in Andrews, *Letters of John Andrews*, 58.

discovered any disposition so to do…the County apprehend this can never justify the seizure of private Property.[466]

Complaining about the arms seizures, a writer in the *Boston Gazette* made the thinly-veiled threat: "Besides the regular trained militia in New-England, all the planters sons and servants are taught to use the fowling piece from their youth, and generally fire balls with great exactness at fowl or beast."[467]

Lord Dartmouth, the British Secretary of State for the Colonies, urged Gage to consider "disarming the Inhabitants of the Massachusetts Bay, Connecticut and Rhode Island," but only if practicable.[468] Gage replied: "Your Lordship's Idea of disarming certain Provinces would doubtless be consistent with Prudence and Safety, but it neither is nor has been practicable without having Recourse to Force, and being Masters of the Country."[469]

The Redcoats reportedly surrounded and disarmed militiamen who were exercising on Boston common; a larger body of militia then pursued the troops and retook their firearms.[470]

Charles Lee wrote in an influential pamphlet, "The Yeomanry of America have, besides infinite advantages, over the peasantry of other countries; they are accustomed from their infancy to fire arms; they are expert in the use of them: – Whereas the lower and middle people of England are, by the tyranny of certain laws, almost as ignorant in the

---

[466] *Boston Gazette*, Oct. 17, 1774, at 2, col. 2–3.
[467] *Id.*, Dec. 5, 1774, at 4, col. 1.
[468] Dartmouth to Gage, Oct. 17, 1774, 2 *Correspondence of General Thomas Gage* 175.
[469] Gage to Dartmouth, Dec. 15, 1774, *id.*, vol. 1, at 387.
[470] *The Massachusetts Gazette*, Dec. 29, 1774, at 2, col. 2.

use of a musket, as they are of the ancient Catapulta."[471] Such Americans obviously did not think that the law prohibited them from carrying their arms outside of their houses.

John Adams wrote that the colonies south of Pennsylvania "have a back country, which is inhabited by a hardy, robust people, many of whom are emigrants from New England, and habituated, like multitudes of New England men, to carry their fuzees[472] or rifles upon one shoulder, to defend themselves against the Indians, while they carry'd their axes, scythes and hoes upon the other to till the ground."[473] However, the colonists sought alliances with friendly tribes. The 1775 address of Massachusetts to the Mohawk and other Eastern Tribes of Indians drafted by Samuel Adams warned that the British Ministry "has laid deep plots to take away our liberty and your liberty" and to "prevent us from having guns and powder to use," but "we hope soon to be able to supply you with both guns and powder, of our own making."[474]

Peter Oliver, the former Chief Justice of the Massachusetts Superior Court, recalled: "The People were continually purchasing Muskets, Powder & Ball in the Town of Boston, & carrying them into the Country; under the Pretence that the Law of the Province obliged

---

[471] Charles Lee, *Strictures on a Pamphlet, Entitled a "Friendly Address to All Reasonable Americans, on the Subject of our Political Confusions"* 12 (Philadelphia: William & Thomas Bradford, 1774).

[472] "Fusee. A small neat musket or firelock. But we now use *fusil*." Noah Webster, *An American Dictionary of the English Language* (New York: S. Converse, 1828).

[473] John Adams, *Novanglus; or, A History of the Dispute with America*, No. III, Feb. 1775, in *The Revolutionary Writings of John Adams*, C. Bradley Thompson ed., 172 (Indianapolis: Liberty Fund, 2000).

[474] 3 *Writings of Samuel Adams*, Harry Alonzo Cushing ed., 213 (N.Y.: G.P. Putnam's Sons, 1907).

every Town & Person to be provided with each of those Articles." As a precaution, Gage "put a Stop to the carrying off any more...."[475]

Lieutenant Frederick MacKenzie of the Royal Welch Fusiliers wrote in his diary that, on the annual memorial of the Boston Massacre: "The towns people certainly expected a Riot, as almost every man had a short stick, or bludgeon, in his hand; and it was confidently asserted that many of them were privately armed."[476]

In October 1774, the British Ministry decreed a ban on "the Exportation of Gunpowder, or any sort of Arms or Ammunition, out of this Kingdom...." In his speech in favor of Conciliation with America, Edmund Burke recalled an earlier epoch in which Parliament "prohibited by statute the sending all sorts of arms into Wales, as you prohibit by proclamation (with something more of doubt on the legality) the sending arms to America. They disarmed the Welsh by statute, as you attempted, (but still with more question on the legality) to disarm New England by an instruction."[477] Burke was referring to Dartmouth's above 1774 instruction to Gage to consider "disarming the Inhabitants of the Massachusetts Bay, Connecticut and Rhode Island."[478] Conciliation was not to be.

---

[475] *Peter Oliver's Origin & Progress of The American Rebellion: A Tory View*, Douglass Adair & John A. Schutz eds. 116–17 (Stanford, CA: Stanford University Press, 1961). The manuscript was written in 1781.

[476] Frederick MacKenzie, *A British Fusilier in Revolutionary Boston*, Allen French ed., 38–39 (Freeport, N.Y.: Books for Libraries Press, 1926, reprint 1969).

[477] 18 William Cobbett, *Parliamentary History of England* 512 (London: T. C. Hansard, 1813).

[478] Dartmouth to Gage, Oct. 17, 1774, 2 *Correspondence of General Thomas Gage* 175.

Patrick Henry's "liberty or death" oration on March 23, 1775, to the Convention of Delegates of Virginia in Richmond, refuted the argument that they were yet too weak to resist:

> But when shall we be stronger?…Will it be when we are totally disarmed, and when a British guard shall be stationed in every house?…Three million people, armed in the holy cause of liberty…are invincible by any force which our enemy can send against us.[479]

Among the resolutions that Patrick Henry proposed and the convention adopted was the following: "That a well regulated Militia, composed of Gentlemen and Yeomen, is the natural Strength, and only Security, of a free Government."[480] It recommended "that every Man be provided with a good Rifle" and "that every Horseman be provided…with Pistols and Holsters, a Carbine, or other Firelock."[481]

E) 1775: A Shot Heard 'Round the World and a Cruel Act of Perfidy

"Disperse you Rebels – Damn you, throw down your Arms and disperse!" shouted British Major John Pitcairn at the militiamen who were assembled on Lexington's common. "Upon which the Troops huzz'd, and immediately one or two Officers discharged their Pistols, which were instantaneously followed by the Firing of four or five of the Soldiers, then there seemed to be a general discharge from the whole Body."[482] So went a widely published American version recounting that fateful day of April 19, 1775.

---

[479] *Journal of Proceedings of Convention Held at Richmond* 34 (Williamsburg: J. Dixon, 1775).
[480] *Id.* at 10.
[481] *Id.* at 17.
[482] *Essex Gazette*, April 25, 1775, at 3, col. 3.

The militiamen of Lexington and Concord consisted of able-bodied males aged sixteen though sixty. All provided their own private arms except for a few poor men who had to borrow them.[483] Militia Colonel James Barrett's fifteen-year-old granddaughter Meliscent taught the other young women of the town how to assemble cartridges.[484] One of the wounded at Lexington was listed as "Prince Easterbrooks (a Negro-Man)."[485]

After the skirmish at Lexington, the Redcoats marched on Concord, where they searched houses and destroyed arms and military stores. One account verified that "even women had firelocks. One was seen to fire a blunderbuss between her father and husband from their windows."[486] As many as three thousand and five hundred militiamen fought the Redcoats. A British officer recorded that, during the British retreat back to Boston, the Americans ambushed them from houses and behind walls and hedges. He conceded, "These fellows were generally good marksmen, and many of them used long guns made for Duck-Shooting."[487]

General Gage's next move was to disarm the inhabitants of Boston. He promised the town committee at their meeting on April 23, "that upon the inhabitants in general lodging their arms in Faneuil Hall, or any other convenient place, under the care of the selectmen, marked with the names of the respective owners, that all such inhabitants as are

---

[483] Robert A. Gross, *The Minutemen and their World* 61, 69–70 (New York: Hill & Wang, 1976).
[484] *Id.* at 69.
[485] *Essex Gazette*, April 25, 1775, at 3, col. 3.
[486] M.L. Brown, *Firearms in Colonial America* 298 (Washington, D.C.: Smithsonian Institution, 1980), quoting letter from unknown author in 10 *Wm. and Mary Quarterly*, 3rd ser., 106 (1953).
[487] MacKenzie, *A British Fusilier in Revolutionary Boston*, 67.

inclined, may depart from the town.... And that the arms aforesaid at a suitable time would be return'd to the owners."[488]

According to the historian Richard Frothingham, "the people delivered to the selectmen 1778 fire-arms [long guns], 634 pistols, 973 bayonets, and 38 blunderbusses."[489] That was a substantial number given that Boston had 16,000 inhabitants, that patriots had already taken many arms outside of the city, and that many arms were likely secreted.[490]

Lexington and Concord, then Boston, were just the first steps to disarm and put the Americans under foot. Newspapers reported "that on the landing of the General Officers, who have sailed for America, a proclamation will be published throughout the provinces inviting the Americans to deliver up their arms by a certain stipulated day; and that such of the colonists as are afterwards proved to carry arms shall be deemed rebels, and be punished accordingly."[491]

The Declaration of Causes of Taking Up Arms of July 6, 1775, drafted by Thomas Jefferson and John Dickinson, protested Gage's seizure of arms from Boston's inhabitants:

> The inhabitants of Boston being confined within that town by the General their Governor, and having, in order to procure their dismission, entered into a treaty with him, it was stipulated that the said inhabitants having deposited their arms with their own magistrates, should have liberty to depart, taking with them their other effects. They

---

[488] Attested Copy of Proceedings Between Gage and Selectmen, Apr. 23, 1775, in *Connecticut Courant*, July 17, 1775, at 4, col. 2.

[489] Richard Frothingham, *History of the Siege of Boston* 95 (Boston: Little Brown and Company, 1903).

[490] See 1 Page Smith, *A New Age Now Begins: A People's History of the American Revolution* 506 (New York: McGraw-Hill, 1976).

[491] *The Virginia Gazette*, June 24, 1775, at 1, col. 1.

accordingly delivered up their arms, but in open violation of honor, in defiance of the obligation of treaties, which even savage nations esteem sacred, the Governor ordered the arms deposited as aforesaid, that they might be preserved for their owners, to be seized by a body of soldiers; detained the greatest part of the inhabitants in the town, and compelled the few who were permitted to retire, to leave their most valuable effects behind.[492]

A Virginia gentleman wrote to a friend in Scotland on September 1, 1775, "We are all in arms, exercising and training old and young to the use of the gun. No person goes abroad without his sword, or gun, or pistols."[493]

The Declaration of Independence, drafted by Thomas Jefferson and signed by the members of the Continental Congress on July 4, 1776, upheld the right of the people to assert their sovereignty over an oppressive government.[494] Just governments are created by the consent of the governed to secure the rights to life, liberty, and the pursuit of happiness, but when a government "becomes destructive to these ends, it is the right of the people to alter or to abolish it, and to institute new government...."

Governments should not be changed "for light and transient causes." "But when a long train of abuses and usurpations...evinces a design to reduce them under absolute despotism, it is their right, it is their duty, to throw off such government, and to provide new guards for their future security." The King "has plundered our seas, ravaged

---

[492] 2 *Journals of the Continental Congress, 1774–1779*, Worthington C. Ford ed., 151 (Washington, D.C.: Government Printing Office, 1905).

[493] 3 Peter Force ed., *American Archives*, 4th Series, 621 (Washington, D.C.: M. St. Claire Clarke & Peter Force, 1840).

[494] See Pauline Maier, *American Scripture: Making the Declaration of Independence* (New York: Alfred A. Knopf, 1997).

our coasts, burnt our towns, and destroyed the lives of our people"; he was "transporting large Armies of foreign Mercenaries to compleat the works of death, desolation, and tyranny"; and he "has endeavoured to bring on the inhabitants of our frontiers, the merciless Indian Savages whose known rule of warfare, is an undistinguished destruction of all ages, sexes and conditions."

Inherent in the Declaration's philosophy is the right of the people to keep and bear arms to defend themselves from such depredations and, as stated, "to throw off such government." And to prevent just that, in 1777, Undersecretary of State William Knox in the British Colonial Office recommended to members of the Ministry, among other measures: "The Militia Laws should be repealed and none suffered to be re-enacted, & the Arms of all the People should be taken away...."[495]

But it was too late either to abolish the militias or confiscate the populace's firearms. While the Americans had suffered defeat after defeat from the end of 1775, that would change at the Battle of Bennington on August 16, 1777. General John Burgoyne sent a party of Hessians, along with some loyalists and Indians under Colonel Friedrich Baum, to seize the town of Bennington, Vermont, near the New York border, to confiscate cattle and other provisions and to intimidate the people in that area. He was met by New Hampshire Militia General John Stark—who had "assembled 1,492 militiamen in civilian clothes with personal firearms"[496]—joined by some of the Green Mountain Boys from Vermont.

---

[495] 1 *Sources of American Independence*, Howard H. Peckham ed., 176 (Chicago: University of Chicago Press, 1978).
[496] "The Battle of Bennington," https://revolutionarywar.us/year-1777/battle-of-bennington/.

Contemporary historian David Ramsay described the outcome: "On this occasion about 800 undisciplined militia, without bayonets, or a single piece of artillery, attacked and routed 500 regular troops advantageously posted behind entrenchments – furnished with the best arms, and defended with two pieces of artillery." This defeat of regulars by the militia greatly encouraged the Americans.[497]

After his defeat, General Burgoyne wrote: "The great bulk of the country is undoubtedly with the Congress, in principle and in zeal; and their measures are executed with a secrecy and dispatch that are not to be equalled. Wherever the King's forces point, militia, to the amount of three or four thousand, assemble in twenty-four hours; they bring with them their subsistence, etc., and, the alarm over, they return to their farms."[498]

The Battle of King's Mountain, fought on October 7, 1780, was another instance in which armed citizens essentially came together as militia to defeat British regulars. After waging campaigns in Pennsylvania and New Jersey, British Major Patrick Ferguson was sent to the Carolinas to lead regulars and loyalist militias against patriot militias, threatening to lay waste to the country with fire and sword. "This aroused to action all who were capable of bearing arms, in opposition to his designs. A body of militia collected in and about the highlands of North Carolina," wrote historian Mercy Otis Warren.[499]

Militias from the Carolinas and Virginia numbering sixteen hundred men under no general command came together to attack

---

[497] Ramsay, *The History of the American Revolution*, 375–76. See also 1 Warren, *History of the Rise*, 228-30.
[498] General Burgoyne to Lord German Germain, Aug. 20, 1777. https://www.historycentral.com/Revolt/battleaccounts/Burgoyne/GenBurg.html.
[499] 2 Warren, *History of the Rise*, 397.

Ferguson at King's Mountain. Behind rocks and trees, the American riflemen repulsed Ferguson's attacks. So accurate was their aim that an unusual number of British were found to be shot in the head. Ferguson and 150 of his men were killed, and the remaining 700 captured, with only a few American losses. As a result of the victory, Royalists in the interior of the Carolinas were demoralized and melted away.[500]

While the American militias suffered their share of defeats, they played a substantial role, along with the Continental Army under the leadership of George Washington, in achieving victory in the American Revolution. Recognition of the right to keep and bear arms and its near universal exercise among the American people contributed greatly to the winning of the Revolutionary War.

Also critical to that victory was a moral philosophy that included as a postulate, as expressed in the pamphlet *Defensive arms vindicated*, "the lawfulness of taking up arms to oppose all tyranny, oppression, and those who abuse and misuse their authority." Written by Revolutionary War soldier Stephen Chase under the pseudonym A Moderate Whig, it argued that when a king "doth really injure, oppress, and invade his subjects civil rights and liberties, and sends out his bloody emissaries, with armed violence against them," then "may a community of such subjects defend themselves and their liberties by arms, in resisting his bloody emissaries."[501] The work was originally written in 1777.

---

[500] 2 Ramsay, *The History of the American Revolution*, 499-501.
[501] A Moderate Whig, *Defensive arms vindicated; and the lawfulness of the American war made manifest* 7-8 (n.p., 1782).

F) Constitutionalizing the Right to Bear Arms

Some of the newly-independent states adopted bills of rights, others adopted written constitutions without such bills, and still others didn't even adopt written constitutions. Most were adopted in 1776. The right to bear arms was a fact on the ground in every state.

South Carolina was the first state to adopt a constitution, which had no bill of rights. Its preamble declared that "a number of peaceable, helpless, and unarmed people were wantonly robbed and murdered" by General Gage's troops in Massachusetts and that "the colonists were therefore driven to the necessity of taking up arms, to repel force by force, and to defend themselves and their properties against lawless invasions and depredations."[502]

The president of the Provincial Congress that adopted the constitution was William Henry Drayton, chief justice of the South Carolina Supreme Court and a member of the Continental Congress. His son wrote: "Mr. Drayton always had about his person, a dirk and a pair of pocket pistols; for the defense of his life."[503]

Virginia was the first of all the colonies to adopt a bill of rights. The Virginia Declaration of Rights, adopted in convention on June 12, 1776, held that all men "have certain inherent Rights," including "the Enjoyment of Life and Liberty, with the Means of...pursuing and obtaining...Safety...."[504] Further, "a well regulated Militia, composed

---

[502] *Extracts from the Journals of the Provincial Congress* 137-38 (Charles-Town: Peter Timothy, 1776).
[503] 1 John Drayton, *Memoirs of the American Revolution...As Relating to South Carolina* 378 (Charleston: A. E. Miller, 1821).
[504] Va. Declaration of Rights, Art. I (1776).

of the Body of the People, trained to Arms, is the proper, natural, and safe Defense of a free State...."[505]

George Mason, author of the Virginia Declaration, a year earlier had helped George Washington organize the Fairfax Independent Militia Company to counter the royal militia. Its members pledged to "constantly keep by us" a firelock, six pounds of gunpowder, and twenty pounds of lead.[506]

Thomas Jefferson also drafted a bill of rights, including the provision: "No freeman shall ever be debarred the use of arms...."[507] When he was ten years old, his father gave him a gun and sent him into the forest to promote self-reliance.[508] In 1768, just before the Redcoats landed to occupy Boston, the 25-year-old Jefferson "won shooting 1/6," i.e., a shilling sixpence, in a target match.[509] He made numerous references throughout his life to the use of firearms.[510]

Jefferson kept a *Commonplace Book* during the years 1774–1776 which has been called "the source-book and repertory of Jefferson's ideas on government."[511] For instance, Jefferson copied passages from Italian Enlightenment intellectual and criminal justice reformer Cesare Beccaria's *Dei delitti e delle pene* (*Crimes and Punishments*). Writing

---

[505] *Id.* Art. XIII.
[506] 1 George Mason, *The Papers of George Mason*, Robert A. Rutland ed., 210–11 (Chapel Hill, N.C.: University of North Carolina Press, 1970).
[507] 1 Thomas Jefferson, *The Papers of Thomas Jefferson*, Julian P. Boyd ed., 344–45 (Princeton, N.J.: Princeton University Press, 1950).
[508] Dumas Malone, *Jefferson the Virginian*, vol. 1 of *Jefferson and His Time* 46–47 (Boston: Little, Brown and Company, 1948).
[509] *Jefferson's Memorandum Books*, James A. Bear, Jr., and Lucia C. Stanton eds., 81 (Princeton, N.J.: Princeton University Press, 1997).
[510] *See* "Firearms" in Index and referenced text in *id.* at 1550. *See also* Ashley Halsey, Jr., "Jefferson's Beloved Guns," *American Rifleman*, Nov. 1969, 17; "Firearms," https://www.monticello.org/site/research-and-collections/firearms.
[511] *The Commonplace Book of Thomas Jefferson: A Repertory of His Ideas on Government*, Gilbert Chinard ed., 4 (Baltimore: Johns Hopkins Univ. Press, 1926).

"*False idee di utilità*" ("false ideas of utility") in the margin, Jefferson copied the following passage in the original Italian:

> The laws that forbid the carrying of arms are laws of such a nature. They disarm those only who are neither inclined nor determined to commit crimes. Can it be supposed that those who have the courage to violate the most sacred laws of humanity, the most important of the code, will respect the less important and arbitrary ones, which can be violated with ease and impunity, and which, if strictly obeyed, would put an end to personal liberty – so dear to men, so dear to the enlightened legislator – and subject innocent persons to all the vexations that the guilty alone ought to suffer? Such laws make things worse for the assaulted and better for the assailants; they serve rather to encourage than to prevent homicides, for an unarmed man may be attacked with greater confidence than an armed man.[512]

Beccaria was highly lauded by the other Founders as well.[513] John Adams began his opening argument in the Boston Massacre trial by quoting Beccaria: "If I can but be the instrument of preserving one life, his blessings and tears of transport, shall be sufficient consolation to me, for the contempt of all mankind."[514] For both Adams and Beccaria, "preserving one life" could be exonerating a defendant facing the death penalty as well as recognizing the right of persons to carry arms to defend their lives.

---

[512] *The Commonplace Book*, Chinard ed., 314; Cesare Beccaria, *On Crimes and Punishments*, Henry Paolucci trans., 87-88 (Englewood Cliffs, N.J.: Prentice Hall, 1963). The original manuscript is in the *Commonplace Book*, No. 53, Jefferson Papers, Library of Congress.

[513] John D. Bessler, "The Italian Enlightenment and the American Revolution: Cesare Beccaria's Forgotten Influence on American Law," 37 *Hamline J. Pub. L. & Pol'y.* 1, 33 (2016).

[514] 3 John Adams, *Legal Papers* 242 (Cambridge, Mass.: Belknap Press/Harvard University Press, 1965).

As chief justice of the New York Supreme Court, John Jay wrote in 1778 that criminals "multiply exceedingly. Robberies become frequent.... Punishment must of course become certain and mercy dormant."[515] Indeed, in New York, "[t]he volume of serious crime was, especially after 1750, clearly greater than the ability of the colony's agencies of law enforcement to cope with."[516] Even so, Judge Jay too was influenced by Beccaria and supported penal reform.[517]

And Beccaria advocated the right to carry arms for self-defense. The armed citizen thus played a vital role in suppression of crime. Reflecting the traditional hue and cry, New York law required "that all men generally be ready, and armed and accoutered...and at the cry of the country, to pursue and arrest felons."[518]

Crime would remain a serious threat during the Founding era. In Philadelphia in 1798, it was said to be dangerous to set foot outside at night, due in part to fighting between street gangs. It was rumored that French agents were plotting to burn the city. John Adams had to have a sentry posted at the presidential mansion.[519]

Pennsylvania was the first state to adopt a Declaration of Rights with an arms guarantee, which provided: "That the people have a right to bear arms for the defense of themselves, and the state...."[520] Its Constitution had a separate militia provision: "The freemen of this

---

[515] George Pellew, *John Jay* 98 (Boston: Houghton, Mifflin, 1890).

[516] Douglas Greenberg, *Crime and Law Enforcement in the Colony of New York, 1691–1776*, at 213 (Ithaca, N.Y.: Cornell University Press, 1974).

[517] *Id.* at 232.

[518] 1 Laws of the State of New York, Comprising the Constitution, and the Acts of the Legislature, Since the Revolution, From the First to the Fifteenth Session, Inclusive 336 (New York: Thomas Greenleaf, 1792).

[519] David McCullough, *John Adams* 501 (New York: Simon & Schuster, 2001).

[520] Pennsylvania Declaration of Rights, Art. XIII (1776).

commonwealth and their sons shall be trained and armed for its defense, under such regulations, restrictions and exceptions as the general assembly shall by law direct."[521]

Benjamin Franklin, who once noted that "most People hav[e] a Firelock of some kind or other already in their Hands,"[522] presided over the convention.[523] One of the drafters of the constitution was Timothy Matlack, who said that he wore a sword "to defend my property and my liberty."[524] Thomas Paine wrote in the *Pennsylvania Magazine* the same month the convention began its deliberations:

> The supposed quietude of a good man allures the ruffian; while on the other hand, arms like laws discourage and keep the invader and the plunderer in awe, and preserve order in the world as well as property....Horrid mischief would ensue were one half the world deprived of the use of them [arms];...the weak will become a prey to the strong.[525]

The North Carolina Declaration of Rights provided: "That the People have a right to bear Arms for the Defense of the State...."[526] North Carolina's members of the Continental Congress earlier wrote, "It is the Right of every English Subject to be prepared with Weapons for his Defense," and "to be in Readiness to defend yourselves against

---

[521] Pa. Const., § 5 (1776).

[522] *The Political Thought of Benjamin Franklin*, Ralph L. Ketcham ed., 49 (New York: Bobbs-Merrill Co., 1965).

[523] J. Paul Selsam, *The Pennsylvania Constitution of 1776: A Study in Revolutionary Democracy* 175–76 (Philadelphia: University of Pennsylvania Press, 1936).

[524] *Id.* at 207 n.6.

[525] 2 *The Complete Writings of Thomas Paine*, Philip S. Foner ed., 53 (New York: The Citadel Press, 1969).

[526] N.C. Declaration of Rights, Art. XVII (1776).

any Violence that may be exerted against your Persons and Properties."[527]

While constantly fleeing the British, New York's convention adopted a constitution without a bill of rights in 1777.[528] Theodore Roosevelt noted that "the members were obliged to go armed, so as to protect themselves from stray marauding parties."[529]

Vermont's Declaration of Rights of 1777 provided: "That the people have a right to bear arms for the defence of themselves and the State...."[530] Ethan and Ira Allen, Vermont's leading founders, carried firearms for self-defense, hunting, and target shooting. On one occasion, while lodging with a Quaker, Ira Allen recalled: "We took our pistols out of our holsters and carried them in with us. He looked at the pistols saying 'What doth thee do with those things?' He was answered 'Nothing amongst our friends,' but we were Green Mountain boys, and meant to protect our persons and property...."[531]

When John Adams sailed to France in 1778, the necessities he took along included a pocket pistol.[532] He authored the Massachusetts Declaration of Rights of 1780, which provided that all men have "certain natural, essential, and unalienable rights," including the rights of "defending their lives and liberties" and of "protecting property."[533]

---

[527] *North Carolina Gazette* (Newbern), July 7, 1775, at 2, col. 3.

[528] Constitution of 1777, in *Reports of the Proceedings and Debates of the Convention of 1821*, Nathaniel H. Carter and William Stone eds., 691–96 (Albany: F. and E. Hansford, 1821).

[529] Theodore Roosevelt, *Gouverneur Morris* 51 (Boston: Houghton, Mifflin, and Co., 1898).

[530] Vermont Constitution, Art. I, Sec. 15 (1777).

[531] Ira Allen, *Autobiography* (1799), in James B. Wilbur, *Ira Allen: Founder of Vermont, 1751–1814*, at 40 (Boston: Houghton Mifflin, 1928).

[532] David McCullough, *John Adams* 177 (New York: Simon & Schuster, 2001).

[533] Mass. Declaration of Rights, Art. I (1780).

It also stated: "The people have a right to keep and bear arms for the common defence."[534]

Two Massachusetts towns commented on the provisions. The town of Northampton resolved that the arms guarantee would harmonize better with Article I if it read: "The people have a right to keep and bear arms as well for their own as the common defence."[535] Similarly, the town of Williamsburg proposed "that the people have a right to keep and to bear Arms for their Own and the Common defence."[536] Others probably assumed these rights were protected by the existing language. On a practical level, in the same period when the Declaration was being drafted, one could freely buy "100 Pair Horseman's Pistols, neatly mounted with Steel," as advertised in a Boston newspaper.[537]

One "Scribble Scrabble" opined that the Declaration "does not prohibit the people, or take from them, the right originally in them of using arms for other purposes than common defense. Who will say that if an honest farmer were to discharge his musket, ten times a day, at pigeons or other game, he thereby becomes an enemy to the constitution?" Since the beginning of time, all men have had "a right to keep and bear arms for their common defense, to kill game, fowl, &c."[538]

---

[534] *Id.* Art. XVII.

[535] *The Popular Sources of Political Authority: Documents on the Massachusetts Constitution of 1780*, Oscar and Mary Handlin eds., 574 (Cambridge: Belknap Press/Harvard University Press, 1966).

[536] *Id.* at 624.

[537] *Independent Chronicle*, June 29, 1780, at 4, col. 3.

[538] "Scribble-Scrabble," *Cumberland Gazette*, Jan. 26, 1787.

Shays' Rebellion in 1786 led to enactment of a law that if 12 or more persons "armed with clubs, or other weapons" gathered, a justice of the peace could order them to disperse and could "require the aid of a sufficient number of persons in arms" to help.[539] Obviously, 11 or fewer persons could go armed together. Other than that, Massachusetts had no laws restricting the peaceable bearing of arms.

To be sure, one law found "[t]he depositing of loaded arms in the houses of the town of Boston" to be dangerous and thus prohibited taking into any building "any cannon, swivel, mortar, howitzer, or cohorn, or fire-arm, loaded with, or having gun powder in the same...."[540] Designed to protect firefighters, that law would not have been applied to the use of a firearm in self-defense; applicable only in a single city, it provides no insight into the public understanding of the right to keep and bear arms.[541] Another law provided that "no person shall...discharge any gun or pistol, charged with shot or ball, in the town of Boston...."[542] Neither law restricted the carrying of firearms in public.

From colonies to independent states, America was now a political reality, founded in no small part on the belief in and exercise of the right to bear arms individually and collectively to protect life, liberty, and the pursuit of happiness. If founding-era armed Americans were told by a zealot from the twenty-first century that they were violating a medieval English statute, they would have been dumbfounded.

---

[539] 1 The Perpetual Laws of the Commonwealth of Massachusetts, From the Establishment of its Constitution in the Year 1780, To the End of the Year 1800, at 346 (1801).

[540] Act of Mar. 1, 1783, ch. 13, § 2, 1783 Mass. Acts 218.

[541] See *District of Columbia v. Heller*, 554 U.S. 570, 631–32 (2008).

[542] Act of May 28, 1746, ch. X, Acts & Laws of Mass. Bay 208.

It remained to adopt a federal constitution with a bill of rights further to protect the right to bear arms and other fundamental liberties.

Chapter Five

ADOPTION OF THE RIGHT TO BEAR ARMS IN THE THE SECOND AMENDMENT

A) On the Eve of the Federal Constitutional Convention

America's Founders carried firearms. And they believed that they had an inherent right to do so. If anyone suggested that some medieval English statute prohibited them from bearing arms, it remains a secret to this day.

George Washington himself owned perhaps 50 firearms during his life, and some of his pistols (typically silver mounted), saddle holsters, and fowlers (shotguns) may be seen today at Mt. Vernon and West Point. His diaries contain numerous entries related to the acquisition of firearms and to "ducking" and other hunting activities.[543]

Not long after the Revolutionary War ended, Washington and his servant Billy were riding on horseback from Mount Vernon to Alexandria, Virginia. The main road was impassable, so the two had to ride through the farm of a man described as "a desperado who had committed murder." The account (which may or may not be accurate) goes as follows:

---

[543] For photographs and detailed descriptions, *see* Ashley Halsey, Jr., "George Washington's Favorite Guns," *American Rifleman*, Feb. 1968, 23.

them, to his saddle. On returning to Mount Vernon, as General Washington was about to enter on this private road, a stranger on horseback barred the way, and said to him, "You shall not pass this way." "You don't know me," said the General. "Yes, I do," said the ruffian; "you are General Washington, who commanded the army in the Revolution, and if you attempt to pass me I shall shoot you." General Washington called his servant, Billy, to him, and taking out a pistol, examined the priming, and then handed it to Billy, saying, "If this person shoots me, do you shoot him;" and cooly passed on without molestation.[544]

In the Virginia General Assembly, a Committee of Revisors drafted restatements of statutory law for the Commonwealth. Thomas Jefferson played the leading role, with George Wythe and Edmund Pendleton also participating. One of the committee's products, the Bill for Preservation of Deer, illustrates the common linguistic usage of the term to "bear arms."[545]

The bill was presented to the whole House in 1785 by James Madison. The bill provided for deer hunting seasons outside one's enclosed land and punished violations as follows:

> Whosoever shall offend against this act, shall forfeit and pay, for every deer by him unlawfully killed, twenty shillings, one half thereof to the use of the commonwealth, and the other half to the informer; and moreover, shall be bound to their good behavior; and, if within twelve months after the date of the recognizance *he shall bear a gun out of his inclosed ground, unless whilst performing military duty,* shall be deemed a breach of the recognizance, and be good cause to bind him

---

[544] Benjamin Ogle Tayloe, *Our Neighbors on LaFayette Square: Anecdotes and Reminiscences* 47 (Washington, D.C.: Library of American Institute of Architects, 1872).
[545] 2 Thomas Jefferson, *The Papers of Thomas Jefferson*, Julian P. Boyd ed., 444 (Princeton, N.J.: Princeton University Press, 1950).

anew, and *every such bearing of a gun* shall be a breach of the new recognizance and cause to bind him again.[546]

The bill would have prohibited the bearing only of "a gun," not of "arms" in general.[547] In the linguistic usage of the time, to *bear arms* meant to carry a gun or other weapon, including when not on military duty; further, "one species of firearms, the pistol, is never called a gun."[548] Given its purpose to protect deer, the bill would not have prohibited violators from bearing pistols, which were unsuitable for hunting deer but which could be lawfully carried for self-defense.

As noted, the law would have been enforceable through an initial fine of twenty shillings. The court would impose a recognizance, which was an obligation that, if violated, would require the forfeiture of a sum of money. However, the House was apparently unwilling to restrict the places where game violators bore their guns, and no further legislative action was taken after the bill was read twice.[549]

Then Minister to France, Jefferson wrote from Paris in 1785 to his 15-year-old nephew, Peter Carr, advising two hours of exercise every day. "As to the species of exercise, I advise the gun. While this gives a moderate exercise to the body, it gives boldness, enterprise, and

---

[546] *Id.* at 443-44 (emphasis added).

[547] Jefferson's Bill for Establishing a Manufactory of Arms, which defined "arms" as muskets, carbines, pistols, and swords, passed in 1779. 3 Thomas Jefferson, *The Papers of Thomas Jefferson*, Julian P. Boyd ed., 132, 135 (Princeton, N.J.: Princeton University Press, 1951).

[548] Noah Webster, *An American Dictionary of the English Language* (New York: S. Converse, 1828) (definition of "gun").

[549] 2 Jefferson, *The Papers of Thomas Jefferson* 444.

independence to the mind....Let your gun therefore be the constant companion of your walks."[550]

While in Europe, Jefferson collected not only books, but also firearms. His journal reflects a shopping spree in London in March 1786 in which he "p[ai]d....for p[ai]r. pocket pistols, £ 1-18 [one pound 18 shillings]," "powder flask 4/.," and "pr. Pistols silvermounted £ 1-18."[551] One set of the pairs, which are screw-barrel, boxlock flintlock pocket pistols, is preserved today at Monticello.[552]

There was no disconnect between the Founders' belief in the right to bear arms, which they well articulated, and their exercise of that right, which is well documented. While humans engage in many activities that may not be considered inherent rights, free speech, bearing arms, and other substantive liberties ended up in the Bill of Rights because they were indeed viewed as unalienable.[553]

---

[550] Thomas Jefferson, *Writings*, Merrill D. Peterson ed., 816–17 (New York: The Library of America, 1984).

[551] *Jefferson's Memorandum Books*, James A. Bear, Jr. and Lucia C. Stanton eds., 615–16 (Princeton, N.J.: Princeton University Press, 1997).

[552] *Id.* at 615 n.55; Ashley Halsey, Jr., "Jefferson's Beloved Guns," *American Rifleman*, Nov. 1969, 17, 20-21.

[553] As Justice Clarence Thomas wrote about a First Amendment issue in *McIntyre v. Ohio Elections Comm'n*, 514 U.S. 334, 360-61 (1995) (Thomas, J., concurring):

> The essays in the Federalist Papers, published under the pseudonym of "Publius," are only the most famous example of the outpouring of anonymous political writing that occurred during the ratification of the Constitution. Of course, the simple fact that the Framers engaged in certain conduct does not necessarily prove that they forbade its prohibition by the government....In this case, however, the historical evidence indicates that Founding-era Americans opposed attempts to require that anonymous authors reveal their identities on the ground that forced disclosure violated the "freedom of the press."

B) A Federal Constitution with No Bill of Rights?

The Constitution as proposed in 1787 vested an enormous amount of power in the central government, and it had no bill of rights. The Federalists immediately went to work minimizing the potential for harm from these two aspects by pointing to the armed populace as the ultimate check on oppression.

Noah Webster published the first pro-Constitution pamphlet in October 1787, *An Examination of the Leading Principles of the Federal Constitution.*[554] He wrote:

> Another source of power in government is a military force. But this, to be efficient, must be superior to any force that exists among the people, or which they can command; for otherwise this force would be annihilated, on the first exercise of acts of oppression. Before a standing army can rule, the people must be disarmed; as they are in almost every kingdom in Europe. The supreme power in America cannot enforce unjust laws by the sword; because the whole body of the people are armed, and constitute a force superior to any band of regular troops that can be, on any pretence, raised in the United States.[555]

Tench Coxe, another rising Federalist star, wrote a series called "An American Citizen" which has been characterized as the first major

---

[554] 13 *Documentary History of the Ratification of the Constitution*, John P. Kaminski, Gaspare J. Saladino, and Merrill Jensen eds., 405–46 (Madison: State Historical Society of Wisconsin, 1981).

[555] Noah Webster, *An Examination of the Leading Principles of the Federal Constitution* 43 (Philadelphia 1787).

defense of the Constitution.[556] In No. IV of the series, Coxe wrote that, should tyranny impend, the "friends to liberty...using those arms which Providence has put into their hands, will make a solemn appeal to 'the power above.'"[557] He added that the militia "will form a powerful check upon the regular troops, and will generally be sufficient to over-awe them...."[558]

In *The Federalist* No. 29, Alexander Hamilton argued that, should a large army ever be raised, "that army can never be formidable to the liberties of the people while there is a large body of citizens, little if at all inferior to them in discipline and the use of arms, who stand ready to defend their rights and those of their fellow citizens."[559]

In *The Federalist* No. 46, Madison argued that any standing army that might oppress the people "would be opposed [by] a militia amounting to near half a million of citizens with arms in their hands, officered by men chosen from among themselves, fighting for their common liberties, and united and conducted by governments possessing their affections and confidence." That was proven by the successful resistance against the British. "Besides the advantage of being armed, which the Americans possess over the people of almost every other nation," the state governments would form a barrier against usurpation. "Notwithstanding the military establishments in the several

---

[556] 2 *Documentary History of the Ratification of the Constitution*, Merrill Jensen ed., 128 (Madison: State Historical Society of Wisconsin, 1976).
[557] Tench Coxe, "An American Citizen IV" (Oct. 21, 1787), in 13 *Documentary History of the Ratification of the Constitution*, John P. Kaminski Gaspare J. Saladino and Merrill Jensen eds., 433 (Madison: State Historical Society of Wisconsin, 1981).
[558] *Id.* at 435.
[559] 15 *Documentary History of the Ratification of the Constitution*, John P. Kaminski and Gaspare J. Saladino eds., 319 (Madison: State Historical Society of Wisconsin, 1984).

kingdoms of Europe, which are carried as far as the public resources will bear, the governments are afraid to trust the people with arms."[560]

All of these advocates for the Constitution presupposed a robust right to bear arms together with a regular exercise of the right. No one thought that they could only carry firearms within their houses.

Stating the case against ratification of the Constitution without a bill of rights was the *Letters from the Federal Farmer,* which was attributed to Richard Henry Lee of Virginia, but may have been authored by Melancton Smith of New York. Letter XVIII argued that "the constitution ought to secure a genuine [militia] and guard against a select militia, by providing that the militia shall always be kept well organized, armed, and disciplined, and include...all men capable of bearing arms...."[561] Instead of a select militia, "to preserve liberty, it is essential that the whole body of the people always possess arms, and be taught alike, especially when young, how to use them...."[562]

A general militia composed of the body of the people would be more likely to protect the public liberty. A select militia, the members of which would be chosen by the officials in power, would be more likely to serve the interests of those to whom they were beholden.

During 1787–88, John Adams published his *Defense of the Constitutions of Government of the United States of America.* He approved of Aristotle's ideal "to place the use of and exercise of arms in the people, because the commonwealth is theirs who hold the

---

[560] *Id.* at 492–93.
[561] 17 *Documentary History of the Ratification of the Constitution,* John P. Kaminski and Gaspare J. Saladino eds., 362 (Madison: State Historical Society of Wisconsin, 1995).
[562] *Id.* at 363.

arms...."[563] Adams recognized the individual right to use arms for personal protection, but looked askance at the kind of armed protest recently exemplified in Shays' Rebellion: "To suppose arms in the hands of citizens, to be used at individual discretion, except in private self-defense, or by partial orders of towns, counties, or districts of a state, is to demolish every constitution, and lay the laws prostrate, so that liberty can be enjoyed by no man – it is a dissolution of the government."[564]

In short, the Founders were unanimous in support of an armed populace that would act as a counterweight to prevent government from becoming oppressive and would ensure that individuals had the means to defend themselves. The looming issue became whether it was necessary to formalize rights such as free speech and bearing arms in a declaration of rights.

C) Demands for a Bill of Rights

When state conventions were called to consider ratification of the Constitution, the Federalists sought a quick approval without any declaration of rights or other amendments. They succeeded at first, but Antifederalist demands for a bill of rights would win out in the end.

The Antifederalists in the Pennsylvania ratification convention proposed a bill of rights, and when it was rejected, published it as the Dissent of the Minority. It declared in part: "That the people have a right to bear arms for the defense of themselves and their own state, or the United States, or for the purpose of killing game; and no law shall

---

[563] 3 John Adams, *A Defense of the Constitutions of Government of the United States of America* 471-72 (1787–88).
[564] *Id.* at 475.

be passed for disarming the people or any of them, unless for crimes committed, or real danger of public injury from individuals...."[565]

Tench Coxe, under the pen name "A Pennsylvanian," argued against the Dissent that no need for amendments existed based on the populace being armed:

THE POWERS OF THE SWORD ARE IN THE HANDS OF THE YEOMANRY OF AMERICA FROM SIXTEEN TO SIXTY. The militia of these free commonwealths, entitled and accustomed to their arms, when compared with any possible army, must be tremendous and irresistible. Who are the militia? are they not ourselves....Congress have no power to disarm the militia. Their swords, and every other terrible implement of the soldier, are the birth-right of an American....[T]he unlimited power of the sword is not in the hands of either the federal or state governments, but, where I trust in God it will ever remain, in the hands of the people.[566]

"A Farmer" wrote in the Philadelphia *Freeman's Journal*: "It is only free republics that can completely and safely form a federal republic: I say free republics, for there are republics who are not free, such as Venice, where a citizen carrying arms is punished with instant death...."[567] Venice's law imposing capital punishment for bearing arms was well known from Montesquieu.[568]

In the Massachusetts convention, Samuel Adams proposed a bill of rights providing "that the said Constitution be never construed to

---

[565] 2 *Documentary History of the Ratification of the Constitution*, 623–24.
[566] "To the Citizens of the United States, III," *Pennsylvania Gazette*, Feb. 20, 1788, in 2 *Documentary History of the Ratification of the Constitution* (microfilm supplement), at 1778–1780.
[567] Philadelphia Freeman's Journal, April 23, 1788, in 17 *Documentary History of the Ratification of the Constitution* 137.
[568] 2 Montesquieu, *The Spirit of the Laws*, Thomas Nugent transl., 79–80 (1899).

authorize Congress, to infringe the just liberty of the press...; or to prevent the people of the United States, who are peaceable citizens, from keeping their own arms...."[569]

It was not adopted, as the Federalists argued that Congress had no such powers. Indeed, when the convention ratified the Constitution, the mass celebrations in Boston included a cart drawn by five horses in which "the British flag was displayed, and insulted by numbers placed in the cart, armed with muskets, who repeatedly discharged the contents of them through the tattered remnant...."[570] For two or three days were heard "Bells – Drums – Guns – Procession &c."[571] The rights to free speech and to bear arms were thus exercised together in very practical ways.

The dam finally broke with the Antifederalist majority in the New Hampshire convention, which ratified the Constitution along with a demand for a bill of rights. It included: "Congress shall never disarm any citizen, unless such as are or have been in actual rebellion."[572] New Hampshire became the ninth state to ratify the Constitution, resulting in the two-thirds of States necessary to make it effective. And it was the first state formally to demand that the new Constitution include a bill of rights.

---

[569] 6 *Documentary History of the Ratification of the Constitution*, John P. Kaminski and Gaspare J. Saladino eds., 1453 (Madison: State Historical Society of Wisconsin, 2000).

[570] *Massachusetts Gazette*, Feb. 8, 1788, in 7 *Documentary History of the Ratification of the Constitution*, John P. Kaminski and Gaspare J. Saladino eds., 1612 (Madison: State Historical Society of Wisconsin, 2001).

[571] *Id.* at 1597.

[572] 18 *Documentary History of the Ratification of the Constitution*, John P. Kaminski and Gaspare J. Saladino eds., 188 (Madison: State Historical Society of Wisconsin, 1995).

In an essay "To the Citizens of Virginia," Alexander White replied to the Pennsylvania Dissent of Minority that there were things "clearly out of the power of Congress," including "the rights of bearing arms for defence, or for killing game...." Such objections were made "merely to induce the ignorant to believe that Congress would have a power over such objects and to infer from their being refused a place in the Constitution, their intention to exercise that power to the oppression of the people."[573]

Once again, the right to bear arms referred to an individual liberty, not a militia function, and its purpose varied from defense to hunting. Similarly, "Common Sense" worried "that the chief power will be in the Congress," and that "a citizen may be deprived of the privilege of keeping arms for his own defence...."[574] One's "own defence" was a purpose of the right to keep and bear arms.

In the Virginia convention in 1788, George Mason recalled that "when the resolution of enslaving America was formed in Great Britain, the British Parliament was advised...to disarm the people; that it was the best and most effectual way to enslave them."[575] And Patrick Henry implored: "The great object is, that every man be armed."[576] The ensuing debate concerned defense against tyranny and invasion.

---

[573] *Winchester Gazette* (Virginia), February 22, 1788, in 8 *The Documentary History of The Ratification of the Constitution*, John P. Kaminski and Gaspare J. Saladino eds., 404 (Madison: State Historical Society of Wisconsin, 1988).

[574] "From the Wilmington Centinel, To the People of North Carolina," *The New York Journal, and Daily Patriotic Register*, April 21, 1788, at 2, col. 2.

[575] 3 *The Debates in the Several State Conventions on the Adoption of the Federal Constitution*, Jonathan Elliot ed., 380 (1836).

[576] *Id.* at 386.

In ratifying the Constitution, the Virginia convention proposed a bill of rights asserting "the essential and unalienable rights of the people," including: "That the people have a right to keep and bear arms; that a well-regulated militia, composed of the body of the people, trained to arms, is the proper, natural, and safe defence of a free state....."[577]

By now, the demand for a bill of rights became ascendant. North Carolina[578] and Rhode Island[579] demanded the same arms guarantee as Virginia. New York proposed slightly different wording: "That the people have a right to keep and bear arms; that a well regulated militia, including the body of the people *capable of bearing arms*, is the proper, natural, and safe defence of a free state.[580] The right to bear arms had universal support.

It has been speculated that the Second Amendment was adopted to protect slavery.[581] Not only is there not a shred of evidence of this, but the Northern states – which abolished or were less reliant on slavery – led the effort to guarantee the right to bear arms. Pennsylvania, which recognized the right to bear arms in its Declaration of Rights of 1776, passed the first state abolition act in 1780.[582] Vermont's Declaration of Rights of 1777 both abolished slavery and declared the right to bear

---

[577] *Id.* at 658–59.
[578] 18 *Documentary History of the Ratification of the Constitution*, 316.
[579] 1 Elliot, *Debates in the Several State Conventions*, 335.
[580] 18 *Documentary History of the Ratification of the Constitution*, John P. Kaminski and Gaspare J. Saladino eds., 298 (Madison: State Historical Society of Wisconsin, 1995).
[581] Carl T. Bogus, "The Hidden History of the Second Amendment," 31 *U.C. Davis L. Rev.* 309 (1998).
[582] An Act for the Gradual Abolition of Slavery (March 1, 1780), http://www.phmc.state.pa.us/portal/communities/documents/1776-1865/abolition-slavery.html.

arms.[583] In Massachusetts, slavery was declared unconstitutional in judicial cases in 1781-83.[584] New Hampshire's 1783 Constitution was read by many to abolish slavery, and its 1790 census counted few slaves.[585] While New York did not enact a law to abolish slavery until 1799, its 1777 constitutional convention resolved to end slavery.[586] Rhode Island abolished slavery in 1784.[587]

As discussed above, the attempt by the British to disarm the Americans and the need to guard against tyranny and invasion were the only concerns voiced during the critical debates in the Virginia convention. No mention of slavery in relation to the right to bear arms was uttered in a single one of the state ratification conventions or in the public discourse.

What became the Second Amendment, as discussed above, was proposed in ratification conventions by Samuel Adams in Massachusetts and by the Antifederalists in Pennsylvania; it was formally demanded by the ratification conventions of New Hampshire, Virginia, North Carolina, New York, and Rhode Island, all during 1787-90. That adds up to five Northern states and only two Southern states where the right to keep and bear arms played a prominent role in the ratification process. To denigrate the Second Amendment by

---

[583] Vt. Const., Ch. I, §§ 1 & 15 (1777).

[584] "Massachusetts Constitution and the Abolition of Slavery," https://www.mass.gov/guides/massachusetts-constitution-and-the-abolition-of-slavery#-the-quock-walker-case-.

[585] "Slavery in New Hampshire," http://slavenorth.com/newhampshire.htm.

[586] "Emancipation in New York," http://slavenorth.com/nyemancip.htm.

[587] An Act authorizing the Manumission of Negroes, Mulattoes and others, & for the gradual Abolition of Slavery (Feb. 26, 1784), https://americasbesthistory.com/abhtimeline1784m.html.

asserting that it was motivated by a secret conspiracy to protect slavery, unsupported by facts, demeans the Bill of Rights itself.

The defect in the early American polity was that, because of slavery, the liberties in the Bill of Rights did not extend to all persons. The remedy was not to deprive everyone of rights such as free speech and bearing arms, but to extend those rights to all Americans.

D) Adopting the Second Amendment to the Federal Constitution, 1789–91

James Madison drafted what became the Bill of Rights. In notes he prepared for introducing the amendments to the House of Representatives in 1789, Madison averred that "[t]hey relate 1[st] to private rights," and observed a fallacy "as to English Decl[aratio]n. of Rights – 1. mere act of parl[iamen]t. 2. no freedom of press –…arms to protest[an]ts."[588] By contrast, in America rights would be protected by the Constitution, not by a "mere act" of Congress that could be repealed, and these rights would be expanded to recognize the press and to extend the arms right to all persons, not just Protestants.

Madison introduced his draft of what became the Bill of Rights to the House of Representatives on June 8, 1789. It included the provision: "The right of the people to keep and bear arms shall not be infringed; a well armed, and well regulated militia being the best security of a free country: but no person religiously scrupulous of bearing arms shall be compelled to render military service in person."[589] While several states had proposed simply "that the people have a right to keep and bear

---

[588] Madison, Notes for Speech in Congress, June 8, 1789, 12 *The Papers of James Madison*, Charles F. Hobson et al. eds., 193–94 (Charlottesville: University Press of Virginia, 1979).
[589] 4 *Documentary History of the First Federal Congress*, Charlene Bangs Bickford ed., 10 (Baltimore: Johns Hopkins University Press, 1986).

arms," Madison inserted the stronger guard that this right "shall not be infringed."

Ten days after Madison proposed his amendments, Tench Coxe—under the pen name "A Pennsylvanian"—published the following explanation: "As civil rulers, not having their duty to the people duly before them, may attempt to tyrannize, and as the military forces which must be occasionally raised to defend our country, might pervert their power to the injury of their fellow-citizens, the people are confirmed...in their right to keep and bear their private arms."[590]

Madison wrote a letter to Coxe complimenting him on the article and commenting that the proposed bill of rights would "be greatly favored by explanatory strictures of a healing tendency, and is therefore already indebted to the co-operation of your pen."[591]

Samuel Nasson, who had been a delegate to the Massachusetts convention, explained the common understanding of the arms guarantee in a letter dated July 9, 1789, to Representative George Thatcher, a Federalist from that state:

> A Bill of Rights well secured that we the people may know how far we may Proceed in Every Department. Then there will be no Dispute Between the people and rulers in that may be secured the right to keep arms for Common and Extraordinary Occasions such as to secure ourselves against the wild Beast and also to amuse us by fowling and for our Defence against a Common Enemy. You know to learn the Use of arms is all that can Save us from a foreign foe that may attempt to subdue us, for if we keep up the Use of arms and become well

---

[590] "Remarks on the First Part of the Amendments to the Federal Constitution," *Federal Gazette*, June 18, 1789, at 2, col. 1.
[591] Madison to Coxe, June 24, 1789, in 12 *Papers of James Madison*, 257.

acquainted with them, we Shall always be able to look them in the face that arise up against us.[592]

In short, the right to keep and bear arms exists for both common and extraordinary occasions, including hunting wild beasts and fowl, and protection from a common foe. The purpose was a citizenry with regular experience in the use of arms.

The House of Representatives revised Madison's draft to state: "A well regulated militia, composed of the body of the people, being the best security of a free state, the right of the people to keep and bear arms shall not be infringed; but no person religiously scrupulous shall be compelled to bear arms."[593] It was considered by the House on August 17, 1789. No one objected to the arms clause, but Elbridge Gerry feared the conscientious-objector clause "would give an opportunity to the people in power to destroy the constitution itself. They can declare who are those religiously scrupulous, and prevent them from bearing arms."[594] Since he opposed giving "a discretionary power to exclude those from militia duty who have religious scruples," he moved that the clause be limited to actual members of religious sects scrupulous of bearing arms.[595]

The House passed the above version of the amendment, but the Senate amended it to read: "A well regulated militia, being the best security of a free state, the right of the people to keep and bear arms,

---

[592] *Creating the Bill of Rights*, Helen E. Veit *et al.* eds., 260-61 (Baltimore: Johns Hopkins University Press, 1991) (letter dated July 9, 1789). Spelling and punctuation corrected.
[593] 4 *Documentary History of the First Federal Congress*, 28.
[594] 11 *Documentary History of the First Federal Congress*, 1285–86.
[595] *Id.* at 1286.

shall not be infringed."[596] The Senate rejected a proposal to add "for the common defence" after "bear arms." It changed "the best security of a free state" to "necessary to the security of a free state." The Senate then passed its final version: "A well regulated militia being necessary to the security of a free state, the right of the people to keep and bear arms shall not be infringed."[597] Other than the adding of two more commas, it would be submitted to the states in that form for ratification.

The proposed amendments were then sent to the states for consideration. At the end of 1791, Virginia's ratification secured the necessary three-fourths of the states for adoption of what then became the Bill of Rights.

E) Self-Defense as the Primary Law of Nature: Justice James Wilson's Lectures

In 1790, Pennsylvania strengthened its guarantee in the Declaration of Rights to state: "That the right of the citizens to bear arms in defense of themselves and the state shall not be questioned."[598] It was drafted in part by James Wilson, who also presided over the convention, and William Findley, who had signed the Dissent of Minority in 1788.[599]

In 1789, James Wilson was appointed by President George Washington as a Justice to the United States Supreme Court, and the following year he became the first law professor at the College of

---

[596] *Journal of the First Session of the Senate of the United States of America*, 71 (Washington, D.C.: Gales & Seaton, 1820).
[597] *Id.* at 77.
[598] Pennsylvania Declaration of Rights, Art. XXI (1790).
[599] *The Proceedings Relative to Calling the Conventions of 1776 and 1790*, at 153–54 (Harrisburg, Pa.: John S. Wiestling, 1825).

Philadelphia.[600] His lectures there exposited the right to have and use arms for self-defense.

"The defence of one's self, justly called the primary law of nature, is not, nor can it be abrogated by any regulation of municipal law," wrote Wilson. The principle extended to the protection of others as well as liberty and property.[601] Wilson quoted Cicero's oration in defense of Milo, which concluded that "a man who has used arms in self-defence is not regarded as having carried them with a homicidal aim."[602]

Wilson further wrote: "Homicide is enjoined [authorized], when it is necessary for the defence of one's person or house."[603] He explained that "the great natural law of self preservation...is expressly recognised in the constitution of Pennsylvania. 'The right of the citizens to bear arms in the defence of themselves shall not be questioned.'" This was a renewal of a Saxon regulation...'to keep arms for the preservation of the kingdom, and of their own persons.'"[604]

Wilson repeated Hawkins' statement that an affray may be committed "where a man arms himself with dangerous and unusual weapons, *in such a manner*, as will naturally diffuse a terrour among the people."[605] A justice of the peace could require a security to keep

---

[600] 1 *The Works of James Wilson*, Robert Green McCloskey ed., 28 (Cambridge, Mass.: Belknap Press/Harvard University Press, 1967).

[601] 2 *The Works of the Honourable James Wilson* 496 (Philadelphia: Lorenzo Press, 1804).

[602] *Id.*, quoting "Cic. pro Mil." (*Cicero pro Milo*) in Latin. The above translation is from Cicero, *Selected Political Speeches*, Michael Grant trans., 222 (New York: Penguin Books, 1969).

[603] 3 *The Works of the Honourable James Wilson*, 84.

[604] *Id.*

[605] *Id.* at 654 (emphasis added). Ignoring the phrase "in such a manner," one writer asserts that passages like this show that "the carrying of dangerous weapons in the public concourse – without the license of government – is what placed the people in great fear or terror...." Patrick J. Charles, "The Statute of Northampton by the Late Eighteenth

the peace of "those who, in his presence, shall make an affray, or shall threaten to kill or beat any person, or shall contend together with hot words, or shall go about with unusual weapons or attendants, to the terrour of the citizens."[606] But citizens had a right peaceably "to bear arms in defense of themselves," as the Pennsylvania Declaration guaranteed.

F) Carrying Arms for Militia Purposes as a Right and a Duty

Under colonial and state militia laws, able-bodied citizens were required to furnish their own arms and to carry them to musters and in service. Like everyone else, militiamen were free to carry their arms at will, regardless of whether they were engaged in militia duties.

Militia training days were filled with exercises, sport, war games, and shooting competitions. Militiamen would come in from the country or from their houses in towns with their arms and gather at the town common for the entire day in a festival-like atmosphere. They were free to roam about town with their muskets and pistols without any restrictions, other than that firearms had to be discharged at safe targets.[607]

The Militia Act that Congress passed in 1792 required able-bodied male citizens to provide themselves with arms, enroll in the militia, and appear armed when called out to exercise or into service. No exemption from any laws prohibiting the carrying of arms was needed to allow them to carry arms when called out, because no such laws existed.

Century: Clarifying the Intellectual Legacy," 41 *Fordham Urb. L.J. City Square* 10, 21 (2013).
[606] *Id.*, vol. 3, at 130 (citing 1 Hawkins 126).
[607] See Marie L. Ahearn, *The Rhetoric of War: Training Day, the Militia, and the Military Sermon* (New York: Greenwood Press, 1989), particularly chapter 2.

Americans were free peaceably to carry muskets, pistols, and other arms for any lawful purpose, whether private or militia related.

"As far as the whole body of the people are necessary to the general defence, they ought to be armed," explained Thomas Fitzsimons of Pennsylvania in debate in 1790 on the militia bill in the House of Representatives.[608] James Jackson of Georgia argued "that the people would never be dissatisfied with bearing arms in their own defence; this right, he observed, was one of the dearest to a freeman."[609] He urged that it was their duty "to provide the means for every man to protect himself as well against tyranny and usurpation, as against assault and invasion."[610]

Roger Sherman of Connecticut "thought there were so few free men in the United States incapable of procuring themselves a musquet, bayonet and cartouchbox, as to render any regulation by the general government respecting them improper." If the arms were provided by Congress, they would be lost or destroyed.[611]

Against a motion to delete the requirement in the bill that every man "provide himself" with arms and insert that every man "shall be provided" with arms,[612] Jackson explained that "most of the citizens of America possessed and used guns. In Georgia and in the back country they were useful to procure food, and were to be met with in every House. He had no doubt but the people would supply themselves fully, without the interference of the Legislature...."[613]

---

[608] 14 *Documentary History of the First Federal Congress*, 73.
[609] *Id.* at 49–50.
[610] *Id.* at 56–57.
[611] *Id.* at 60.
[612] 5 *Documentary History of the First Federal Congress*, 1461 n.3.
[613] 14 *Documentary History of the First Federal Congress*, 63–64.

Sherman "conceived it to be the privilege of every citizen, and one of his most essential rights, to bear arms, and to resist every attack upon his liberty or property, by whomsoever made. The particular states, like private citizens, have a right to be armed, and to defend, by force of arms, their rights, when invaded."[614] Jackson agreed "that every citizen was not only entitled to carry arms, but also in duty bound to perfect himself in the use of them, and thus become capable of defending his country."[615]

In these remarks, made during the 1790 debate, to "bear arms" was synonymous with to "carry arms," and bearing arms was seen as an individual right to arms to defend life, liberty, and property as well as a right to associate with others to defend the country. This linguistic usage was not very remarkable because it was so commonplace.

The Militia Act slowly worked its way through both houses of Congress and was signed by President Washington on May 8, 1792.[616] The Act began by requiring that "each and every free able-bodied white[617] male citizen of the respective states," aged 18 to 44, be enrolled in the militia.[618] Each militiaman was required to arm himself as follows:

> That every citizen so enrolled and notified, shall, within six months thereafter, provide himself with a good musket or firelock, a sufficient bayonet and belt, two spare flints, and a knapsack, a pouch with a box therein to contain not less than twenty-four cartridges, suited to the

---

[614] *Id.* at 92-3.
[615] *Id.* at 95.
[616] Chap. 33, 1 Hening, *Statutes at Large* 271 (1792).
[617] In 1867, the term "white" was deleted so as to include the now-freed blacks in the militia. 14 Stat. 422, 423 (1867).
[618] § 1, 1 Stat. at 271.

bore of his musket or firelock, each cartridge to contain a proper quantity of powder and ball: or with a good rifle, knapsack, shot-pouch and powder-horn, twenty balls suited to the bore of his rifle and a quarter of a pound of powder; and shall appear, so armed, accoutred and provided, when called out to exercise, or into service....[619]

In his 1828 dictionary, Noah Webster—who had been a leading Federalist pamphleteer (see above)—defined "musket" as "a species of fire-arms used in war, and fired by means of a lighted match." That ignition system was obsolete, but the term "in common speech, is yet applied to fusees or fire-locks fired by a spring lock."[620] A "firelock" was defined as "a musket, or other gun, with a lock, which is discharged by striking fire with flint and steel."[621] A "fusee" was "a small neat musket or firelock."[622] The rifle was the most accurate arm, which Webster defined as "a gun about the usual length and size of a musket, the inside of whose barrel is *rifled*, that is, grooved, or formed with spiral channels."[623]

The Act provided that "the commissioned officer shall severally be armed with a sword or hanger and espontoon" (a half pike),[624] but that such officers in troops of horses must furnish themselves with a horse and "be armed with a sword and pair of pistols, the holsters of which to be covered with bearskin caps." Dragoons, who were trained

---

[619] *Id.*
[620] Noah Webster, *An American Dictionary of the English Language* (New York: S. Converse, 1828).
[621] *Id.*
[622] *Id.*
[623] *Id.*
[624] *Id.*

to fight on horseback and on foot, must also be armed with a pair of pistols along with a sabre.[625]

Regarding the above provision that the militiaman "shall appear, so armed, accoutred and provided, when called out to exercise, or into service,"[626] no need existed for exempting him from any laws against carrying firearms, because no such laws existed. By contrast, it was necessary to provide that the militiaman "shall hold the same [arms] exempted from all suits, distresses, executions or sales, for debt or for the payment of taxes."[627]

Militiamen, "during the time of their being under arms," were subject to having their arms and equipment inspected to ensure compliance with the requirements, and officers of different corps in the state would report "the actual situation of their arms" and equipment to the adjutant general.[628] Since inspection of arms took place only when the militiaman was on duty and extended only to the required arms, the Act was not a precedent for a registration system in which authorities kept records on all arms owned by the citizens.

The Act recognized that "sundry corps of artillery, cavalry, and infantry now exist in several of the said states, which by the laws, customs, or usages thereof have not been incorporated with, or subject to the general regulations of the militia...." It declared that "such corps retain their accustomed privileges, subject, nevertheless, to all other duties required by this act, in like manner with the other militia."[629]

---

[625] § 4, 1 Stat. at 272.
[626] § 1, *Id.* at 271.
[627] § 1, *Id.* at 272.
[628] §§ 6 & 10, *Id.* at 273.
[629] § 11, *Id.* at 274.

That accommodated various militias in the states, some of which were voluntary and independent.

G) Last Words from the Founders on the Right to Be Armed

Many of America's Founders carried pistols mostly for self-defense in everyday life, and carried long guns when desired, such as for self-defense, hunting, target shooting, and militia service. Pistols were and are designed to be easily carried. No question exists that they believed that their right to bear arms entitled them to do so. As if to speak from the grave, they bequeathed their arms to be borne by their survivors.

George Washington died in 1799, and the inventory of his estate listed 7 swords and 7 guns in the study, "1 pr Steel Pistols" and "3 pr Pistols" in an iron chest, "1 Old Gun" in the storehouse, and one gun at the River Farm.[630] His last will and testament included the following: "To General de la Fayette I give a pair of finely wrought steel pistols, taken from the enemy in the Revolutionary war."[631]

Patrick Henry died a few months earlier, also in 1799, and the inventory of his estate includes "1 large Gun" and "1 pr. pistols."[632] As an attorney, Henry had regularly carried a firearm while walking from his home to the courthouse.[633]

Thomas Jefferson's memorandum books kept between 1768 and 1823 show numerous references to the acquisition of pistols, guns,

---

[630] Eugene E. Prussing, *The Estate of George Washington, Deceased* 416, 418, 486, 441 (Boston: Little, Brown, & Co., 1927).

[631] *Copies of the Wills of General George Washington…and Other Interesting Records of the County of Fairfax, Virginia* 20 (publisher not identified).

[632] George Morgan, *The True Patrick Henry* 464 (Philadelphia: J.B. Lippincott, 1907).

[633] Harlow Giles Unger, *Lion of Liberty* 30 (Boston: Da Capo Press, 2010).

muskets, rifles, and fusils.[634] In an 1803 letter to Paul Verdier, innkeeper at Orange Courthouse, Jefferson wrote: "I left at your house, the morning after I lodged there, a pistol in a locked case, which no doubt was found in your bar after my departure. I have written to [illegible] Mr. Randolph or Mr. Eppes to call on you for it, as they come on to Congress, to either of whom therefore be so good as to deliver it."[635]

In an 1816 letter, Jefferson informed John Payne Todd of his gift of a pair of Turkish pistols with 20 inch barrels, "so well made that I never missed a squirrel at 30 yards with them. I fixed one in a wooden holster to hang in the loop of the pommel of [my saddle] to be handily taken out and in....I had other holsters also made for both [to] hang them at the side of my carriage for road use, and with locks and staples to secure them from being handled by curious people."[636]

In an 1822 letter, Jefferson wrote to Peter Minor that he was sending him a keep-sake, "an article of the tackle of a gunman, offering the convenience of carrying the powder & shot together." "Every American who wishes to protect his farm from the ravages of quadrupeds & his country from those of biped invaders" ought to be a

---

[634] *See* "Firearms" in Index and referenced text in *Jefferson's Memorandum Books*, 1550. *See also* Ashley Halsey, Jr., "Jefferson's Beloved Guns," *American Rifleman*, Nov. 1969, 17.

[635] 41 *Papers of Thomas Jefferson*, ed. Barbara B. Oberg, 486 (Princeton University Press 2014). See original letter at http://memory.loc.gov/cgi-bin/ampage?collId=mtj1&fileName=mtj1page029.db&recNum=210.

[636] 10 *Papers of Thomas Jefferson* (Retirement Series), ed. J. Jefferson Looney, 320–21 (Princeton University Press, 2013).

gunman, he added. "I am a great friend to the manly and healthy exercises of the gun."[637]

In an 1824 missive to English Whig Major John Cartwright, Jefferson wrote: "The constitutions of most of our States assert, that all power is inherent in the people...that it is their right and duty to be at all times armed...."[638] The "right" to be armed "at all times" surely precludes the modern fiction that the Founders thought that no right to be armed existed other than in the home or in the militia.

As noted earlier in this chapter, just after Madison proposed the Bill of Rights in Congress in 1789, Tench Coxe explained that what became the Second Amendment confirmed the right of the people "to keep and bear their private arms."[639] Coxe would go on to serve in the Washington, Adams, and Jefferson administrations. As late as 1823, Coxe found himself still writing newspaper articles on the right to keep and bear arms, this time on behalf of the Republican Party against the Presidential campaign of John Quincy Adams.[640] He referred to "the right to own and use arms and consequently of self-defense and of the public militia power...."[641]

Decrying the English game laws that were intended to disarm the populace, Coxe wrote that "his own firearms are the second and better

---

[637] Jefferson to Peter Minor, July 20, 1822, quoted by Monticello archivist James A. Bear, Jr., "Guns, Exercise, and Hunting," 3 (Charlottesville: Monticello, n.d. mimeograph).

[638] Jefferson, *Writings*, 1491–92.

[639] "Remarks on the First Part of the Amendments to the Federal Constitution," *Federal Gazette*, June 18, 1789, at 2, col. 1.

[640] *See* Stephen P. Halbrook & David B. Kopel, "Tench Coxe and the Right to Keep and Bear Arms, 1787–1823," 7 *William & Mary Bill of Rights Journal*, Issue 2, 347-99 (Feb. 1999).

[641] *Democratic Press* (Philadelphia), Jan. 23, 1823, at 2, col. 2.

right hand of every freeman…."[642] He made the following observation that having arms is sometimes a duty, but is ever a right:

> So prudent, faithful and provident have our people and constitutions been, that we find in their precious bills of rights, schedules of duties, reasons of powers, and declarations recognizing the right to own, keep and use arms, provisions preventing and forbidding the legislatures to interfere with and to abrogate, that all important right of the citizens.[643]

Thomas Jefferson and John Adams both died on July 4, 1826, but James Madison would persist another decade. In his final years, Madison warned against the replacement of a republic by an aristocracy, which could not take place "without a standing Army, an enslaved press, and a disarmed populace."[644]

By now the Founders had faded away. America's Founding era had ended. The new Republic was in full swing.

---

[642] Sherman [Coxe's pen name], "To the People of the United States," No. IX, apparently published in the *Democratic Press* or in the *Philadelphia Sentinel and Mercantile Advertiser* in 1823, or possibly 1824. *Papers of Tench Coxe in the Coxe Family Papers at the Historical Society of Pennsylvania*, Microfilm Reel 113, at 716. (Philadelphia: Historical Society of Pennsylvania, 1977).

[643] *Id.* at 717.

[644] James Madison, "James Madison's Autobiography," 2 *William & Mary Quarterly* 191, 208 (1945).

Part Three

THE RIGHT TO BEAR ARMS IN THE NINETEENTH CENTURY

Chapter Six

GOING ARMED IN THE EARLY AMERICAN REPUBLIC

Throughout the early American Republic, ordinary Americans used and carried firearms as a regular part of their lives as citizens. But even beyond these lived experiences, the right to bear arms was being progressively recognized in most new state constitutions as the United States grew. Then-contemporary legal commentaries explained the right as an individual liberty to carry arms for self-defense and as a guard against tyranny.

However, going armed offensively in a manner to terrorize one's fellow citizens was prohibited by statute or by the common law. Persons doing so were ordered to find sureties to keep the peace.

While at the Founding the peaceable carrying of arms was unrestricted, beginning in 1813 a minority of states made it an offense to carry weapons concealed. These laws were upheld because they did not outlaw the right and ability to continue to carry firearms for self-defense or other lawful purposes. All of these states continued to recognize the right to carry arms openly.

Selective bans on bearing arms were tools of oppression. In some states, slaves and African Americans were prohibited from possessing or carrying arms without a license or at all. Free persons of color were required to obtain a license to carry a firearm that an official had discretion to issue or withhold.

The following analyzes the broad right peaceably to carry arms and the restrictions on doing so offensively, together with the bans on concealed weapons and on the bearing of arms by black persons, in the early American Republic.

A) New States Entering the Republic in the Antebellum Period Recognize the Right to Bear Arms

Just a year after the Bill of Rights was ratified in 1791, new states began to be admitted to the Union, and most adopted a guarantee of the right to bear arms.[645] While the wording varied, the influence of the state bills of rights adopted beginning in 1776 as well as of the Second Amendment is clear. After all, the right to carry arms was seen as a preexisting, fundamental right. Unchallenged recognition of the right to bear arms precludes a depiction of that era as one in which carrying arms was generally prohibited.

Kentucky became a state in 1792, and it copied Pennsylvania's language from two years before: "That the right of the citizens to bear arms in defense of themselves and the State shall not be questioned."[646] Next came Tennessee in 1796, and it declared: "That the freemen of this State have a right to keep and to bear arms for their common

---

[645] For a compilation of all arms guarantees and years of adoption, see State Constitutional Right to Keep and Bear Arms Provisions. https://www2.law.ucla.edu/volokh/beararms/statecon.htm.
[646] Ky. Const., Art. XII, § 23 (1792).

defence."[647] Ohio, in 1802, affirmed: "That the people have a right to bear arms for the defence of themselves and the State...."[648]

Of the states admitted between 1816 and 1820, Indiana declared: "That the people have a right to bear arms for the defense of themselves and the State...."[649] Mississippi's provision was almost identical, except its use of "every citizen" rather than "the people": "Every citizen has a right to bear arms, in defence of himself and the State."[650] Although already a state, Connecticut adopted its first constitution in 1818 and copied Mississippi's language.[651] So did Alabama.[652] Maine's wording varied as follows: "Every citizen has a right to keep and bear arms for the common defence; and this right shall never be questioned."[653] Finally, Missouri combined two rights in the same section: "That the people have the right peaceably to assemble...and that their right to bear arms in defence of themselves and of the State cannot be questioned."[654]

No more states were admitted to the Union from 1821 until the mid-1830s. Starting with the admission of new states again in 1835, the right to bear arms continued to be recognized formally. The first new state was Michigan, which declared: "Every person has a right to bear arms for the defence of himself and the State."[655] But three states limited the right to whites. Tennessee amended its guarantee, which

---

[647] Tenn. Const., Art. XI, § 26 (1796).
[648] Ohio Const., Art. VIII, § 20 (1802).
[649] Ind. Const., Art. I, § 20 (1816).
[650] Miss. Const., Art. I, § 23 (1817).
[651] Conn. Const., Art. I, § 17 (1818).
[652] Ala. Const., Art. I, § 23 (1819).
[653] Me. Const., Art. I, § 16 (1819).
[654] Mo. Const., Art. XIII, § 3 (1820).
[655] Mich. Const., Art. I, § 13 (1835).

Arkansas and Florida copied, to state: "That the free white men of this State shall have a right to keep and to bear arms for their common defence."[656] While already a state, Rhode Island adopted its first constitution in 1842, declaring simply: "The right of the people to keep and bear arms shall not be infringed."[657]

Of the last three arms guarantees adopted in the antebellum period, Texas declared in 1845: "Every citizen shall have the right to keep and bear arms in lawful defence of himself or the State."[658] In 1859, Oregon adopted this wording: "The people shall have the right to bear arms for the defence of themselves, and the State...."[659] Finally, the same year, Kansas declared: "The people have the right to bear arms for their defense and security...."[660]

In sum, while the wording varied, all of the above recognized a "right," not a legal duty, to "bear arms," meaning to carry them. This "right" was held by "the citizens," "the freemen," "the people," "every citizen," "every person," or most narrowly, "the free white men of this State." The purpose of bearing arms was specified as "defense of themselves and the State," "defence of himself and the State," "common defence," and "defense and security," with one state merely saying that the right "shall not be infringed."

In no sense were any of the above guarantees limited to the militia, which was not even mentioned. None of these guarantees was consistent with a general ban on carrying arms in public. The plain text

---

[656] Tenn. Const., Art. I, § 26 (1834); Ark. Const., Art. II, § 21 (1836); Fla. Const., Art. I, § 21(1838).
[657] R.I. Const., Art. I, § 22 (1842).
[658] Tex. Const., Art. I, § 13 (1845).
[659] Ore. Const., Art. I, § 28 (1857).
[660] Kan. Const., Art. I, § 4 (1859).

of each—*the right* to bear arms—was not some kind of secret code for *no right* to bear arms. No Illuminati-like conspiracy was afoot surreptitiously to incorporate a misinterpreted version of England's Statute of Northampton of 1328 into these constitutions to turn the right to bear arms into the crime of bearing arms.

At the same time that new states were entering the young Republic and adopting bills of rights that included the right to bear arms, legal minds were authoring commentaries on that right as expressed in the state constitutions and the Second Amendment. The right to carry arms outside the home in public was an unquestioned premise. The following analysis of those commentaries gives context to the constitutional texts that were being adopted.

B) Constitutional Commentaries Agreed that the Right to Bear Arms Included Carrying Arms in Public

Law professor and judge St. George Tucker, known as "the American Blackstone," wrote the first ever commentaries on the United States Constitution. His importance and influence spanned the period from the Founding to the early Republic. He fought in the Revolution, was an Antifederalist when the Constitution was being debated, and would serve as both a state and a federal judge. His commentaries on the Constitution have been repeatedly cited by the U.S. Supreme Court.[661]

Tucker's 1803 edition of Blackstone's *Commentaries* contrasted the Second Amendment from the English Declaration of Rights: "The right of the people to keep and bear arms shall not be infringed...and this without any qualification as to their condition or degree, as is the

---

[661] E.g., *Horne v. Department of Agriculture*, 576 U.S. 350, 359 (2015).

case in the British government...."[662] Tucker called the Second Amendment "the true palladium of liberty," explaining:

> The right of self defence is the first law of nature: in most governments it has been the study of rulers to confine this right within the narrowest limits possible. Wherever standing armies are kept up, and the right of the people to keep and bear arms is, under any colour or pretext whatsoever, prohibited, liberty, if not already annihilated, is on the brink of destruction.[663]

By contrast, the people of England had been disarmed under the pretext of preserving game animals. Moreover, in England "the right of bearing arms is confined to protestants, and the words suitable to their condition and degree, have been interpreted to authorise the prohibition of keeping a gun...to any farmer, or inferior tradesman, or other person not qualified to kill game."[664]

Tucker asserted the inherent power of judicial review under the U.S. Constitution two years before Chief Justice John Marshall's famous decision on the subject.[665] Tucker wrote that if Congress passed a law abridging "the right of the people to assemble peaceably, or to keep and bear arms; it would...be the province of the judiciary to pronounce whether any such act were constitutional, or not; and if not, to acquit the accused from any penalty which might be annexed to the breach of such unconstitutional act."[666]

---

[662] 1 St. George Tucker, *Blackstone's Commentaries* *143 n.40 (1803).
[663] *Id.*, Appendix, 300. See Stephen P. Halbrook, "St. George Tucker's Second Amendment: Deconstructing 'The True Palladium of Liberty,'" 3 *Tenn. J. of Law & Pol'y*, No. 2, at 120 (Spring 2007).
[664] *Id.*
[665] *Marbury v. Madison*, 5 U.S. (1 Cranch) 137 (1803).
[666] 1 Tucker, *Blackstone's Commentaries*, Appendix 357.

Strict judicial review was particularly warranted if Congress relied on the "necessary and proper" clause to restrict Bill of Rights guarantees. "If, for example, congress were to pass a law prohibiting any person from bearing arms, as a means of preventing insurrections, the judicial courts, under the construction of the words necessary and proper, here contended for, would be able to pronounce decidedly upon the constitutionality of these means." If Congress could use any means to exercise a power, "the provision in the constitution which secures to the people the right of bearing arms, is a mere nullity; and any man imprisoned for bearing arms under such an act, might be without relief...."[667]

As noted above, Tucker viewed the Second Amendment right to bear arms to be broader than the right to have arms under the English Declaration of Rights. To illustrate further, the Englishman Sir Matthew Hale, in *The History of the Pleas of the Crown*, noted a presumption of warlike force in the use of weapons by an assembly without the king's license, other than in a lawful case.[668] Tucker found no such rule in America:

> But ought that circumstance of itself, to create any such presumption in America, where the right to bear arms is recognized and secured in the constitution itself? In many parts of the United States, a man no more thinks, of going out of his house on any occasion, without his rifle or musket in his hand, than an European fine gentleman without his sword by his side.[669]

---

[667] *Id.* at 289.

[668] 1 Matthew Hale, *The History of the Pleas of the Crown* 150 (London: E. & R. Nutt, 1776).

[669] 5 Tucker, *Blackstone's Commentaries*, App'x, at 19.

In support of an argument that the Second Amendment guarantees no right of a citizen to carry firearms for self-defense, Professor Saul Cornell suggests that Tucker was referring only to militiamen carrying military arms, excluding pistols, and that the practice was limited to Virginia.[670] But Tucker referred simply to a man leaving his house "on any occasion" with a firearm, contrasting him with a European gentleman carrying a sword, neither without any military context. And the notion that Tucker's observation was confined to Virginia is flatly contradicted by his reference to "many parts of the United States."

Nor did Tucker's statement conflict with the views of any other American jurist. Indeed, far from some regional, Virginia-centric work, *Tucker's Blackstone* was "one of the most influential legal works of the early nineteenth century." It quickly became "the leading legal text in the United States, enjoying wide circulation throughout the country," and the book "was also one of the legal texts most frequently cited by the United States Supreme Court and relied upon by lawyers appearing before the Court during the first few decades of the nineteenth century."[671] One suspects that St. George Tucker may have had a better grasp on the practices of early nineteenth century Americans "[i]n many parts of the United States" than Professor Cornell.

Tucker's observation that many Americans typically went armed was factual. Hunting was nearly universal, and anyone could go or ride armed from one's house through public places on the way to the woods unrestricted. English journalist William Cobbett, who came to the

---

[670] Saul Cornell, "The Right to Carry Firearms Outside of the Home: Separating Historical Myths from Historical Realities," 39 *Fordham Urb. L.J.* 1695, 1710-11 (2012).
[671] Davison M. Douglas, "Foreword: The Legacy of St. George Tucker," 47 *Wm. and Mary L. Rev.* 1111, 1114 (2006).

United States in 1792, wrote: "As to game-laws, there are none, except those which appoint the times for killing. People go where they like, and, as to wild animals, shoot what they like."[672]

In 1807, Aaron Burr was tried for treason, of which he would be acquitted, based on an alleged conspiracy to create a separate country in the Southwest. In response to claims that he met with a number of armed men in the course of the conspiracy, his defense attorney made an argument that illustrated the widespread use of firearms in the United States:

> Rifles, shot guns and fowling pieces are used commonly by the people of this country in hunting and for domestic purposes; they are generally in the habit of pursuing game. In the upper country every man has a gun; a majority of the people have guns everywhere, for peaceful purposes. Rifles and shot guns are no more evidence of military weapons than pistols or dirks used for personal defence, or common fowling pieces kept for the amusement of taking game. It is lawful for every man in this country to keep such weapons.[673]

Like their English forebears, American commentators distinguished the peaceable carrying of arms from going armed in a manner to terrify others. U.S. District Court Judge John Haywood wrote in his 1800 treatise on North Carolina law that while "riding or going armed with dangerous or unusual weapons, is a crime against the public peace, by terrifying the good people of the land," the ordinary "[w]earing of arms, however, is not within the meaning of the statute,

---

[672] William Cobbett, *Cobbett's America*, ed. J.E. Morpugo, 200 (London: Folio Society, 1985).
[673] David Robertson, *Reports of the Trials of Colonel Aaron Burr, (Late Vice President of the United States,) for Treason, and for a Misdemeanor* 582 (Philadelphia: Hopkins & Earle, 1808).

unless accompanied with such circumstances as are apt to terrify the people."[674] Similarly, Harry Toulmin, a judge of the superior court for the eastern district of Mississippi Territory, wrote that "there may be an affray, where there is no actual violence; as when a man arms himself with dangerous and unusual weapons, in such a manner as will naturally cause terror to the people."[675]

Judge Charles Humphreys' often-cited *Compendium of the Common Law in Force in Kentucky* (1822) analyzed Blackstone and sought to determine what in English law was still valid and what had become obsolete in America. On the subject at hand he wrote:

> Riding or going armed with dangerous or unusual weapons, is a crime against the public peace, by terrifying the people of the land, which is punishable by forfeiture of the arms, and fine and imprisonment. But here it should be remembered, that in this country the constitution guaranties to all persons the right to bear arms; then it can only be a crime to exercise this right in such a manner, as to terrify the people unnecessarily.[676]

It has been argued that the above statements deviate from the common law and were unique to the South.[677] To the contrary, Humphreys (like Haywood) stated the traditional rule that going armed was a crime only when done in a manner to terrify the people, and the

---

[674] John Haywood, *The Duty and Office of Justices of the Peace, and of Sheriffs, Coroners, Constables, &c. According to the Laws of the State of North Carolina* 10 (Halifax: Abraham Hodge, 1800).
[675] Harry Toulmin, *The Magistrate's Assistant* 5 (Natchez, Miss.: Samuel Terrell, 1807).
[676] Charles Humphreys, *Compendium of the Common Law in force in Kentucky* 482 (Lexington, Ky.: William Gibbes Hunt, 1822).
[677] Saul Cornell, "The Right to Keep and Carry Arms in Anglo-American Law: Preserving Liberty and Keeping the Peace," 80 *Law & Contemp. Probs.* 11, 35 (2017).

Second Amendment and state guarantees confirmed the right to bear arms peaceably.

William Rawle, who served as U.S. district attorney for Pennsylvania and was president of the Pennsylvania Abolition Society, authored *A View of the Constitution*, the first edition of which appeared in 1825. It became a popular textbook that was used at the U.S. Military Academy at West Point and other schools. Rawle viewed the Second Amendment as a general prohibition on both the federal and state governments acting "to disarm the people."[678] In England, he observed, "the right was secured to protestant subjects only…and it is cautiously described to be that of bearing arms for their defence, 'suitable to their conditions, and as allowed by law.'"[679]

However, Rawle added, the right to bear arms may not be "abused to the disturbance of the public peace." Thus, "the carrying of arms abroad by a single individual, attended with circumstances giving just reason to fear that he purposes to make an unlawful use of them, would be sufficient cause to require him to give surety of the peace."[680] In other words, while carrying a firearm with the perceived intent to make an unlawful use of it did not constitute a basis for the deprivation of the right to bear arms, it did provide the basis for requiring one to obtain a surety, which is equivalent to posting a bond today.

Similarly, in his 1846 *Treatise on the Criminal Law*, Francis Wharton wrote that "there may be an affray where there is no actual violence; as where a man arms himself with dangerous and unusual

---

[678] William Rawle, *A View of the Constitution*, 2d ed., 125–26 (Philadelphia: Philip H. Nicklin, 1829).
[679] *Id.*
[680] *Id.* at 126, citing 3 Coke's Inst. 160. Hawkins, b. 1. c.60.

weapons, in such a manner as will naturally cause a terror to the people, which is said to have been always an offense at common law, and is strictly prohibited by the statute."[681] He went on the quote the Statute of Northampton, once again expressing the understanding that only going armed in a terrorizing manner constituted the offense.[682]

Henry St. George Tucker Sr., son of St. George Tucker and president of the Virginia Supreme Court, also published commentaries. Among the rights that protect personal security, personal liberty, and private property is: "The right of bearing arms – which with us is not limited and restrained by an arbitrary system of game laws as in England; but is particularly enjoyed by every citizen, and is among his most valuable privileges, since it furnishes the means of resisting as a freeman ought, the inroads of usurpation."[683]

Joseph Story, associate justice of the U.S. Supreme Court (1811-1845), saw the right as necessary to deter oppression:

> The right of the citizens to keep and bear arms has justly been considered, as the palladium of the liberties of the republic; since it offers a strong moral check against usurpation and arbitrary power of the rulers; and will generally, even if these are successful in the first instance, enable the people to resist and triumph over them.[684]

---

[681] Francis Wharton, *A Treatise on the Criminal Law of the United States* 527–28 (Philadelphia: James Kay, 1846).

[682] Wharton added that "[a] man cannot excuse wearing such armour in public, by alleging that such a one threatened him," but "such armour" referred to dangerous and unusual weapons, not to common arms. *Id.*

[683] 1 Henry St. George Tucker, *Commentaries on the Laws of Virginia* 43 (Winchester: Office of the Winchester Virginian, 1831).

[684] 3 Joseph Story, *Commentaries on the Constitution* 746 (Boston: Hilliard, Gray & Co., 1833).

Justice Levi Woodbury, who replaced Justice Story on the U.S. Supreme Court bench, explained the origins of the Second Amendment in terms of the practical exercise of the right and the imperative of resisting tyranny:

> The dragon's teeth of oppression, which had been sowed by England started up armed men everywhere; men accustomed to the rifle from the cradle; restrained by no game laws from a free chase; claiming a natural, afterwards a constitutional right to keep and bear arms; drilled as militia to the smell in gunpowder; able, in practice no less than theory, to defend their homes as their castles, and prosecute bloody strifes in behalf of the mother country, till they thus learned how to protect themselves even against her wrongs.[685]

Further evidence comes from the "law dictionaries" that began to be published in the late eighteenth century. Several such dictionaries, in defining the legal meaning of the words "affray" or "arms," reproduced William Hawkins' influential description of the Northampton law as applying only where arms were carried "with such circumstances as are apt to terrify the people."[686]

In sum, the antebellum commentators were unanimous in their view of the right to keep and bear arms as an individual liberty which existed for a variety of purposes, from personal self-defense to protection from invasion and tyranny. While arms could be peaceably carried for any lawful purpose, the following discusses laws under which persons who went armed in a manner that would terrorize others could be required to find sureties to keep the peace.

---

[685] 3 Capen L. Woodbury, ed., *Writings of Levi Woodbury* 214 (Boston: Little, Brown, 1852).
[686] Affray, T. Cunningham, *A New and Complete Law Dictionary* (1764); Affray, G. Jacob, *A New Law Dictionary* (1750); Arms, *id.*

C) Surety Laws for Keeping the Peace Applied to Persons Who Went Armed in a Manner to Terrorize Others

When the states became independent of Great Britain, they generally adopted reception statutes declaring that the common law of England and acts of Parliament made in aid of the common law would be recognized unless inconsistent with the constitutions and laws of each state.[687] As will be seen below, some state legislatures drafted their own version of the Statute of Northampton, while the courts in other states debated whether it applied as part of the common law. Either way, the Statute was read to apply only to going armed in a manner to terrorize others.

In the Founding and Early American periods, carrying arms in public for lawful purposes was widely practiced and uniformly accepted. However, some states did impose limits on public arms-bearing by individuals who were determined to pose a risk of misusing them. Even for such a potentially dangerous individual, these laws did not forbid carrying arms in public; they only required him to post a surety, or bond, as security for his peaceable conduct—unless he himself had some particular need to carry firearms for self-defense. If the person failed to keep the peace, he would forfeit the amount of money covered by the surety, and would answer to the court for his misconduct.

---

[687] For example, the Maryland Declaration of Rights, Art. III (1776), stated in part that "the inhabitants of Maryland are entitled to the common law of England, . . . and to the benefit of such of the English statutes, as existed at the time of their first emigration, and which, by experience, have been found applicable to their local and other circumstances...." No specific statutes were listed. See further "State Statutes Adopting the Common Law of England," Institute for U.S. Law. https://www.iuslaw.org/common-law-reception-statutes/.

1. Virginia's Acts on Affrays

In Virginia, a Committee of Revisors—of which Thomas Jefferson played the leading role—drafted a restatement of Virginia's statutory law which included the common law and elements of such English statutes as were deemed applicable.[688] One of the provisions reported by the Committee, presented to the General Assembly by James Madison, would be passed as an Act Forbidding and Punishing Affrays (1786).[689] It provided in pertinent part that no man shall "come before the Justices of any court, or other of their ministers of justice doing their office, with force and arms...nor go nor ride armed by night nor by day, in fairs or markets, or in other places, in terror of the country...."[690] This offense had three pertinent elements: (1) going or riding armed, (2) in fairs, markets or "other places," which according to the canon of *noscitur a sociis* (associated words) meant other places like fairs and markets, and (3) in terror of the country.

A sufficient indictment of the above could not simply allege the first element, but would have been required to allege all three. As Virginia courts held, it was "an established rule, that in general, if an Indictment pursues the words of a Statute in describing an offence...it is sufficient...."[691] A demurrer (motion to dismiss) would be sustained

---

[688] Edward Dumbauld, *Thomas Jefferson and the Law* 134–36 (1978).
[689] 2 Jefferson, *The Papers of Thomas Jefferson*, Julian P. Boyd ed., 519-20 (Princeton: Princeton University Press, 1951). "This Bill is a good example of TJ's retention of the language of early English statutes, with its archaic provision for the forfeiture of 'armour,' &c." *Id.* at 520 (note by editor).
[690] A Collection of All Such Acts of the General Assembly of Virginia, of a Public and Permanent Nature, as Are Now in Force, ch. 21, at 30 (1803).
[691] *Rasnick v. Commonwealth*, 4 Va. (2 Va. Cas.) 356, 357 (1823).

for an insufficient indictment.[692] And all three elements of the offense would have to be proven at trial.

It is unclear how long the Virginia law remained on the books, and no judicial decision exists reciting its language. Had it been read to ban the mere carrying of firearms, its draftsman Thomas Jefferson would have been one of its biggest violators, as he regularly went armed and defended the right to do so.[693]

In 1820, the Grand Jury for Richmond, Virginia, denounced "the practice of carrying arms secreted, in cases where no personal attack can reasonably be apprehended," even though it was not unlawful. But it added: "The Grand Jury would not recommend any legislative interference with what they conceive to be one of the most essential privileges of freemen, the right of carrying arms...."[694]

If it was still law in 1838, Virginia's enactment on affrays was not interpreted to prohibit the habitual carrying of concealed weapons, as in that year the Virginia legislature for the first time saw the need to provide: "If a free person, habitually, carry about his person hid from common observation, any pistol, dirk, bowie knife, or weapon of the like kind, he shall be fined fifty dollars."[695] This provision would have been unnecessary if going armed was already an offense, not to mention that it only restricted going armed habitually and hiding the arms.

---

[692] *Commonwealth v. Lodge*, 43 Va. (2 Gratt.) 579, 580–81 (1845).
[693] See Stephen P. Halbrook, *The Founders' Second Amendment* 131, 260, 316–18 (Lanham, Md.: Rowman & Littlefield, 2008).
[694] "On Wearing Concealed Arms," *Daily Nat'l. Intelligencer*, Sept. 9, 1820, at 2.
[695] Virginia Code, tit. 54, ch. 196, § 7 (1849).

In 1847, Virginia enacted a surety law: "If any person shall go armed with any offensive or dangerous weapon, without reasonable cause to fear an assault or other injury, or violence to his person, or to his family or property, he may be required to find sureties for keeping the peace."[696] If anyone complained, any person engaging in that conduct could continue to do so if the court did not find that keeping the peace required sureties. If sureties were required, he could simply obtain them. If he failed to keep the peace, he would forfeit the amount of money covered by the surety. The court might then impose a further surety requirement or commit him to jail.

There are no published judicial decisions on the provision. That suggests that it was enforced infrequently or leniently. An analogy might be made to typical practices in misdemeanor courts today of not entering a judgment of guilty of some offense but continuing the case for a year and then dismissing the charge if no further violations occurred. If a further violation occurred, the court might sentence the person to pay a fine and/or impose a jail term.

At a more general level than just the above statute, courts could require a person to enter into a recognizance with sureties to keep the peace, particularly in regard to a specified person who was threatened, for a given period.[697] If a person violated the recognizance, a writ of *scire facias* could be issued alleging the violation with specificity and requiring the person to answer in court.[698] Specific threats or harm were required for a judicial finding that sureties were needed to ensure that the person kept the peace.

---

[696] 1847 Va. Laws 127, 129, § 16.
[697] *Welling's Case*, 47 Va. (6 Gratt.) 670 (1849).
[698] *Randolph v. Brown*, 4 Va. (2 Va. Cas.) 351 (1823).

2. Tennessee's Act on Disorderly Persons

In Tennessee, a person could go armed peaceably. The exception to the rule was set forth in that state's Act for the restraint of idle and disorderly persons of 1801, which provided that going armed aggressively required persons to be bound to their good behavior. It stated:

> That if any person or persons shall publicly ride or go armed to the terror of the people, or privately carry any dirk, large knife, pistol or any other dangerous weapon, to the fear or terror of any person, it shall be the duty of any judge or justice, on his own view, or upon the information of any other person on oath, to bind such person or persons to their good behavior, and if he or they fail to find securities, commit him or them to jail, and if such person or persons shall continue so to offend, he or they shall not only forfeit their recognizance, but be liable to an indictment, and be punished as for a breach of the peace, or riot at common law.[699]

The law thus distinguished between (a) "publicly" or openly going armed to the terror of "the people," and (b) "privately" carrying certain weapons to the terror of "any person." Going armed with a weapon hidden from view would not terrorize the people, while doing so could terrorize a specific person, perhaps if attended with threats. If either occurred, the judge was to bind the person to his good behavior by requiring sureties. If the person continued to terrorize others, he could be indicted and punished the same as for a breach of the peace or riot. Depending on its severity, that could include fines and/or incarceration.

Forbidding a person to "publicly ride or go armed to the terror of the people" contrasted with the proscription that "[n]o slave shall go

---

[699] Tenn. Laws, c.22, § 6 (1801).

armed with gun, sword, club or other weapon" without a certificate from the county court, in which the master gave bond for the good behavior of the slave.[700] A free person could go armed as long as not done so "to the terror of the people"; a slave could not go armed at all, even without creating terror, without a judicial certificate.

The meaning of "to the terror of the people" was explained by the Tennessee Supreme Court in cases involving affrays and riots. "It is because the violence is committed in a public place, and to the terror of the people, that the crime is called an affray, instead of assault and battery," noted the court.[701] Because "every fact and circumstance necessary to constitute the offence must be specifically set forth in the indictment," the court found an indictment insufficient for not alleging that an affray took place in a public place, for an assault "in a private place out of the hearing or seeing of any except the parties concerned, in which case it cannot be to the terror of the people."[702] Nor could carrying a weapon privately in a peaceable manner do so.

"In some cases of riot the gist of the offence consists alone in the terror to the public, inspired by the conduct of the parties.... [I]n indictments for riots, which consists in going about armed, etc., the words *in terrorem populi* are essential...."[703] By the same token, in an indictment for going armed, the element of terrorizing others must be alleged and proven.

The Tennessee Supreme Court upheld an indictment alleging that the defendant "unlawfully did privately carry a certain large knife, to

---

[700] Acts 1741, c. 24, in 1 Statute Laws of the State of Tennessee of a Public & General Nature, 314 (Knoxville: F.S. Heiskell, 1831).
[701] *Cash v. State*, 2 Tenn. 198, 199 (1813).
[702] *State v. Heflin*, 27 Tenn. 84, 85–86 (1845).
[703] *State v. Whitesides*, 31 Tenn. 88, 89 (1851).

the fear and terror of *certain persons then and there being*, which said knife was then and there a dangerous weapon." The court rejected the argument that the indictment was insufficient because it did not give the names of the specific persons who were terrorized, because it followed the language of the statute.[704] The law did not proscribe peaceably going armed, and proof was required of fear and terror by persons actually present: "But the object of the whole section was to prevent the practices mentioned, whenever it occasioned fear, whether in one or many. The offense is committed whether the carrying of the dangerous weapon be to the terror of several persons or of one person."[705]

In sum, the constitutional right to bear arms peaceably went unquestioned. Tennessee only proscribed going armed in a manner that terrorized or caused fear in others.

3. The Massachusetts Models

The right to carry arms in public was not questioned under Massachusetts law. However, Massachusetts would enact two statutes on going armed in a manner to terrorize others, one in 1795 and the other in 1836. The Act of 1795 incorporated a version of the Statute of Northampton in the following words:

> That every Justice of the Peace, within the county for which he may be commissioned, may cause to be staid and arrested, all affrayers, rioters, disturbers, or breakers of the peace, and *such as shall ride or go armed offensively, to the fear or terror of the good citizens of this Commonwealth*, or such others as may utter any menaces or threatening speeches, and upon view of such Justice, confession of the

---

[704] *State v. Bentley*, 74 Tenn. 205, 206 (1880) (emphasis added).
[705] *Id.* at 206–07.

223

delinquent, or other legal conviction of any such offence, shall require of the offender to find sureties for his keeping the Peace, and being of the good behaviour; and in want thereof, to commit him to prison until he shall comply with such requisition....[706]

Elements of the offense included (1) riding or going armed, (2) offensively, i.e., not peaceably, and (3) to the fear or terror of the good citizens. Just peaceably riding or going armed alone was not an offense. As the Massachusetts Supreme Judicial Court ruled, "an indictment shall set forth, with technical particularity, every allegation necessary to constitute the offence charged," since the state constitution provided "that no subject shall be held to answer for any crime or offence, until the same is fully, substantially and formally described to him."[707]

The explicit definition of the crime as riding or going armed "offensively, to the fear or terror of the good citizens" is given further meaning and context by the statute's references to "affrayers, rioters, disturbers, or breakers of the peace," and those who "utter any menaces or threatening speeches."

There are no judicial opinions on the 1795 enactment. However, the court ruled in another matter that the phrase *in terrorem populi* must be used "in indictments for that species of riots which consist in going about armed, &c., without committing any act...because the offence

---

[706] 1795 Mass. Acts 436, ch. 2; 2 *Perpetual Laws of the Commonwealth of Massachusetts*, Chap. 25, 259 (1801) (emphasis added). After Maine broke off from Massachusetts to become a state in 1820, it adopted a similar provision. 1821 Me. Laws 285.

[707] *Commonwealth v. Eastman*, 55 Mass. (1 Cush.) 189, 223 (1848). The court added: "If an indictment for murder, should allege merely that the accused had committed the crime of murder upon the person of one A. B., or, if an indictment for larceny should simply set forth, that the defendant had stolen from C. D., in neither case would the offence be set forth with the particularity and precision required by law." *Id.*

consists in terrifying the public...."[708] Further, the court differentiated being armed from the misuse of arms, by referring to "the right to keep fire arms, which does not protect him who uses them for annoyance or destruction."[709]

Today's advocates of the strict liability view of such Statute of Northampton analogues—that the offense included no *mens rea* or criminal intent element—argue that the terror element was redundant and that anyone going armed peaceably by definition did so in a manner to terrorize the subjects, i.e., that "terrorizing the public was the consequence of going armed."[710] Judge Diarmuid O'Scannlain refuted that argument: "What an odd way it would be to write a criminal statute! To interpret such language as merely purposive is to remove its operative effect, for if going armed was itself unlawful then clarifying the consequences of going armed adds not an iota of substance to the crime."[711]

Recall that the law refers first to affrayers and other breakers of the peace, then to those who went armed offensively to the terror of the citizens, and finally to those who uttered menaces. Why announce that going armed inherently terrorized the citizens, while not saying something similar about affrayers and those who utter menaces? The

---

[708] *Commonwealth v. Runnels*, 10 Mass. 518, 520 (1813).
[709] *Commonwealth v. Blanding,* 20 Mass. (3 Pick.) 304, 314 (1825).
[710] Eric M. Ruben & Saul Cornell, "Firearm Regionalism and Public Carry," 125 *Yale L.J. Forum* 121, 129–30 (2015).
[711] *Young v. Hawaii*, 896 F.3d 1044, 1067 (9th Cir. 2018), overruled, 2021 WL 1114180 (9th Cir. 2021) (en blanc).

reason is that the terror element meant something; it was an element of the offense.[712]

Massachusetts' enactment of 1795 was superseded by the Act of 1836, entitled "Of Proceedings to Prevent the Commission of Crimes," which provided:

> If any person shall go armed with a dirk, dagger, sword, pistol, or other offensive and dangerous weapon, without reasonable cause to fear an assault or other injury, or violence to his person, or to his family or property, he may, on complaint of any person having reasonable cause to fear an injury, or breach of the peace, be required to find sureties for keeping the peace, for a term not exceeding six months, with the right of appealing as before provided.[713]

This Act did not prohibit a person from peaceably going armed with the specified weapons. It required an aggrieved person to file a complaint and to show reasonable cause to fear injury or breach of the peace, and such a finding by the court would have to entail threats or other bad behavior. Even then, the subject person could show reasonable cause to fear injury. And if the court found otherwise and determined that his keeping the peace required sureties, the person could simply find sureties and continue going armed. The following explains the procedures required by the Act.

---

[712] Nor was the plain text of the law changed by unartful newspaper accounts, such as the statement that it was "well known to be an offence against law to ride or go with…firelocks, or other dangerous weapons…." *Salem Gazette*, June 2, 1818, quoted in Patrick J. Charles, "The Faces of the Second Amendment Outside the Home," 60 *Clev. St. L. Rev.* 1, 33 n.1 (2012).

[713] 1836 Mass. Laws 748, 750, ch. 134, § 16; Revised Statutes of the Commonwealth of Massachusetts 750 (1836).

Reasonable cause to fear an injury. What would be required of a complainant to show "reasonable cause to fear an injury"? The mere presence of ordinary weapons, without more, would not suffice. By analogy, a magistrate had to have "reasonable cause" to believe certain things to get a search warrant. "The oath to the complainant's belief, and not to his suspicion, is one of 'the formalities prescribed by the laws,' without which 'no warrant ought to be issued.'"[714] Here, reasonable cause to fear an injury, not speculation or suspicion, was required.

Similar language was used in a decision regarding an indictment for a forcible entry, which "must be accompanied with circumstances tending to excite terror": "There must at least be some apparent violence; or *some unusual weapons*; or the parties attended with an unusual number of people; some menaces, or other acts giving *reasonable cause to fear*, that the party making the forcible entry will do some bodily hurt to those in possession, if they do not give up the same."[715]

Reasonable cause to fear a breach of the peace. Again, the mere presence of a weapon would not be a breach of the peace. A breach of the peace was not considered a minor matter—one case referred to "breaches of the peace or other great disorder and violence, being what

---

[714] *Commonwealth v. Lottery Tickets*, 59 Mass. 369, 372 (1850) (citation omitted).
[715] *Commonwealth v. Shattuck*, 58 Mass. 141, 145 (1849) (emphasis added). Similarly, see *Commonwealth v. Dudley*, 10 Mass. 403, 409 (1813) ("There must be some apparent violence offered, in deed or in word, to the person of another; or the party must be furnished with unusual offensive weapons, or attended by an unusual multitude of people; all which circumstances would tend to excite terror in the owner").

are usually considered *mala in se* or criminal in themselves...."[716] Reasonable cause to fear such would entail anticipated violence or related unlawful conduct: "Breaches of the peace comprise not only cases of actual violence to the person of another, but any unlawful acts, tending to produce an actual breach of the peace...."[717] Under a 1783 enactment, "justices of the peace had power to bind over to keep the peace those who are complained of as having a present intent to commit a breach of the peace, as well as those who are charged with having committed such an offence...."[718]

On complaint of any person. When a complaint was made that "any person has threatened to commit an offence against the person or property of another," the magistrate was required to examine the complainant and any witnesses under oath and to prepare a written complaint.[719] If the magistrate determined that "there is just cause to fear that any such offence may be committed," he issued a warrant reciting the substance of the complaint and directed an officer to apprehend the person.[720]

Professor Saul Cornell describes the 1836 Massachusetts enactment as "a sweeping law that effectively prohibited the right to travel armed."[721] Other than quoting the statute, Cornell is mum – as if

---

[716] *Commonwealth v. Willard*, 39 Mass. 476, 478 (1839). See *Fifty Associates v. Howland*, 59 Mass. 214, 218 (1849) (reference to "such a degree of force, as would tend to a breach of the peace").

[717] *Pearce v. Atwood*, 13 Mass. 324, 332 (1816), citing 4 Blackstone, *Commentaries* 255.

[718] *Commonwealth v. M'Neill*, 36 Mass. 127, 141 (1837).

[719] 1836 Mass. Laws 748, § 2. See *Commonwealth v. Wallace*, 80 Mass. 382 (1860) (a complaint would have one's full name, a sworn statement of the complaint, and a signature. It would be certified by the appropriate authority, which was "an averment by him that the signature and oath were those of the complainant....").

[720] *Id.* § 3.

[721] Saul Cornell, "The Right to Carry Firearms Outside of the Home," 39 *Fordham Urb. L.J.* 1695, 1720 (2012).

no one would notice – on the requirement that the statute only applies "on complaint of any person having reasonable cause to fear an injury, or breach of the peace.". He goes on to claim: "In Massachusetts and those states emulating its model, the scope of the right to arm oneself defensively outside of the home was extremely limited."[722] Not so. Without a complaint and proof of reasonable cause to fear injury or breach of the peace, a person could go armed peaceably at will.

Finding sureties. The Act reflected general remedies available to a person who was injured or feared injury or breach of the peace by another. "When the person complained of is brought before the magistrate, he shall be heard in his defense, and he may be required to enter into a recognizance, with sufficient sureties, in such sum as the magistrate shall direct, to keep the peace" towards all persons but "especially towards the person requiring such security," for no more than six months.[723] As applied in a similar scenario, a threatened person "may apply to a magistrate, and ask that sureties to keep the peace may be required of one from whom he may apprehend any serious personal injury."[724]

Appeal. The defendant could appeal to the court of common pleas, which would hear the witnesses and could either discharge him or require him to enter into a new recognizance in a sum determined to be proper.[725]

Insufficient cause. Alternatively, if on examination the magistrate determined that it did "not appear that there is just cause to fear that

---

[722] *Id.* at 1721.
[723] 1836 Mass. Laws 748, § 4.
[724] *Mason v. Mason*, 36 Mass. (19 Pick.) 506, 508 (1837).
[725] 1836 Mass. Laws 748, §§ 9-11.

any such offence will be committed," the person was to be discharged. If the magistrate deemed the complaint "unfounded, frivolous or malicious," he could order the complainant to pay the costs of the prosecution.[726] A groundless complaint could have further consequences: "A false complaint, made with express malice, or without probable cause, to a body having competent authority to redress the grievance complained of, may be the subject of an action for a libel; and the question of malice is to be determined by the jury."[727]

These procedures were not required for certain offenses committed in the presence of a magistrate, who could issue a summons or make an arrest. Any person who would "make an affray, or threaten to kill or beat another, or to commit any violence or outrage against his person or property," or would "contend with hot and angry words, to the disturbance of the peace," could be ordered to keep the peace or be of good behavior. No further process or other proof was required.[728] This provision identifies the types of analogous behavior included in the next section about going armed in a manner causing a person to have "reasonable cause to fear an injury, or breach of the peace."[729]

Failing to keep the peace. Generally, if a person violated his recognizance to keep the peace such as by assaulting the complainant, the Commonwealth could prosecute an action of debt upon this forfeited recognizance, or bring a writ of *scire facias*.[730] It was decided in one case: "Where one, being under a recognizance to keep the peace,

---

[726] *Id.* § 7.
[727] *Bodwell v. Osgood*, 20 Mass. 379 (1825).
[728] 1836 Mass. Laws 748, § 15.
[729] *Id.* § 16.
[730] *Commonwealth v. Green*, 12 Mass. 1 (1815).

committed a breach of the peace, for which he was indicted and fined, it was *held* that he was nevertheless liable to an action for the penalty of the recognizance."[731] The severity of the penalties obviously depended on whether the breach of the peace was minor or major.

Just after passage of the Massachusetts law in 1836, Judge Peter Oxenbridge Thacher of the Boston Municipal Court told a grand jury that "no person may go armed with a dirk, dagger, sword, pistol, or other offensive and dangerous weapon, without reasonable cause to apprehend an assault or violence to his person, family, or property."[732] He left out the statutory requirement that it had to be "on the complaint of any person having reasonable cause to fear an injury, or breach of the peace." Had he been actually instructing a grand jury about a specific case before him, a complainant would have been necessary to give such evidence to establish reasonable cause to fear an injury or breach of the peace. Otherwise a charge would have had no foundation.

Professor Saul Cornell asserts: "Thacher's account of the Massachusetts law prohibiting the right to carry arms unambiguously interprets this law as a broad ban on the use of arms in public."[733] There are three things wrong with this statement. First, as discussed above, the "right to carry arms" was widely recognized—and exercised— throughout the young Nation, during this period, making Cornell's interpretation of Thacher's grand jury charge extremely implausible. Second, Thacher made no pretense of "interpret[ing] this law" but only

---

[731] *Commonwealth v. Braynard*, 23 Mass. (6 Pick.) 113 (1828).

[732] Peter Oxenbridge Thacher, *Two Charges to the Grand Jury of the County of Suffolk, for the Commonwealth of Massachusetts, at the Opening of the Terms of the Municipal Court of the City of Boston, on Monday, December 5th, A. D. 1836, and on Monday, March 13th, A. D. 1837*, at 27 (1837).

[733] Saul Cornell, "The Right to Carry Firearms Outside of the Home," *39 Fordham Urb. L.J.* 1695, 1721 (2012).

gave a snippet of part of the law. Third, and conclusively, the *explicit text* of the Massachusetts law unambiguously required that a complainant establish "reasonable cause to fear an injury or breach of the peace" as an element of the offense, a fact of which Judge Thacher must be presumed to have been aware. The law simply did not ban the carrying of arms in public.

An even less reliable substitute for the actual language of a statute would be newspaper articles that mention criminal charges. A riot in Charlestown, Massachusetts, involving a mob of as many as three hundred persons took place on March 4, 1853.[734] Arrests were made for everything from "refusing to leave scene of riot" and "throwing a brick at a policeman" to "creating a false alarm of fire" and "carrying a concealed weapon."[735] Like throwing the brick, carrying a concealed weapon did not name a criminal offense, but described the facts supporting the arrests in the context of the riot. Massachusetts had no law on the books at that time against carrying a firearm, either openly or concealed.

An 1860 Massachusetts law made it a crime for a person to possess a dangerous weapon when arrested for another offense. A defendant who was armed with a loaded pistol was found not to have violated the law because it was not lawful to arrest a person for mere drunkenness, and there was thus "nothing in the complaint which shows that the defendant was unlawfully armed with a dangerous weapon at the time

---

[734] "The Riot at Charlestown, Mass.," *New York Times*, Mar. 4, 1853, at 4.
[735] "City Intelligence," *Boston Courier*, Mar. 7, 1853, at 4.

of a lawful arrest by the officer."[736] Obviously, just being armed, even when drunk, was not unlawful.

In 1893, Massachusetts banned the parading of armed bodies of persons in cities without authorization. In what may have been a test case to challenge the law, a dozen or so men paraded with Springfield rifles that had been rendered inoperative. Affirming their convictions, the Supreme Judicial Court —the highest court of Massachusetts—held that the legislature could "regulate the bearing of arms, so as to forbid such unauthorized drills and parades," adding that it also "may regulate and limit the mode of carrying arms," citing out-of-state decisions upholding concealed weapon bans.[737] But it did not suggest that carrying arms per se could be banned.

A person could freely and peaceably carry a handgun, openly or concealed, in Massachusetts until 1906, when it was provided that a person who "carries on his person a loaded pistol or revolver" without a license was subject to imprisonment for up to one year. A license would be issued if "the applicant has good reason to fear an injury to his person or property, and that he is a suitable person to be so licensed."[738] This was a radical break from the tradition in the Commonwealth of recognition of the right to bear arms.

---

[736] *Commonwealth v. O'Connor*, 89 Mass. 583, 584–85 (1863) (citing 1860 Gen. Sts. c.164, § 10). See also *Commonwealth v. Doherty*, 103 Mass. 443, 444 (1869) (indictment void for failure to allege lawful arrest; defendant possessed loaded pistol).
[737] *Commonwealth v. Murphy*, 166 Mass. 171, 172, 44 N.E. 138 (1896), citing, e.g., *Andrews v. State*, 50 Tenn. (3 Heisk.) 165 (1871) (holding that the state could not ban both the open and concealed carrying of an army revolver, *id.* at 177, 186–87).
[738] Ch. 172, § 1, 1906 Mass. Acts 150.

4. Other States Follow the 1836 Massachusetts Model

As explained, Massachusetts made it an offence to go armed *only* on proof by a person with "reasonable cause to fear an injury, or breach of the peace."[739] Nothing in the Massachusetts law made it a crime to carry firearms, open or concealed, peaceably. However, several states adopted variants of the Massachusetts model of 1836 in the antebellum period.

Following the Massachusetts approach, an 1840 Maine law provided:

> Any person, going armed with any dirk, dagger, sword, pistol, or other offensive and dangerous weapon, without a reasonable cause to fear an assault on himself, or any of his family or property, may, on the complaint of any person having cause to fear an injury or breach of the peace, be required to find sureties for keeping the peace for a term, not exceeding one year, with the right of appeal as before provided.[740]

Peaceably carrying a gun could not give rise to reasonable cause to fear injury or breach of the peace. Justices of the peace were empowered to try persons for "all assaults and batteries and other breaches of the peace,"[741] and, as a Maine court held, a forced entry "with a dangerous weapon, putting peaceable citizens in jeopardy or fear, is a breach of the peace...."[742]

---

[739] 1836 Mass. Laws 748, 750, ch. 134, § 16.

[740] Revised Statutes of the State of Maine 709 (1840).

[741] *State v. Furlong*, 26 Me. (13 Shep.) 69, 70–71 (1846).

[742] *In re Harding*, 1 Me. (1 Greenl.) 22, 24–25 (1820). "An individual enters into a recognizance to keep the peace as to all the good citizens of the State, but particularly as to A B, and after giving such recognizance commits a breach of the peace by making an assault upon him. He is liable on his recognizance, he is responsible to the person assaulted in damages, but he is none the less liable to indictment." *State v. Keen*, 34 Me. 500, 507 (1852).

In 1858, Wisconsin adopted almost identical language as Maine, including the requirement of a complaint by a person "having reasonable cause to fear an injury or breach of the peace...."[743] As a Wisconsin court held in a purported self-defense case, regarding terms like "reasonable cause to fear," "the apprehension or belief or appearances must be *reasonable*...."[744] A breach of the peace was associated with conduct involving "force" or "riot."[745]

The Territory of Oregon adopted as part of its Organic Law in 1845 a guarantee that "[n]o person shall be deprived of the right of bearing arms in his own defence...."[746] Eight years later, it adopted a law requiring a person who went armed without reasonable cause to fear injury, on complaint of a person with "reasonable cause to fear an injury, or breach of the peace," to get sureties to keep the peace.[747] "The statute specifically requires as an element that the actor act 'without reasonable cause to fear an assault, injury, or other violence to his person' and in such a manner as to cause another to 'fear an injury.' Thus, by its terms, the statute would have been inapplicable to an individual who openly carried arms for the purpose of self-defense."[748]

When it became a state in 1857, Oregon adopted a Constitution that provided: "The people shall have the right to bear arms for the

---

[743] Revised Statutes of the State of Wisconsin 985 (1858). A prior Wisconsin terrirorial law had similar language. 1838 Wis. Sess. Laws 381, § 16.

[744] *State v. Clifford*, 58 Wis. 477, 17 N.W. 304, 308 (1883).

[745] *Ferrell v. Lamar*, 1 Wis. 8, 14 (1853).

[746] Organic Law of the Provisional Government of Oregon, Art. I, § 5 (1845).

[747] Ore. Laws 1853, ch. 16, § 17; Statutes of Oregon 220 (1854).

[748] *State v. Christian*, 249 Or. App. 1, 32, 274 P.3d 262 (2012) (Edmonds, S.J., dissenting).

defense of themselves, and the state...."[749] That was held to include "an individual's right to bear arms to protect his person and home."[750]

Almost identical surety laws were adopted by Michigan, Minnesota, and the District of Columbia, none of which limited the right peaceably to go armed and all of which required a complaint by a person "having reasonable cause to fear an injury or breach of the peace."[751] As noted above, Virginia and Tennessee had similar surety laws, and as discussed below, North Carolina recognized the common law offense of going armed to the terror of the people. It would be inaccurate to suggest that surety laws were limited to the Northern states, and that the Southern states, because of slavery, represented an "exceptional model of permissive gun carrying...."[752]

Delaware law authorized a justice of the peace to arrest "all who go armed offensively to the terror of the people, or are otherwise disorderly and dangerous."[753] Simply going armed did not suffice. Indeed, it was an offense for a slave to "go armed with any dangerous weapon" only if he did so "without the special permission of his master."[754] Obviously the master had authority to go armed.

Virtually all of the Massachusetts-inspired surety laws use the terms "armed with" and "complaint of any" in the same sentence. A

---

[749] Ore. Const., Art. I, § 27.

[750] *State v. Kessler*, 289 Or. 359, 367, 614 P.2d 94 (1980).

[751] Revised Statutes of the State of Michigan 692 § 16 (1846) ("on complaint of any person having reasonable cause to fear an injury or breach of the peace"); Revised Statutes of the Territory of Minnesota 528 § 18 (1851) (complainant must possess "reasonable cause to fear an injury or breach of the peace"); Revised Code of the District of Columbia 567, 570 (1857) ("on complaint of any person having reasonable cause to fear an injury or breach of the peace").

[752] Saul Cornell, "History, Text, Tradition, and the Future of Second Amendment Jurisprudence," 83 *Law & Contemp. Probs.* 73, 88 (2020).

[753] Ch. 97, § 13, Revised Statutes of the State of Delaware 333 (1852).

[754] § 30, *id.* at 336.

Westlaw search in all state and federal cases does not reveal a single judicial decision applying those terms in a case where such laws were applied. That suggests that such surety-type laws were not enforced much, or that most persons required to get sureties behaved themselves thereafter, leaving no adverse judicial orders that could lead to an appeal. If these laws were wrongly enforced against persons who were merely carrying arms without the required proof of reasonable cause to fear an injury or breach of the peace, presumably there would have been appeals and subsequent judicial opinions that could be found today. The only decisions where such laws are analyzed are the twenty-first century opinions about whether carry bans violate the Second Amendment.

Three twentieth century Pennsylvania decisions concern that state's Surety of Peace Act of 1860, which had two parts, the first relating to threats in general, and the second relating to going armed in a manner to threaten a breach of the peace. Part one provided that if a person threatened to harm another and the person threatened appeared before a justice of the peace and on oath testified to being endangered, the person making the threat was bound over to the next term of court with a surety to appear and to be on good behavior. Part two provided:

> If any person, not being an officer on duty in the military or naval service of the state or of the United States, shall go armed with a dirk, dagger, sword or pistol, or other offensive or dangerous weapon, without reasonable cause to fear an assault or other injury or violence to his family, person or property, he may, on complaint of any person having reasonable cause to fear a breach of the peace therefrom, be required to find surety of the peace as aforesaid.[755]

---

[755] Act of March 31, 1860, P.L. 427, section 6, 19 P.S. § 23.

Under part one of the statute, "the person threatened" must appear and attest to being threatened, while under part two, "the prosecution of a person for going armed with an offensive or dangerous weapon may be made 'on complaint of *any* person having reasonable cause to fear a breach of the peace therefrom.'"[756]

A 1909 amendment added that before binding a person over, the justice of the peace shall "enter into a full hearing and investigation of the facts; and shall only bind over the defendant when the evidence shows...that the prosecutor's or prosecutrix's danger of being hurt in body or estate is actual, and that the threats were made by the defendant maliciously and with intent to do harm."[757] That established "a standard under which the Act of 1860 should operate. This standard established that the complaining party's danger of being hurt in body or estate be actual and that the threats made be malicious and with intent to do harm."[758]

There are a handful of judicial decisions on part one, but none on part two, of the Pennsylvania law. The following applied to both parts: "Where the evidence is clear, the court under general authority to preserve the peace has a right to require a surety bond for such time as it would answer the ends of the public justice."[759] However: "If the prosecutor fails to prove any element of the offense to the satisfaction of the justice or judge, the action is dismissed."[760]

---

[756] *Commonwealth v. Rice*, 8 Pa. D. & C. 295, 297–98 (Quarter Sess. 1926).
[757] Act of March 18, 1909, P.L. 42, sec. 1, 19 P.S. § 24.
[758] *Commonwealth v. Cushard*, 184 Pa. Super. 193, 198, 132 A.2d 366 (1957).
[759] *Id.* at 196-97.
[760] *Commonwealth v. Miller*, 452 Pa. 35, 40, 305 A.2d 346 (1973).

Some states apparently adopted no statutory provisions like the above but relied on the common law to keep order. No provisions could be found for Connecticut, but John Niles' 1833 manual for that state's justices of the peace stated that a justice may arrest "those who go about armed with dangerous or offensive weapons, to the terror and disquiet of the people,"[761] and that those "who go armed offensively . . . to the terror of the people, may be required to give sureties of the peace . . . ."[762]

A historical evolution may be observed about these types of laws. The late eighteenth century Virginia and Massachusetts laws simply made it an offense, derived from how the Statute of Northampton was interpreted, to go armed to the terror of the people. While justices of the peace may have used their general authority to require sureties to keep the peace, that was not part of these specific laws. Both states, and more so Massachusetts, then refined those laws explicitly to adopt procedural mechanisms requiring sureties to keep the peace. Other states followed this evolution.

This evolution is inconsistent with an interpretation of the Statute of Northampton analogues adopted in the colonies and early states as broadly banning public carriage. To begin, if these Northampton-style laws broadly prohibited carrying firearms in public, more narrow surety requirements for carriage by dangerous individuals would have been unnecessary. And even more perversely, the effect of these surety laws, on this interpretation of the Northampton-style laws, would have been to allow those people who were deemed so dangerous to society

---

[761] John M. Niles, *The Connecticut Civil Officer* 12 (Hartford: Huntington & Hopkins, 1833).
[762] *Id.* at 146. And see *id.* at 190 ("Such persons as go armed with offensive and dangerous weapons . . . to the terror of the people, may be arrested").

that they were required to post a surety—and apparently no one else— to carry. That makes no sense at all.

In sum, the statutory offense of going armed to the terror of the people required proof that the defendant did so in an offensive manner that terrified actual persons. It is inaccurate to describe the Massachusetts model as having made it unlawful to carry dangerous weapons in public per se, not to mention the requirement that a complainant must prove reasonable cause to fear an injury or breach of the peace.[763] Nothing about the existence of these laws altered the key historical fact of American life found in all these jurisdictions: individuals peaceably carrying arms was accepted and entirely lawful.

D) Going Armed at Common Law: Judicial Precedents in Tennessee and North Carolina

To what extent was the prohibition of the Statute of Northampton recognized as a common law offense in the early Republic? The courts of Tennessee and North Carolina grappled with the issue, the former holding that it was not applicable and the latter holding that it was. The latter also provided significant detail regarding how both going armed and doing so to the terror of the people were separate elements of the offense, both of which must be alleged in the indictment and proven to the jury.

In *Simpson* v. *State* (1833), the Supreme Court of Tennessee dismissed an indictment alleging that "William Simpson, laborer, with force and arms being arrayed in a warlike manner, in a certain public street or highway situate, unlawfully, and to the great terror and

---

[763] See Patrick Charles, *Armed in America* 142, 390 & n.108 (Amhurst, N.Y.: Prometheus, 2018).

disturbance of divers good citizens, did make an affray…."[764] The court held that the indictment was insufficient as it failed to allege the elements of an affray of fighting between two or more persons.

The issue was whether the above was recognized as a common law offense. The prosecution apparently did not rely on Tennessee's 1801 enactment on going armed to the terror of the people (discussed above) because it created an indictable offense only if the person was previously bound to his good behavior for such conduct and violated his recognizance.[765]

The Attorney General sought to rely on English commentator William Hawkins' statement that "there may be an affray…where a man arms himself with dangerous and unusual weapons, in such a manner as will naturally cause terror to the people, which is said always to have been an offence at common law, and is strictly prohibited by many statutes."[766] That doctrine, averred the court, relied "upon ancient English statutes, enacted in favor of the king, his ministers and other servants, especially upon the statute of the 2d Edward III," which provided that no man "shall go or ride armed by night or by day, etc."[767]

The *Simpson* court repeated Hawkins' comment about the Statute of Northampton "that persons of quality are in no danger of offending against this statute by wearing their common weapons" in places and on occasions where common.[768] The court held the English statute not to be incorporated into American common law:

---

[764] *Simpson v. State*, 13 Tenn. Reports (5 Yerg.) 356, 361 (1833).

[765] Tenn. Laws, c. 22, § 6 (1801).

[766] *Simpson*, 13 Tenn. Reports at 357-58, citing Hawkins, *Pleas of the Crown*, book 1, ch. 28, sec. 4.

[767] *Id.* at 358.

[768] *Id.* at 358–59.

It may be remarked here, that ancient English statutes, from their antiquity and from long usage, were cited as common law; and though our ancestors, upon their emigration, brought with them such parts of the common law of England, and the English statutes, as were applicable and suitable to their exchanged and new situation and circumstances, yet most assuredly the common law and statutes, the subject-matter of this fourth section [of Hawkins],[769] formed no part of their selection.[770]

The *Simpson* court held in the alternative that if the Statute of Northampton had been brought to America, "our constitution has completely abrogated it; it says, 'that the freemen of this state have a right to keep and to bear arms for their common defence.'"[771] That guarantee precluded recognition of "a man's arming himself with dangerous and unusual weapons" as part of the crime of an affray. "By this clause of the constitution, an express power is given and secured to all the free citizens of the state to keep and bear arms for their defence, without any qualification whatever as to their kind or nature...." The constitution having thus said that "the people may carry arms," doing so in itself could not be the basis of the element of "terror to the people" necessary for an affray.[772]

In the twenty-first century, the curious argument has been made by some that the Statute of Northampton somehow supersedes the right to bear arms under the federal and state constitutions. An adherent of

---

[769] I.e., Hawkins, book 1, ch. 28, sec. 4.

[770] *Id.* at 359.

[771] *Id.* at 360, quoting Tenn. Const., Art. 11, § 26.

[772] *Id. Simpson* was followed by *Aymette v. State*, 2 Humph. (21 Tenn.) 154 (1840), which upheld a conviction for carrying a concealed Bowie knife under the test that the right protected the arms used in "civilized warfare," noting: "If the citizens have these arms in their hands, they are prepared in the best possible manner to repel any encroachments upon their rights, etc."

this view states, "The [*Simpson*] court *never* answered whether the Tennessee Constitution superseded the Statute of Northampton or whether there was a right to armed carriage in public."[773] Yet as quoted above, the court held that the Constitution "abrogated" the Statute and guaranteed that "the people may carry arms."

In North Carolina, a justice of the peace manual by James Davis published in 1774 stated that "Justices of the Peace . . . may apprehend any person who shall go or ride armed with unusual and offensive Weapons, in an Affray, or among any great Concourse of the People . . . ."[774] And a manual by Henry Potter published in 1816 stated that a recognizance for keeping the peace may be required of a person for "riding or going armed with dangerous or unusual weapons, under such circumstances as are apt to terrify the people . . . ."[775]

However, Potter continued, a slave was prohibited from going armed with *any* weapon under *any* circumstances without a certificate so permitting: "No slave shall go armed with gun, sword, club, or other weapon, or shall keep any such weapon, or shall hunt or range with a gun in the woods, upon any pretence whatsoever, (except such slave or slaves, who shall have a certificate, as is herein after provided) . . . ."[776] The master had to give bond and the county court had to issue the certificate, which the slave was required to carry when going armed.[777] If the master could thus empower his slave to go armed with a

---

[773] Charles, *Armed in America*, 399 n.165.

[774] James Davis, *The Office and Authority of a Justice of the Peace* 13 (New Bern, N.C: James Davis, 1774).

[775] Henry Potter, *The Office and Duties of a Justice of the Peace . . . According to the Laws of North-Carolina* 39 (Raleigh: Henry Potter, 1816).

[776] *Id.* at 291.

[777] *Id.* at 292.

certificate, obviously the master could go armed as long as not done in a manner to terrify others.

In contrast to the approach by the Tennessee court in the *Simpson* case, the Supreme Court of North Carolina upheld indictments with language and under reasoning reflecting the legacy of the Statute of Northampton, as including both going armed and doing so in a concrete manner to terrorize specific people.[778] In *State v. Langford* (1824), the indictment alleged that the defendants "with force and arms, at the house of one Sarah Roffle, an aged widow woman…did then and there wickedly, mischievously and maliciously, and to the terror and dismay of the said Sarah Roffle, fire several guns…."[779] As the court stated, "men were armed with guns, which they fired at the house of an unprotected female, thus exciting her alarm for the safety of her person and her property. This is the *corpus delicti*…."[780] The court recalled the words of Hawkins that "there may be an affray when there is no actual violence: as when a man arms himself with dangerous and unusual weapons, in such a manner as will naturally cause a terror to the people…."[781]

---

[778]What is misleadingly cited today as "1792 N.C. Laws 60, 61 ch. 3" was never passed by the legislature. That the citation is fake should have been a dead giveaway, since the quotation repeatedly refers to "the King." In 1792, a lawyer published what he thought to be the English statutes in force in North Carolina, including the Statute of Northampton. François-Xavier Martin, *A Collection of the Statutes of the Parliament of England in Force in the State of North-Carolina 60–61* (1792). Later compilers wrote that this work "was utterly unworthy of the talents and industry of the distinguished compiler, omitting many statutes, always in force, and inserting many others, which never were, and never could have been in force, either in the Province, or in the State." "Preface of the Commissioners of 1838," *Revised Code of North Carolina*, xiii (1855).

[779] *State v. Langford*, 10 N.C. (3 Hawks) 381 (1824).

[780] *Id.* at 383.

[781] *Id.*, quoting 1 Hawkins 136.

Similarly, in *State v. Huntley* (1843), the North Carolina Supreme Court upheld an indictment alleging that the defendant, "with force and arms…did arm himself with pistols, guns, knives and other dangerous and unusual weapons, and, being so armed," publicly threatened before various citizens "to beat, wound, kill and murder" another person and others, causing citizens to be "terrified," and all "to the terror of the people…."[782] The court quoted Blackstone's references to "the offence of riding or going armed with dangerous or unusual weapons…by terrifying the good people of the land," and to the Statute of Northampton (which the court noted was not in effect in North Carolina).[783] It further quoted Hawkins' reference to an affray as including "where a man arms himself with dangerous and unusual weapons in such a manner, as will naturally cause a terror to the people…."[784] It also noted the statement in Sir John Knight's case that the Statute of Northampton was made in affirmance of the common law.[785]

The *Huntley* court next turned to the guarantee of the North Carolina bill of rights securing to every man the right to "bear arms for the defence of the State." While this "secures to him a right of which he cannot be deprived," he has no right to "employ those arms…to the annoyance and terror and danger of its citizens…."[786] That said, "the carrying of a gun *per se* constitutes no offence. For any lawful purpose

---

[782] *State v. Huntley*, 25 N.C. (3 Ired.) 418, 419 (1843).
[783] *Id.* at 420-21, quoting 4 Blackstone, *Commentaries* *149. "[W]hether this statute [Northampton] was or was not formerly in force in this State, it certainly has not been since the first of January, 1838, at which day it is declared in the Revised Statutes, (ch. 1st, sect. 2,) that the statutes of England or Great Britain shall cease to be of force and effect here." *Id.* at 420.
[784] *Id.* at 421, quoting Haw. P. C. B. 1, ch. 28, sect. 1.
[785] *Id.* at 421, citing 3 Mod. Rep. 117.
[786] *Id.* at 422.

– either of business or amusement – the citizen is at perfect liberty to carry his gun."[787] However, he may not carry a weapon "to terrify and alarm, and in such manner as naturally will terrify and alarm, a peaceful people."[788]

Decisions on affrays were rendered by courts of other states that used some of the above familiar language without mentioning the English antecedents. *O'Neill v. State* (1849), a decision by the Alabama Supreme Court, reversed a conviction for an affray in which the apparently unarmed defendant rode up to the witness and called him a "thief, liar, rascal, &c., whereupon the witness caned him," but the defendant did not resist other than to "to throw up his hands to protect his head...."[789] The court held that quarrelsome words did not constitute an affray, adding in *dictum*: "It is probable, however, that if persons arm themselves with deadly or unusual weapons for the purpose of an affray, and in such manner as to strike terror to the people, they may be guilty of this offence, without coming to actual blows."[790]

E) Prohibitions on Carrying Concealed Weapons in the Antebellum Era

Before the Civil War, citizens in every state of the union had a right to carry a firearm. In every state, it was lawful to carry openly. And in most states, it was also lawful to carry a concealed firearm. A minority of states restricted the carrying of concealed weapons. No state attempted to ban carriage on both an open and a concealed basis. Any

---

[787] *Id.* at 422–23.
[788] *Id.* at 423.
[789] *O'Neill v. State*, 16 Ala. 65, 65 (1849).
[790] *Id.* at 67, citing 1 *Russell on Crimes* 271.

such restriction would have been totally foreign to the Founding generation.

It was not an offense at common law or in the statutes of any state at the Founding peaceably to bear arms openly or concealed. Going armed without the arm being seen inherently could not cause terror to anyone, and carrying firearms openly was normal and commonplace. Before 1846, only eight states—seven Southern states and Indiana—of the 29 states in the Union enacted laws prohibiting the carrying of pistols (or small pistols) in a concealed manner. They included, in order of enactment: Kentucky, Louisiana, Tennessee, Indiana, Alabama, Georgia, Virginia, and Arkansas.[791]

By 1861, when there were 34 states in the Union, Ohio was the only additional state to regulate concealed pistols. Instead of banning the practice, Ohio made it an affirmative defense that the circumstances would "justify a prudent man in carrying the weapon...for the defense of his person, property or family...."[792] By the twenty-first century, because police would sometimes arrest a person openly carrying a firearm for disorderly conduct, the prohibition was declared violative of the right to bear arms.[793]

Of the 34 states, none of the other 26 states, Northern or Southern, restricted the carrying of concealed firearms before the Civil War.

---

[791] See compilation in Clayton E. Cramer, *Concealed Weapon Laws of the Early Republic* 143–52 (1999). See also Tenn. Laws, c. 13, § 1 (1821) (imposing fine for "carrying a dirk, sword cane, Spanish stiletto, belt or pocket pistols, either public or private," except while on a journey).

[792] An Act to Prohibit the Carrying or Wearing of Concealed Weapons, Acts of the State of Ohio 56 (1857).

[793] *Klein v. Leis*, 146 Ohio App.3d 526, 531, 535, 767 N.E.2d 286 (2002).

Other than a law struck down by the Georgia Supreme Court discussed below, no state prohibited the open carrying of firearms in this period.

Kentucky enacted the first restriction on carrying concealed weapons.[794] It did so in 1813, an unlikely year in that the War of 1812 was being waged and the carrying of arms would have been commonplace and perhaps encouraged. Gun ownership was so pervasive that, when Kentucky volunteers arrived without rifles to help defend New Orleans from the British assault at the end of the war, Andrew Jackson famously said in astonishment: "I have never seen a Kentuckian without a gun and a pack of cards and a bottle of whiskey in my life."[795]

Moreover, the Kentucky Constitution plainly stated: "That the right of the citizens to bear arms in defense of themselves and the State *shall not be questioned.*"[796] That compared with the more general language of the Second Amendment that "the right of the people to keep and bear arms, *shall not be infringed.*"

Given the declaration that the right "shall not be questioned" and that a ban on concealed carry was unprecedented, it was no small wonder that the first judicial decision thereon by a state court declared it unconstitutional. In *Bliss v. Commonwealth* (1822), the Kentucky Supreme Court reasoned that "in principle, there is no difference between a law prohibiting the wearing concealed arms, and a law forbidding the wearing such as are exposed; and if the former be

---

[794] Acts Passed at the First Session of the Twenty First General Assembly for the Commonwealth of Kentucky 100-01 (Frankfort: Gerard & Berry, 1813).
[795] "1815 One Hundred And Seventy-five Years Ago," https://www.americanheritage.com/1815-one-hundred-and-seventy-five-years-ago.
[796] Ky. Const., Art. XII, § 23 (1792) (emphasis added).

unconstitutional, the latter must be so likewise."[797] What if the legislature banned open carry, the court asked? It reasoned that the rule could not be that whichever mode of carry was banned first was thereby constitutional.[798] "Diminish that liberty, therefore, and you necessarily restrain the right; and such is the diminution and restraint, which the act in question most indisputably imports, by prohibiting the citizens wearing weapons in a manner which was lawful to wear when the constitution was adopted."[799]

In reaction to *Bliss*, the Kentucky Constitution was amended to add, after declaring that the right to bear arms shall not be questioned, the clause "but the General Assembly may pass laws to prevent persons from carrying concealed arms."[800] That made clear that the right to bear arms openly could not be prohibited. The arms guarantees of some other state constitutions would later declare that the right to bear arms did not extend to carrying concealed weapons.[801]

Despite its logic, the *Bliss* opinion that carrying concealed weapons could not be restricted would not be followed by the courts in the other handful of states with such restrictions, largely on the basis that the open carry of firearms in those states was freely available and legally allowed. The Supreme Court of Indiana, the next court to opine

---

[797] *Bliss v. Commonwealth*, 2 Litt. 90, 92 (Ky. 1822).
[798] *Id.* at 93.
[799] *Id.* at 92.
[800] Ky. Const., Art. XIII, § 25 (1850).
[801] See Colo. Const., Art. II, § 13 (1876); La. Const., Art. III, § 3 (1879); Miss. Const., Art. III, § 12 (1890); Mo. Const., Art. II, § 17 (1875); Mont., Const., Art. II, § 12 (1889); New Mex. Const., Art. II, § 6 (1912). Other states authorized the legislature to prescribe "the manner" in which arms may be borne, Fla. Const., Art. I, § 20 (1885), Ga. Const., Art. I, § 14 (1868); "to regulate the wearing of arms with a view to prevent crime," Tenn. Const., Art. I, § 26 (1870), Tex. Const., Art. I, § 23 (1876); or simply "the carrying of weapons." Okla. Const., Art. II, § 26 (1907).

on the issue, held in a one sentence opinion that a statute "prohibiting all persons, except travelers, from wearing or carrying concealed weapons, is not unconstitutional."[802] Perhaps being unable to articulate how to refute the logic of the Kentucky court's decision, this judicial *ipse dixit* offered no reasoning to justify the prohibition.

No consensus existed that the court got it right. The Indiana constitution provided: "That the people have a right to bear arms for the defense of themselves and the State...."[803] At the 1850 Indiana constitutional convention, Robert Dale Owen—"the most diligent, prominent, and influential delegate in the convention"[804]—explained that "to prohibit the carrying of weapons it would be necessary to change the language of the old Constitution. For if it were declared by Constitutional provision that the people should have the right to bear arms, no law of the Legislature could take away that right."[805] Motions were made and rejected to rephrase the right as to "bear arms openly" or as "[n]o person shall be restricted in the right to carry visible arms."[806]

The Alabama Supreme Court upheld a concealed weapon ban because open carry was allowed, cautioning: "A statute which, under the pretence of regulating, amounts to a destruction of the right, or which requires arms to be so borne as to render them wholly useless for the purpose of defence, would be clearly unconstitutional."[807]

---

[802] *State v. Mitchell*, 3 Blackf. 229 (Ind. 1833).
[803] Ind. Const., Art. I, § 20 (1816).
[804] Richard W. Leopold, *Robert Dale Owen* 269 (New York: Octagon Books, 1969).
[805] *Report of the Debates and Proceedings of the Convention of the Revision of the Constitution of the of the State of Indiana* 1385 (1850).
[806] *Id.* at 574, 1931.
[807] *State v. Reid*, 1 Ala. 612, 616–17 (1840).

That was followed by *Nunn v. State* (1846), in which the Georgia Supreme Court held that the right to bear arms expressed in the Second Amendment was an inalienable right and thus applied to the states.[808] Invalidating a ban on open carry of pistols, the court wrote: "The right of the whole people, old and young, men, women and boys, and not militia only, to keep and bear *arms* of every description, and not *such* merely as are used by the militia, shall not be *infringed*, curtailed, or broken in upon, in the smallest degree...."[809]

While holding that a statute prohibiting the carrying of concealed weapons was not in violation of the Second Amendment, the Louisiana Supreme Court reasoned that the right to carry arms openly "placed men upon an equality. This is the right guaranteed by the Constitution of the United States, and which is calculated to incite men to a manly and noble defense of themselves, if necessary, and of their country...."[810] As this suggests, the open carry rule was tied into the social norms of the day.

It has been argued that *Nunn* and the other above decisions, except for the Indiana case, are tainted because they were from "the slaveholding South" and that no right peaceably to carry firearms was recognized in the North.[811] That is false. While concealed carry bans were predominantly a Southern phenomenon during the antebellum period, the only restrictions on carriage in most Northern states were the surety laws such as the 1836 Massachusetts enactment analyzed

---

[808] *Nunn v. State*, 1 Ga. 243, 250 (1846).
[809] *Id.* at 251.
[810] *State v. Chandler*, 5 La. Ann 489, 490 (1850). And see *State v. Smith*, 11 La. Ann. 633 (1856) ("The arms there spoken of [in the Second Amendment] are such as are borne by a people in war, or at least carried openly."); *State v. Jumel*, 13 La Ann. 399 (1858).
[811] Eric M. Ruben and Saul Cornell, "Firearm Regionalism and Public Carry: Placing Southern Antebellum Case Law in Context," 125 *Yale L.J. Forum* 121, 123 (2015).

above. Those laws, which existed in several Northern and Southern states, only applied where a person filed a complaint that he or she had "reasonable cause to fear an injury, or breach of the peace" by the person going armed—and even then, only required that person to post a bond to continue carrying.[812] Apart from that modest limitation, both open and concealed carry were freely allowed in all Northern states except Indiana and Ohio.

To the extent that the "slaveholding South" had a unique approach to gun control before the Civil War, then, it was *more restrictive* than the predominant approach north of the Mason-Dixon line. The relative lack of restrictions in the Northern states explains the dearth of judicial decisions by Northern courts equivalent to *Nunn*.

Indeed, it was still an open question whether a prohibition on carrying concealed weapons violated the right to bear arms. The edition of James Kent's celebrated *Commentaries on American Law* edited by Oliver Wendell Holmes stated: "As the Constitution of the United States, and the constitutions of several of the states, in terms more or less comprehensive, declare the right of the people to keep and bear arms, it has been a subject of grave discussion, in some of the state courts, whether a statute prohibiting persons…from wearing or carrying concealed weapons, be constitutional. There has been a great difference of opinion on the question."[813]

---

[812] *Id.* at 130.

[813] 2 James Kent, *Commentaries on American Law*, O. Holmes ed., *340 n.2 (12th ed. 1873). See also 2 Joel Prentiss Bishop, *Commentaries on the Criminal Law* § 103 (2d ed. 1858) ("There are provisions in the statutes of some of the States against carrying concealed weapons….A point of embarrassment has been, whether these statutes are constitutional.").

Rejection of state bans on carrying concealed arms in the North was exemplified at the Pennsylvania constitutional convention in 1873. A delegate moved to amend the state arms guarantee to read: "The right of the citizens *openly* to bear arms in defence of themselves and the State, shall not be questioned." Some localities banned concealed carry, noted another delegate, who explained that some courts held such bans to be violative of the right to bear arms.[814]

Isaac W. MacVeagh, who would later serve as U.S. Attorney General, opposed the amendment, arguing that "the present Constitution is perfectly explicit and satisfactory on this subject," and noting that a man might "be under the necessity of protecting himself by carrying a weapon of defence." He explained that sometimes he arrived in Philadelphia from Washington on late trains, and "to tell me that I am to walk the streets of this city at night without any protection whatever from ruffians, is to state something to which I will never agree."[815]

A "law against carrying concealed weapons does not interfere with the habit among the dangerous classes," MacVeagh continued, adding that "I believe in the right of self-defence of the weak against the strong, and I do not propose to allow any man to maltreat me at his pleasure, as long as there are any weapons of defence to be had by which I can equalize my strength with his." In short, "I cannot see why the Constitution should prohibit a man from carrying weapons to

---

[814] 7 *Debates of the Convention to Amend the Constitution of Pennsylvania* 258 (Harrisburg: Benjamin Singerly, 1873) (emphasis added).
[815] *Id.*

defend himself unless he carries them openly, why you should require him to sling a revolver over his shoulder."[816]

Delegate Beebe recalled times when "no man's life would have been safe had it not been well understood that every man carried concealed weapons....Thieves and murderers never would and never do regard any law of this kind, and the revolver under such circumstances is the best conservator of the public peace in the hands of law-abiding men."[817]

It was pointed out that Pennsylvania law at the time "restrain[ed] persons from carrying concealed weapons with malicious intent."[818] In fact, an 1864 law prohibited "carrying upon the person...a concealed deadly weapon...with an intent, unlawfully and maliciously, to do bodily harm to another," as summarized by the Pennsylvania Supreme Court, holding that doing so "has no protection under the 21st section of the Bill of Rights, saving the right of the citizens to bear arms in defence of themselves and the state."[819]

George M. Dallas supported the amendment, arguing that it would leave it to the legislature to decide whether to ban the carrying of concealed weapons. It could allow such carrying in some parts of the state, but in Philadelphia he did "not believe that the carrying of concealed deadly weapons is necessary for the protection of orderly people."[820] When delegate Ewing noted repeated instances "when it has been unsafe for people to go abroad in Philadelphia upon the public

---

[816] *Id.* at 258–59.
[817] *Id.* at 259.
[818] *Id.* at 260.
[819] *Wright v. Commonwealth*, 77 Pa. 470, 471 (1875) (citing Act of May 5, 1864, § 1, 1 Brightly 323, pl. 40).
[820] 7 *Debates of the Convention to Amend the Constitution of Pennsylvania* 260.

streets without carrying deadly weapons," Dallas responded that while "men have been assaulted and robbed on the street," Ewing "has no right to ask that he may exercise a power outside of the law to protect himself, when the law itself is sufficient for his protection."[821]

Dallas concluded that limiting the right only to "openly to bear arms" would "make clear a constitutional provision in regard to which there has been some conflict of opinion." In other words, the constitutionality of a ban on concealed carry was open to question. Some two-thirds of the convention must have thought it would be unconstitutional and wanted to keep it that way, as the amendment was defeated by a vote of 54 to 23.[822]

Most states in the first half of the nineteenth century and beyond allowed open or concealed carry, and all states allowed open carry. The passage of prohibitions in a minority of states on carrying concealed weapons and the decisions thereon upholding open carry again proves that there was no recognized common law offense simply of going armed without more. It would have been unnecessary to restrict concealed carry if both concealed and open carry were already crimes under the common law. Moreover, other than the above Indiana decision, there were no decisions on the right to bear arms from courts in the North because, other than Indiana and Ohio, none of the Northern states had restrictions on the peaceable carrying of arms, concealed or openly.

In sum, every citizen in every state could carry a firearm in public. In a minority of states, open carry was required. In most states, one

---

[821] *Id.* at 260–61.
[822] *Id.* at 261.

could carry either openly or concealed. The right peaceably to bear arms was the rule and there were no complete prohibitions.

F) African Americans: Prohibitions and Licensing Requirements

From colonial times until slavery was abolished, slaves were prohibited from keeping and bearing arms in most circumstances or altogether. In the same period, several states prohibited free blacks from carrying arms unless they obtained a license, which was subject to an official's discretion. Such laws reflected that African Americans were not trusted or recognized to be among "the people" with the rights of citizens.

The Virginia slave code provided that "[n]o negro or mulatto slave whatsoever shall keep or carry any gun, powder, shot, club or other weapon whatsoever, offensive or defensive," punishable by no more than thirty-nine lashes, except those living at a frontier plantation could be licensed to "keep and use" such weapons by a justice of the peace.[823] Further, "[n]o free negro or mulatto, shall be suffered to keep or carry any fire-lock of any kind, any military weapon, or any powder or lead, without first obtaining a license from the court" where he resided, "which license may, at any time, be withdrawn by an order of such court."[824]

As a Virginia court held in 1824, among the "numerous restrictions imposed on this class of people [free blacks] in our Statute Book, many of which are inconsistent with the letter and spirit of the Constitution, both of this State and of the United States," were "the restriction upon the migration of free blacks into this State, and upon

---

[823] Va. 1819, c. 111, § 7.
[824] *Id.* § 8.

their right to bear arms."[825] But white persons had a right to carry arms and needed no license to do so.

After Nat Turner's slave revolt in 1831, Virginia law was amended to provide: "No free negro or mulatto shall be suffered to keep or carry any firelock of any kind, any military weapon, or any powder or lead...." It repealed the prior law that authorized justices of the peace "to permit slaves to keep and use guns or other weapons," and that also authorized courts "to grant licenses to free negroes and mulattoes to keep or carry any firelock of any kind, any military weapon, or any powder or lead...."[826]

In Georgia, it was unlawful "for any slave, unless in the presence of some white person, to carry and make use of fire arms," unless the slave had a license from his master to hunt.[827] It was also unlawful "for any free person of colour in this state, to own, use, or carry fire arms of any description whatever...."[828] Georgia's high court held: "Free persons of color have never been recognized here as citizens; they are not entitled to bear arms, vote for members of the legislature, or to hold any civil office."[829]

Delaware forbade "free negroes and free mulattoes to have, own, keep, or possess any gun [or] pistol," except that such persons could apply to a justice of the peace for a permit to possess a gun or fowling piece, which could be granted if "the circumstances of his case justify his keeping and using a gun...."[830] The police power was said to justify

---

[825] *Aldridge v. Commonwealth*, 2 Va. 447, 449 (Gen. Ct. 1824).
[826] Va. 1831, c. 22, § 4.
[827] Digest of the Laws of the State of Georgia 424 (1802).
[828] § 7, 1833 Ga. Laws 226, 228.
[829] *Cooper v. Savannah*, 4 Ga. 72 (1848).
[830] Ch. 176, § 1, 8 Laws of the State of Delaware 208 (1841).

restrictions such as "the prohibition of free negroes to own or have in possession fire arms or warlike instruments."[831]

The above is just a sampling of some of the slave code provisions and how they also applied to restrict the rights of free blacks from enjoying all the rights of free white citizens. Licensing was discretionary based on the issuing authority's determination of the applicant's circumstances or need to keep or carry a firearm.

North Carolina judicial decisions explained in more detail the basis of discretionary licensing for free persons of color. The state made it unlawful "if any free negro, mulatto, or free person of color, shall wear or carry about his or her person, or keep in his or her house, any shot gun, musket, rifle, pistol, sword, dagger or bowie-knife, unless he or she shall have obtained a licence" from the court.[832] This was upheld in *State v. Newsom* (1844) as constitutional partly on the ground that "the free people of color cannot be considered as citizens...."[833]

The court added: "It does not deprive the free man of color of the right to carry arms about his person, but subjects it to the control of the County Court, giving them the power to say, in the exercise of a sound discretion, who, of this class of persons, shall have a right to the licence, or whether any shall."[834] This is reminiscent of today's judicial jargon that the right of the people to bear arms is not infringed by laws granting officials discretion to deny them that very right.

---

[831] *State v. Allmond*, 7 Del. 612, 641 (Gen. Sess. 1856).
[832] *State v. Newsom*, 27 N.C. 250, 250 (1844) (quoting Act of 1840, ch. 30).
[833] *Id.* at 254.
[834] *Id.* at 253.

Averring that having weapons by "this class of persons" was "dangerous to the peace of the community," a later decision explained the basis of the discretionary-issuance policy:

> Degraded as are these individuals, as a class, by their social position, it is certain, that among them are many, worthy of all confidence, and into whose hands these weapons can be safely trusted, either for their own protection, or for the protection of the property of others confided to them. The County Court is, therefore, authorised to grant a licence to any individual they think proper, to possess and use these weapons.[835]

The court could not only deny a license outright, but also could limit a license to carry to certain places. In *State v. Harris* (1859), a free person of color had a license to carry a gun only on his own land, but he was caught hunting with a shotgun elsewhere with white companions.[836] Upholding the conviction, the court held that "the county court might think it a very prudent precaution to limit the carrying of arms to the lands of the free negro" and that the act did not "prevent the restriction from being imposed."[837]

Maryland made it unlawful "for any negro or mulatto...to keep any...gun, except he be a free negro or mulatto...."[838] It was unlawful "for any free negro or mulatto to go at large with any gun,"[839] but that did not prevent him "from carrying a gun...who shall...have a certificate from a justice of the peace, that he is an orderly and

---

[835] *State v. Lane*, 30 N.C. 256, 257 (1848).

[836] *State v. Harris*, 51 N.C. 448 (1859).

[837] *Id.* at 449.

[838] Chap. 86, § I (1806), in 3 Laws of Maryland 297 (1811).

[839] § II, *id.* at 298.

peaceable person...."[840] The Court of Appeals of Maryland described "free negroes" as being treated as "a vicious or dangerous population," as exemplified by laws "to prevent their migration to this State; to make it unlawful for them to bear arms; to guard even their religious assemblages with peculiar watchfulness."[841]

Despite the above, it was routine for some free blacks to obtain licenses to carry firearms. Historian Martha Jones examined court records in Baltimore, Maryland, and described how in 1858 Samuel Hardy and Nathan Bowers, free persons of color, presented their applications, both endorsed by two lawyers, to Superior Court Judge Z. Collins Lee, who granted each permission "to keep and carry a gun for one year."[842] The 1859 court docket also reflected: "Permission is granted to Alexander Henry Martin a free negro to keep and carry a gun and dog for one year."[843] Permit holders were thereby authorized to carry firearms for self-defense and hunting. Professor Jones found:

> Permits were routinely granted, with no commentary in the court records or the local newspapers about concerns or fears. Statutory restrictions on black gun ownership enacted in Annapolis never suppressed black gun ownership and never led to prosecutions for illicit, unlicensed gun possession.[844]

Free blacks also obtained permits to travel, even interstate, and with gun licenses they thereby were able to assemble a bundle of rights associated with citizenship. "As they traveled with a permit or carried

---

[840] *Id.*
[841] *Waters v. State*, 1 Gill 302, 309 (Md. 1843).
[842] Martha S. Jones, *Birthright Citizens: A History Of Race and Rights in Antebellum America* 104 (Cambridge: Cambridge University Press, 2018).
[843] *Id.* at 105.
[844] *Id.* at 104.

a licensed gun," Professor Jones concludes, "they were that much closer to citizenship."[845]

Other antebellum African Americans carried guns as part of their effort to *gain* their freedom. Harriet Tubman, heroine of the Underground Railroad, famously carried a pistol as part of her work transporting escaped slaves to freedom.[846] Her pistol remains a family heirloom owned by her descendants to this day.[847] Indeed, the carrying of firearms by fleeing slaves was apparently common enough to be captured in contemporary fiction: in a memorable scene of *Uncle Tom's Cabin*, escaped slaves George and Eliza Harris use a pistol to fend off a party of pursuing slave hunters.[848]

In short, free persons of color were not entitled to the right to keep and bear arms, because they were not considered to be American citizens. That status was reflected in the requirement that they obtain a license, subject to the issuing authority's subjective decision as to whether the applicant was a proper person with a proper reason.

These state laws were bolstered by the U.S. Supreme Court in *Dred Scott v. Sanford* (1857), which notoriously held that African Americans were not citizens and had no rights that must be respected.[849] Chief Justice Roger Taney wrote that, if African Americans were considered citizens, "it would give them the full

---

[845] *Id.* at 106–07.

[846] Kate C. Larson, *Bound for the Promised Land: Harriet Tubman: Portrait of an American Hero* 101 (New York: Random House, 2003).

[847] Marina Brown, "Florida family cherishes Harriet Tubman memories—and her pistol," *Florida Times-Union* (Dec. 2, 2019), https://www.jacksonville.com/zz/news/20191202/florida-family-cherishes-harriet-tubman-memories-mdash-and-her-pistol.

[848] Harriet Beecher Stowe, *Uncle Tom's Cabin* 284–86 (1852).

[849] *Scott v. Sanford*, 60 U.S. (19 How.) 393 (1857).

liberty of speech…; to hold public meetings upon political affairs, and to keep and carry arms wherever they went."

Yet there was an irony about Taney's statement that Professor Martha Jones juxtaposed in light of the issuance of permits to carry firearms to free blacks:

> Wasn't it true that in Baltimore City black residents did "keep and carry arms wherever they went." They did so pursuant to court issued licenses. Surely Taney's view would be that a license requirement marked black gun possession as a badge of degradation which cut against the view that such gun possession was a sign of citizenship. But even as Taney sat on the Circuit Court bench on St. Paul Street, his reach did not extend around the corner into the City courthouse where new meanings were being attached to the possibility of keeping and carrying a gun.[850]

The abolitionists Lysander Spooner and Joel Tiffany argued in favor of that very concept of citizenship. They wrote treatises contending that slavery was unconstitutional; after all, the Second Amendment and other guarantees protected "the people." Spooner wrote that the Second Amendment protects "the natural right of all men 'to keep and bear arms' for their personal defence…."[851] Tiffany argued that " the right to keep and bear arms, also implies the right to use them if necessary in self defence; without this right to use the guaranty would have hardly been worth the paper it consumed."[852]

---

[850] Martha S. Jones, *Bearing Arms in Baltimore City: From Claims-making to Citizenship in the Era of* Dred Scott 15 (2010), available at http://lawweb.usc.edu/centers/clhc/events/feature/documents/Jones.pdf.

[851] Lysander Spooner, *The Unconstitutionality Of Slavery* 97-98 (1860).

[852] Joel Tiffany, *A Treatise on the Unconstitutionality of Slavery* 117-18 (1849).

Their arguments would influence John Bingham and the other framers of what would become the Fourteenth Amendment.[853]

* * *

At the Founding and in the Antebellum period, the right to bear arms was constitutionalized. Going armed was no offense unless done so in a manner to terrorize others. In most states, one could carry firearms openly or concealed in public. Laws in a minority of states prohibiting the carrying of concealed weapons were upheld on the basis that open carry was allowed and lawful.

Slaves were generally prohibited from having arms altogether, and in the Southern states free persons of color were prohibited from carrying arms unless they had a license issued at the discretion of the government. As discussed in the next chapter, the abolition of slavery and the adoption of the Fourteenth Amendment would extend Second Amendment rights to African Americans.

---

[853] Jacobus tenBroek, *Equal Under Law* 110-13, 146 (New York: Collier Books, 1965).

Chapter Seven

THE FOURTEENTH AMENDMENT
AND ITS AFTERMATH

A) The Black Codes and Discretionary Licensing

"In the aftermath of the Civil War, there was an outpouring of discussion of the Second Amendment in Congress and in public discourse, as people debated whether and how to secure constitutional rights for newly free slaves," the Supreme Court noted in *District of Columbia v. Heller*.[854] The slave codes were reenacted as the black codes, including prohibitions on the unlicensed keeping and the carrying of firearms by African Americans. As Frederick Douglass explained in 1865, "the black man has never had the right either to keep or bear arms."[855]

The first state law noted by the Supreme Court in *McDonald v. Chicago* as typical of what the Fourteenth Amendment would invalidate required a license to have a firearm that an official had discretion to limit or deny. Mississippi provided that "no freedman, free negro or mulatto, not in the military service of the United States

---

[854] *District of Columbia v. Heller*, 554 U.S. 570, 614 (2008), citing S. Halbrook, *Freedmen*, the Fourteenth Amendment, and the Right to Bear Arms, 1866—1876 (1998). An updated version of Freedmen was issued as *Securing Civil Rights*.
[855] "In What New Skin Will the Old Snake Come Forth?" Address delivered in New York City, May 10, 1865, 4 *The Frederick Douglass Papers* 84 (1991).

government, and not licensed so to do by the board of police of his or her county, shall keep or carry fire-arms of any kind, or any ammunition, dirk or bowie knife."[856]

That law was attacked by the media as violative of the Second Amendment. The *Chicago Tribune* wrote: "The word people is the very broadest term that can be used to cover all classes of population. Worcester [A Dictionary of the English Language] defines people as follows: 'Those who compose a community, persons or men in general; folks; population.'"[857] It added in a later issue: "Hence, every negro in Mississippi has the right to keep and bear arms. They are now a part of the People of Mississippi."[858] *Harper's Weekly* noted that "the statute laws of Mississippi do not recognize the negro as having any right to carry arms."[859]

Second Amendment deprivations were debated in bills leading to the enactment of the Freedmen's Bureau Act and the Civil Rights Act of 1866. Rep. Thomas Eliot, sponsor of the former, explained that the bill would invalidate laws like that of Opelousas, Louisiana, providing that no freedman "shall be allowed to carry fire-arms" without permission of his employer and as approved by the board of police.[860] He noted that in Kentucky "[t]he civil law prohibits the colored man from bearing arms...."[861] Accordingly, the Freedmen's Bureau bill guaranteed the right "to have full and equal benefit of all laws and

---

[856] Certain Offenses of Freedmen, 1865 Miss. Laws p. 165, § 1, quoted in *McDonald v. City of Chicago*, 561 U.S. 742, 771 (2010).
[857] "Disarming the Negroes," *Chicago Tribune*, Nov. 14, 1865, at 2.
[858] "Barbarism in Mississippi," *Chicago Tribune*, Nov. 17, 1865, at 2.
[859] *Harper's Weekly*, Jan. 13, 1866, at 3.
[860] Cong. Globe, 39th Cong., 1st Sess. 517 (1866).
[861] *Id.* at 657.

proceedings for the security of person and estate, including the constitutional right to bear arms."[862]

Senator Garret Davis said that the Founding Fathers "were for every man bearing his arms about him and keeping them in his house, his castle, for his own defense.[863] Senator Samuel Pomeroy counted among the "safeguards of liberty" "the right to bear arms for the defense of himself and family and his homestead."[864] Yet violations persisted, such as in Alexandria, Virginia, which continued "to enforce the old law against them [freedmen] in respect to whipping and carrying fire-arms...."[865]

Representative William Lawrence of Ohio discussed the need to protect freedmen, quoting General D. E. Sickles' General Order No. 1 of January 1, 1866, for the Department of South Carolina, which negated the state's prohibition on possession of firearms by blacks and, at the same time, recognized the right of all peaceable persons to carry arms:

> The constitutional rights of all loyal and well disposed inhabitants to bear arms, will not be infringed; nevertheless this shall not be construed to sanction the unlawful practice of carrying concealed weapons; nor to authorize any person to enter with arms on the premises of another without his consent.[866]

---

[862] Id. at 654.
[863] Id. at 371.
[864] Id. at 1182.
[865] Report of the Joint Committee on Reconstruction, H.R. Rep. No. 30, 39th Cong., 1st Sess., pt. 2, at 21 (1866).
[866] Cong. Globe, 39th Cong., 1st Sess., 908–09 (1866). See McDonald, 561 U.S. at 773 & n.21 (citing this order and commenting that "Union Army commanders took steps to secure the right of all citizens to keep and bear arms").

This order was repeatedly printed in the *Loyal Georgian*, a black newspaper.[867] One issue of the paper included the following:

Have colored persons a right to own and carry fire arms?

A Colored Citizen

Almost every day we are asked questions similar to the above....

Article II, of the amendments to the Constitution of the United States, gives the people the right to bear arms, and states that this right shall not be infringed.... All men, without distinction of color, have the right to keep and bear arms to defend their homes, families or themselves.[868]

While General Sickles' order upheld the right of individuals openly to bear arms, South Carolina was under military occupation, and extra-legal, organized groups were not allowed to exercise power. He issued General Order No. 7, which provided: "Organizations of white or colored persons bearing arms, or intended to be armed, not belonging to the military or naval forces of the United States, are unauthorized, and will not be allowed to assemble, parade, patrol, drill, make arrests, or exercise any authority."[869]

The first Reconstruction Act of 1867 abolished the civilian governments in the South and provided that specified "rebel States shall be divided into military districts, and made subject to the military authority of the United States...."[870] General Sickles' General Orders No. 10, applicable in the Second Military District (North and South

---

[867] *Loyal Georgian*, Feb. 3, 1866, at 1.
[868] *Id.* at 3.
[869] 1 Walter L. Fleming, *Documentary History of Reconstruction* 211 (1906).
[870] An Act to Provide for the More Efficient Government of the Rebel States, March 2, 1867, 14 Stat. 428.

Carolina), substituted military orders for civilian law. One such rule provided:

> The practice of carrying deadly weapons, except by officers and soldiers in the military service of the United States, is prohibited. The concealment of such weapons on the person will be deemed an aggravation of the offense. A violation of this order will render the offender amenable to trial and punishment by military commission.[871]

That suspended not only the Second Amendment right to bear arms, but also the Sixth Amendment right to trial by jury. Military rule replaced guarantees under the Bill of Rights as well as ordinary civilian government. While the military authority deemed such harsh measures necessary, such actions should not be interpreted as reasonable interpretations of the constitutional provisions at issue. To the contrary, those provisions were superseded.

B) The Freedmen's Bureau Act and the Fourteenth Amendment

Introducing the Fourteenth Amendment in the Senate, Jacob Howard referred to "the personal rights guaranteed and secured by the first eight amendments of the Constitution; such as…the right to keep and bear arms…."[872] He averred: "The great object of the first section of this amendment is, therefore, to restrain the power of the States and compel them at all times to respect these great fundamental guarantees."[873] The Amendment was needed, Rep. George W. Julian argued, because Southern courts declared the Civil Rights Act void and some states

---

[871] General Orders No. 10, April 11, 1867, in *Tri-Weekly Standard* (Raleigh, N.C.), May 23, 1867.
[872] Cong. Globe, 39th Cong., 1st Sess. 2765 (1866).
[873] *Id.* at 2766.

made it "a misdemeanor for colored men to carry weapons without a license."[874]

James Lewis, a freedman in Mississippi, was arrested for carrying a musket without the required license. Chief Justice Alexander Hamilton Handy of Mississippi's highest court upheld the conviction, declaring the federal Civil Rights Act unconstitutional and holding that the state arms guarantee protected only citizens.[875] In a separate case, Judge R. Bullock acquitted Wash Lowe and other freedmen for carrying firearms without a license, holding the requirement violative of the right to bear arms for self-defense, which was "a natural and personal right – the right of self-preservation."[876] General Ulysses S. Grant noted these decisions in a report stating: "The statute prohibiting the colored people from bearing arms, without a special license, is unjust, oppressive, and unconstitutional."[877]

The *New York Times*, after publishing both decisions in full, editorialized about the proposed Fourteenth Amendment that "the necessity of some such protection for the freedmen is plainly evidenced by the decision" by Justice Handy "in the case of JAMES LEWIS, a freedman convicted of carrying firearms contrary to a law passed by the Legislature of the State in November 1865."[878] The Second Amendment did not help Mr. Lewis under the view that it only applied to the federal government, and the state guarantee did not help him under the view that he was not a citizen. Commented the *Times*:

---

[874] *Id.* at 3210.

[875] "Mississippi…The Civil Rights Bill Declared Unconstitutional by a State Court," *New York Times*, Oct. 26, 1866, at 2; see *McDonald*, 561 U.S. at 775 n.24.

[876] *Id.*

[877] Cong. Globe, 39th Cong., 2d Sess., 33 (1866).

[878] "Mr. Browning's Letter & Judge Handy's Decision," *New York Times*, Oct. 28, 1866, at 4.

This decision practically disarms the whole freed population of Mississippi, and leaves them unprotected....

It is against just such legislation and such judicial decisions that the first section of the Amendment is designed to furnish a protection. If the States, or any of them design to have such laws, they ought to be prevented by the power of the Federal Government....[879]

A common theme in the media was that freedmen had the right to bear arms because they were part of "the people." The *American Citizen*, a Pennsylvania newspaper, quoted the Second Amendment and wrote: "Now what is here meant by 'the people' – Webster defines it as 'the body of persons who compose a community, town, city or nation....'" So defined, "not a black person in the South, or anywhere else in the country, can be excluded under it from the right to bear arms," and "if the negro be not included in the militia, they are peculiarly the 'people' of the nation, and under the words of the Constitution are entitled to bear arms."[880]

The Freedmen's Bureau Act was passed by the same more than two-thirds majority of members of Congress who voted for the Fourteenth Amendment.[881] The Act declared that:

the right...to have full and equal benefit of all laws and proceedings concerning personal liberty, personal security, and the acquisition, enjoyment, and disposition of estate, real and personal, including the constitutional right to bear arms, shall be secured to and enjoyed by all the citizens of such State or district without respect to race or color or previous condition of slavery.[882]

---

[879] *Id.*
[880] "The Right to Bear Arms," *American Citizen* (Butler, Penn.), Nov. 7, 1866, at 4.
[881] Halbrook, *Freedmen*, 41–43.
[882] §14, 14 Stat. 173, 176–77 (1866).

Opposition to extension of the arms right to freedmen was starkly illustrated in the Maryland constitutional convention of 1867, where a delegate proposed adding to the state bill of rights that "every citizen has the right to bear arms in defence of himself and the State." Another delegate moved to weaken that to refer only to "every white citizen," while still another chimed in, "Every citizen of the State means every white citizen, and none other." Given the opposition to recognizing a right of non-whites to bear arms, it was proposed that "the citizen shall not be deprived of the right to keep arms on his premises." Even that was rejected.[883]

Similar debates played out in the newspapers. The Springfield *Republican* praised the existence of blacks with "a veritable gun, carried in hand, in open view, bravely before the eyes of all," adding that it "is part of the first amendments to the original law of the nation, 'the right of the people to keep and bear arms shall not be infringed.'" The Louisville *Daily Journal* denounced this advocacy for "'every negro' to show himself with his musket or his rifle on his shoulder."[884]

C) Protection Under the Civil Rights Act of 1871

The Civil Rights Act of 1871, which remains law today, provides for a civil action against a person who, under color of state law, subjects a citizen to "the deprivation of any rights, privileges, or immunities secured by the Constitution and laws."[885] The right to bear arms was one of the rights intended to be protected by the enactment.[886]

---

[883] Phillip B. Perlman, *Debates of the Maryland Constitutional Convention of 1867*, at 150-51 (1867).
[884] *Louisville Daily Journal*, Jan. 25, 1868, at 1 (quoting the Springfield Republican).
[885] 17 Stat. 13 (1871). Section 1 survives as 42 U.S.C. § 1983.
[886] *McDonald*, 561 U.S. at 776, citing Halbrook, *Freedmen* 120–131.

In debate, Rep. Henry Dawes explained that the citizen "has secured to him the right to keep and bear arms in his defense." And the federal courts would protect "these rights, privileges, and immunities."[887] Rep. John Coburn observed: "A State may by positive enactment cut off from some the right…to bear arms…. How much more oppressive is the passage of a law that they shall not bear arms than the practical seizure of all arms from the hands of the colored men?"[888]

Rep. Washington Whitthorne objected to the bill on the basis that "if a police officer…should find a drunken negro or white man upon the streets with a loaded pistol flourishing it, & c., and by virtue of any ordinance, law, or usage, either of city or State, he takes it away, the officer may be sued, because the right to bear arms is secured by the Constitution…."[889] Yet no one suggested that brandishing a firearm would be actionable; supporters of the bill were concerned that police would arrest a law-abiding African American peaceably carrying a pistol.

After passage of the Act, a Congressional investigation found widespread disarming of African Americans and a continuation of the old black codes whereby "a free person of color was only a little lower than a slave…[and hence] forbidden to carry or have arms."[890] President Grant reported that Ku Klux Klan groups continued "to deprive colored citizens of the right to bear arms and of the right to a

---

[887] Cong. Globe, 42nd Cong., 1st Sess., 475-76 (1871). See *McDonald*, 561 U.S. at 835 (Thomas, J., concurring).
[888] *Id.* at 459.
[889] *Id.* at 337.
[890] 1 *Report of the Joint Select Committee to Inquire into the Condition of Affairs in the Late Insurrectionary States* 261–62 (Feb. 19, 1872).

free ballot...."[891] The Klan targeted the black person, Senator Daniel Pratt noted, who would "tell his fellow blacks of their legal rights, as for instance their right to carry arms and defend their persons and homes."[892]

In sum, the Civil Rights Act of 1871 was understood to provide a remedy to persons who were deprived of the right to bear firearms, including in public. No one suggested that the right was limited to one's house or that the state could limit licenses to carry arms only to persons it deemed to have a "need" to do so. The laws that subjected the African Americans to such a discretionary licensing system were among the deprivations that prompted Congress to act.

D) Carry Laws in Reconstruction, 1865–1877

The post-Civil War period of Reconstruction ran from 1865 to 1877. During Reconstruction, most Northern states did not restrict an individual's right or ability to carry a firearm in public, whether it be concealed or openly, as long as they carried the weapon peaceably. Most Southern states continued to restrict the carrying of concealed weapons, and two of these states had open carry restrictions that the courts reined in. Texas stood alone as the only state to prohibit the carrying of pistols in public other than while traveling.

In 1870, California repealed its ban on carrying concealed weapons that it had passed only seven years earlier.[893] Repeal had been advocated by the *Daily Alta California*, a leading San Francisco newspaper, on the basis of the Second Amendment, explaining: "As the sovereignty resides in the people in America, they are to be

---

[891] Ex. Doc. No. 268, 42nd Cong., 2d Sess. 2 (1872).
[892] Cong. Globe, 42nd Cong., 2d Sess., 3589 (1872).
[893] Statutes of California, Ch. 63, p. 67 (1870), repealing *id.*, ch. 485, p. 748 (1863).

permitted to keep firearms and other weapons and to carry them at their pleasure." The restriction "disarms the orderly citizen and places no obstruction in the way of the robber."[894]

Going armed in a manner that terrorized others continued to be an offense in some states. An 1870 South Carolina law authorized the arrest of "all who go armed offensively, to the terror of the people...."[895] The separate elements of being armed, offensively, and to terrorize, were required to be proven. In a decision about another provision of the same law, the court held that the crime alleged in an indictment "should be clearly and distinctly set forth," and that the jury must understand the question "they were passing upon."[896]

The South Carolina law is still on the books today,[897] and yet South Carolina has a robust shall-issue handgun carry licensing system.[898] When they carry, license holders are obviously not considered as going armed offensively to the terror of the people.

However, a law requiring one who went armed in certain circumstances to give a recognizance did not thereby make such going armed a crime. West Virginia enacted the following in 1870: "If any person go armed with a deadly or dangerous weapon, without reasonable cause to fear violence to his person, family, or property, he may be required to give a recognizance...."[899] Under that provision, "a

---

[894] "The Carrying of Concealed Weapons," *Daily Alta California*, March 13, 1869, at 2.
[895] S.C. Acts 402, no. 288, § 4 (1870).
[896] *State v. McKettrick*, 14 S.C. 346, 353–54 (1880).
[897] "Magistrates may cause to be arrested (a) all affrayers, rioters, disturbers and breakers of the peace, (b) all who go armed offensively, to the terror of the people...." S.C. Code § 22-5-150 (Supp. 2013).
[898] S.C. Code 1976 § 23-31-215.
[899] W. Va. Code 703, For Preventing the Commission of Crimes, ch. 153, § 8.

person armed with such dangerous or deadly weapon can be required to give a recognizance for good behavior and to keep the peace."[900]

Giving the recognizance was thus equivalent to getting a license to carry as long as one did so peaceably. A separate provision imposed a fine on a person who would "habitually, carry about his person, hid from common observation, any pistol, dirk, bowie knife, or weapon of the like kind...."[901] A person who gave the recognizance could carry openly or even concealed if not done habitually. And against a charge for carrying a concealed weapon, "a statutory acquittal is mandatory in favor of persons who prove ... that they were in good faith armed only for self-defense...."[902]

Since the Fourteenth Amendment prohibited the states from infringing on the right to bear arms based on race or color, some states passed discretionary licensing schemes or even bans on the carrying of handguns altogether. That allowed for selective enforcement against disfavored classes while extending privileges to favored classes. The following analyzes some of those laws and judicial reactions to them.

An 1870 Tennessee law made it unlawful "to publicly or privately carry a dirk, swordcane, Spanish stiletto, belt or pocket pistol or revolver," except for law enforcement or on a journey.[903] In *Andrews v. State*, the state Supreme Court held this law to violate the right of the

---

[900] *Claiborne v. Chesapeake & O. Ry. Co.*, 46 W. Va. 363, 364, 33 S.E. 262 (1899). The court felt it necessary to add the following stereotypical comment: "The razor was undoubtedly added to this section on account of the proneness of the Americanized African to carry and use the same as a deadly weapon." *Id.*
[901] 1870 W. Va. Code 692, Of Offenses against the Peace, ch. 148, § 7.
[902] *State v. Workman*, 35 W. Va. 367, 14 S.E. 9, 10-11 (1891). See also *State v. Barnett*, 34 W. Va. 74, 11 S.E. 735 (1890) (another concealed weapon cased based on W. Va. Code, ch. 148, § 7).
[903] *Andrews v. State*, 50 Tenn. (3 Heisk.) 165, 171 (1871).

citizens "to bear arms for their common defense" as applied to a "pistol known as the repeater," which "is a soldier's weapon – skill in the use of which will add to the efficiency of the soldier."[904] The court did not limit the right to military use, and rejected the argument that the legislature could "prohibit absolutely the wearing of all and every kind of arms, under all circumstances," as "[t]he power to regulate, does not fairly mean the power to prohibit...."[905] Further, the legislature could not prohibit wearing arms in "circumstances essential to make out a case of self-defense."[906]

In a further decision, the Tennessee court held that a certain intent was required for the crime of carrying a small pistol that was not protected as "an arm for war purposes":

> To constitute the carrying criminal, the intent with which it is carried must be that of going armed .... In the case before us, the intent with which Page was carrying his pistol was ... that he might be armed, as was shown by his threatened assault upon the prosecutor. It would probably be difficult to enumerate all the instances in which one of these weapons could be carried innocently, and without criminality. It is sufficient here to say, that, without the intent or purpose of being or going armed, the offense described in this statute can not be committed.[907]

Similarly, in an 1876 case, the Arkansas Supreme Court agreed that army and navy repeaters were protected as "necessary and suitable to a free people, to enable them to resist oppression, prevent usurpation,

---

[904] *Id.* at 177, 186–87.
[905] *Id.* at 180–81.
[906] *Id.* at 191. See *State v. Wilburn*, 66 Tenn. (7 Bax.) 57 (1872) (upholding ban on carrying army pistol about the person other than "carrying of the army pistol openly in the hands").
[907] *Page v. State*, 50 Tenn. 198 (1871).

repel invasion, etc.," but that carrying pocket pistols could be banned because they were not "effective as a weapon of war or "useful and necessary for 'the common defense.'"[908] But in 1878, that court overturned a conviction for carrying a revolver, reasoning thus: "But to prohibit the citizen from wearing or carrying a war arm...is an unwarranted restriction upon his constitutional right to keep and bear arms.... If cowardly and dishonorable men sometimes shoot unarmed men with army pistols or guns, the evil must be prevented by the penitentiary and gallows, and not by a general deprivation of a constitutional privilege."[909]

The limitation of pistols that could be carried to "war arms" was based on the above states' guarantees of the right to bear arms "for the common defense." Army pistols were expensive and thus not affordable by poor persons, including many African Americans. Also, they were large, thus not easily usable by females with smaller hands. Most state guarantees protected bearing arms for self-defense and were not limited to military arms.[910]

---

[908] *Fife v. State*, 31 Ark. 455, 458, 461 (1876). *Fife* was preceded by *State* v. *Buzzard*, 4 Ark. 18 (1842), which upheld a ban on carrying concealed weapons but which featured separate opinions by three judges, one writing that individuals may bear arms suitable for militia use, another that the right to bear arms applies only to the militia, and the third that the individual may bear arms of any variety.

[909] *Wilson v. State*, 33 Ark. 557, 559-60 (1878). See *Haile v. State*, 38 Ark. 564 (1882) (upholding ban on carrying army or navy pistol "except uncovered, and in the hand").

[910] See *People v. Brown*, 253 Mich. 537, 540, 235 N.W. 245, 246 (1931) ("The protection of the Constitution is not limited to militiamen nor military purposes, in terms, but extends to 'every person' to bear arms for the 'defense of himself' as well as of the state."). The militia-centric view was set forth by Dean Pomeroy, who stated that "a militia would be useless unless the citizens were enabled to exercise themselves in the use of warlike weapons.... This constitutional inhibition is certainly not violated by laws forbidding persons to carry dangerous or concealed weapons...." John Norton Pomeroy, *An Introduction to the Constitutional Law of the United States* 152–53 (1868).

An 1871 Texas law punished a person for "carrying on or about his person...any pistol...unless he has reasonable grounds fearing an unlawful attack on his person," with an exception for persons traveling and "carrying arms with their baggage...."[911] In *English v. State* (1871), the Texas Supreme Court upheld the law under the Texas Constitution, which recognized the right to bear arms only "under such regulations as the legislature may prescribe."[912]

No other state nationwide had such a broad ban or such sweeping authorization to regulate. Those tempted to cite this case as precedent today may not like its recognition of "the right to 'keep' such 'arms' as are used for purposes of war," which included not just the musket and pistol, but also "the field piece, siege gun, and mortar."[913]

The *English* court saw "the early customs and habits of the people of this state" as conflicting with "the ideas of intelligent and well-meaning legislators." Texas traditions derived from "the Spanish codes" and blended inferior laws and customs that did not compare with the "pure morality of the common law."[914] The court seemed to suggest that carrying arms was a Hispanic habit that the refined Anglo culture eschewed.

The *English* opinion was written by Justice Moses B. Walker from Ohio who had been a Union officer in the Civil War and worked in the military occupation of Texas after the war. A judge in the modern Texas Court of Appeals characterized *English* as having been decided

---

[911] Tex. Gen. Laws 1322, art. 6512 (1871).

[912] *English v. State*, 35 Tex. 473 (1871). Even so, the law did not prevent travelers "from placing arms in their vehicles for self-defense...." *Maxwell v. State*, 38 Tex. 170, 171 (1873).

[913] *Id.* at 476–77.

[914] *Id.* at 480.

by "a court established by a State constitution (that of 1869) which was the product of military occupation and the disfranchisement of most of the State's inhabitants...."[915] That suggests that selective enforcement of the law may have been the rule.

Such outlier laws and opinions provide no guidance for interpretation of other constitutional rights, such as a free press. For instance, a Texas court upheld a ban on selling "the illustrated *Police News*" and similar "indecent" publications.[916] That ban was likely as unenforceable as the ban on carrying a pistol. William C. Brann, a journalist in Waco toward the end of the century, wrote:

> The law prohibiting the carrying of concealed weapons has ever been a dead letter.... It is about as difficult to punish a man in Texas for carrying a pistol as for purveying whiskey in a local option precinct. If a conviction is secured, the chances are that the court of criminal appeals will reverse the verdict.... A man may carry a pistol in Texas for a decade and never be molested unless he makes a "gun-play".... The "tough" element pays absolutely no attention to the statute, and the result is that the law-abiding are placed at the mercy of the lawless.[917]

The Georgia Supreme Court in 1874 upheld a ban on carrying a pistol in a court of justice on the basis that the state's arms guarantee authorized the legislature "to prescribe the manner in which arms may be borne."[918] Yet there were limits to that authority: "If the legislature were to say arms shall not be borne on the shoulder, nor in the hands,

---

[915] *Masters v. State*, 653 S.W.2d 944, 947 (Tex. App. 1983) (Powers, J., concurring).
[916] *Thompson v. State*, 17 Tex. App. 257 (1884).
[917] 4 William C. Brann, *The Works of Brann, The Iconoclast* 51–53 (New York: Brann Publishers, 1898).
[918] *Hill v. State*, 53 Ga. 472 (1874).

or on the arms, but they shall only be borne strapped or fastened upon the back, this would be prescribing only the manner, and yet, it would, in effect, be a denial of the right to bear arms altogether."[919] In short, a restriction may not "interfere with the ordinary bearing and using arms, so that the 'people' shall become familiar with the use of them."[920]

E) *United States v. Cruikshank* (1876): The Bill of Rights Does Not Protect from Private Action

The Enforcement Act of 1870 made it a crime to conspire to injure a citizen with intent to prevent exercise of a right "granted or secured" by the Constitution or laws of the United States.[921] Federal authorities prosecuted Klansmen under the Act for violation of the freedmen's rights to assemble, to bear arms, and to be secure from unreasonable searches and seizures. It would eventually be held that private persons cannot violate these constitutional rights, although they obviously could be prosecuted under state law for crimes like assault on persons in an assembly or robbery of firearms. Throughout these prosecutions, the right to carry firearms was considered a Second Amendment right of all persons unconnected to militia service.[922]

In *United States v. Cruikshank* (1876), the Supreme Court held as defective under the Enforcement Act indictments alleging that private individuals had violated First and Second Amendment rights. The first count alleged a conspiracy to hinder persons "of African descent and persons of color" in "their lawful right and privilege to peaceably assemble together," and the second count alleged an intent to "prevent

---

[919] *Id.* at 481.
[920] *Id.* at 483.
[921] 16 Stat. 140, 141 (1870).
[922] See Halbrook, *Freedmen*, chapters 6 and 7.

the exercise by the same persons of the 'right to keep and bear arms for a lawful purpose.'"[923] The case arose out of the Colfax Massacre, in which blacks in Louisiana who had assembled and were carrying arms had been intimidated and murdered by whites.[924]

When the case was tried, Justice William B. Woods, sitting as a Circuit Judge, instructed the jury that "peaceable assembly is one of the rights secured by the constitution and laws of the United States," even if persons "assemble with arms" peaceably, and further:

The right to bear arms is also a right secured by the constitution and laws of the United States. Every citizen of the United States has the right to bear arms, provided it is done for a lawful purpose and in a lawful manner. A man who carries his arms openly, and for his own protection, or for any other lawful purpose, has as clear a right to do so as to carry his own watch or wear his own hat.[925]

But the Supreme Court found both counts to be defective on the basis that these rights were not "granted or secured" by the Constitution. The right to assemble "existed long before the adoption of the Constitution," was "one of the attributes of citizenship under a free government," and "was not, therefore, a right granted to the people by the Constitution. The government of the United States when established found it in existence...."[926] Similarly, "bearing arms for a lawful purpose...is not a right granted by the Constitution. Neither is it

---

[923] *United States v. Cruikshank*, 92 U.S. 542, 544–45 (1876).
[924] See Halbrook, *Freedmen*, chapter 7.
[925] "The Grant Parish Prisoners," *New Orleans Republican*, March 14, 1874, at 1.
[926] *Cruikshank*, 92 U.S. at 551.

in any manner dependent upon that instrument for its existence. The second amendment declares that it shall not be infringed...."[927]

The Court thus held it not to be a federal crime for a private individual to violate the above rights, and that victims must look to state law for protection.[928] But it recognized that the rights to assemble and to bear arms pre-existed the Constitution. The Court in *Heller* (2008) would recall that holding in *Cruikshank*, and add that "there was no pre-existing right in English law 'to use weapons for certain military purposes' or to use arms in an organized militia."[929] Indeed, African Americans in the case were said to be "bearing arms for a lawful purpose," without any mention of militia activity.

F) *Presser v. Illinois* (1886): Armed Marches in Cities Not Protected

A decade later, in 1886, the United States Supreme Court would distinguish the right of the people to bear arms from associating as military companies and conducting armed marches. It grew out of labor troubles in Illinois. The background to the case illustrates the public understanding that individuals have the right to bear arms, while states have the power to decide the rules for bearing arms in a militia.

Workers groups like the *Lehr und Wehr Verein* (Education and Defense Society), which consisted of German immigrants, were conducting peaceable, armed marches in Chicago to protest what they perceived to be police repression. Illinois passed a law that required a

---

[927] *Id.* at 553.
[928] *Id.* at 551-53.
[929] *District of Columbia v. Heller,* 554 U.S. 570, 592 & n.16 (2008).

permit for such marches in cities and established a select militia in the form of a national guard.[930]

The Chicago *Daily Times Herald* defended the law as not violating the Second Amendment, explaining that the "right of the citizen to bear arms…has long been recognized as a necessary part of, and indispensable to, the full right of self-defense.… The new law does not affect their right to bear arms as individuals. It is directed only against the maintenance of their military organization." It described that organization as "communist."[931]

Judge William H. Barnum of the Criminal Court of Cook County held the law unconstitutional and dismissed charges against *Verein* members who conducted a military parade. He wrote that "the right to keep and bear arms…was pre-existent and older than any and all constitutions." Blackstone had described the "right of having and using arms for self-preservation and defense," which meant that "the people's right to keep and use arms was a barrier against the encroachments of rulers as well as others." He added that the right "existed for the individual subjects' own and only sake. There is not a word in the English Bill of Rights concerning the militia."[932]

Judge Barnum held that the right of the people to bear arms may be "exercised in their collective no less than in their individual capacity," and is "an unconditioned undeniable right…militia or no militia." However, the new law "empowers the Governor in the

---

[930] See Stephen P. Halbrook, "The Right of Workers to Assemble and to Bear Arms: *Presser v. Illinois*, One of the Last Holdouts Against Application of the Bill of Rights to the States," 76 *U. Det. Mercy L. Rev.* 943 (Summer 1999).
[931] *Chicago Daily Times Herald*, July 3, 1879, at 4.
[932] "Militia Law," *Chicago Tribune*, Sept. 2, 1879, at 6.

granting or withholding of licenses to make odious discriminations based on politics, religion, class interests, nationality, place, or similar considerations repugnant to the genius of our institutions and subversive of constitutional equality."[933]

While it is unclear if this decision was appealed, in a separate case the Illinois Supreme Court upheld the requirement of a license to parade in a city with arms, noting: "The right of the citizen to 'bear arms' for the defense of his person and property is not involved, even remotely, in this decision."[934]

A test case was brought in which Hermann Presser, without a license, led a peaceful march in Chicago of 400 members of the *Verein* carrying unloaded rifles.[935] It reached the U.S. Supreme Court, which decided in *Presser v. Illinois* (1886) that "the sections under consideration, which only forbid bodies of men to associate together as military organizations, or to drill or parade with arms in cities and towns unless authorized by law, do not infringe the right of the people to keep and bear arms."[936]

* * *

Every citizen was considered as having the right to bear arms outside the home in public, openly if not concealed. However, the black codes gave discretionary powers to local governmental officials to decide whether to license African Americans the right to bear arms. The Freedmen's Bureau Act of 1866 found that the rights to personal security and personal liberty included "the constitutional right to bear

---

[933] *Id.*
[934] *Dunne v. People*, 94 Ill. 120, 140, 34 Am. Dec. 213, 228 (1879).
[935] *Presser v. Illinois*, 116 U.S. 252, 255 (1886).
[936] *Id.* at 264–65.

arms." The Fourteenth Amendment was designed to guarantee that right from state violation, and the Civil Rights Act of 1871 was passed to provide a remedy to protect that right.

A handful of Southern states passed carry restrictions that could be selectively enforced, but were reined in by the courts. The Texas high court stood alone in the nineteenth century in upholding a general carry ban that was passed when the state was under military occupation. In *Cruikshank*, the Supreme Court held that the rights to assemble and to bear arms preexisted the Bill of Rights, but provided no protection from private violation. And in *Presser*, the Court held that a licensing requirement for armed marches in cities did not implicate the individual right to bear arms.

The extent to which the promise of the right to bear arms would be respected as applied to all of "the people" would be tested in the coming decades. While the right generally would be upheld, unpopular groups would be targeted and stripped of the right.

Part Four

HISTORY MARCHES ON

Chapter Eight

THE "WILD WEST," JIM CROW, AND ANTI-IMMIGRANT ABERRATIONS TO THE RIGHT TO BEAR ARMS

There have been epochs or phases in the latter part of the nineteenth and early part of the twentieth centuries in which the right to bear arms was impaired or denied to selected groups of people. In the "Wild West," some localities banned the carrying of firearms in town without a permit, which could be made available to favored persons. In the Jim Crow era in the South, laws were enacted with exorbitant fees and arbitrary criteria to ensure that African Americans could not carry firearms, effectively in the same way that poll taxes were instituted to deny them the right to vote. And in New York, a ban on carrying without a permit was enacted with the support of Timothy "Big Tim" Sullivan, who had ties to organized crime, and targeted Italian American immigrants.

These outlier laws and policies did not exist in the vast majority of the United States, and were neither widespread nor longstanding. They do nothing to alter the explicit text of the Second Amendment or to contribute to its original public understanding from the eighteenth century. Instead, these laws provide lessons for what it means for the right to be "infringed" without redress; in other words, they teach the realities of the old saying that "there is no right where there is no remedy."

The following explores the details of this sordid history.

A. "Wild West" Carry Bans

Some advocates have attempted to invoke the experience of the so-called Wild West to cast doubt on the constitutional right to bear arms. This effort is misguided for a variety of reasons. The small smattering of laws to which they point were enacted almost a century after the Second Amendment was adopted. Given how far removed they are from the time of the Founding, they tell us precisely nothing about the public meaning of the Second Amendment when it was adopted.

In addition, these laws were outliers—"needles in a legal haystack"—in the words of one federal judge,[937] even when they were adopted. They were not widespread. They were often enacted as tools of political oppression. Several were struck down as unconstitutional. And all were subsequently repealed.

Territorial legislatures and local towns in the Old West had no state constitutional guarantees to constrain their enactments. Some passed laws prohibiting the carrying of pistols on the person in settlements and towns. Such bans would be precluded by constitutional protection accorded to the right to bear arms after the territories became states.[938]

---

[937] *Grace v. District of Columbia*, 187 F. Supp.3d 124, 139 n.14 (D. D.C. 2016), *aff'd*, *Wrenn v. District of Columbia*, 864 F.3d 650 (D.C. Cir. 2017).

[938] While Texas may be considered part of the "Wild West," it had entered the Union in the antebellum period. As discussed in the previous chapter, a court upheld an 1871 Texas law that banned the carrying of a pistol absent "reasonable grounds fearing an

Tombstone, Territory of Arizona, passed Ordinance No. 9 in 1880 making it "unlawful for any person to carry deadly weapons, concealed or otherwise (except the same be carried openly in sight, and in the hand) within the limits of the City of Tombstone." It then amended the ordinance in 1881 to make it "unlawful to carry in the hand or upon the person or otherwise any deadly weapon within the limits of said city of Tombstone, without first obtaining a permit in writing."[939]

Town marshal Virgil Earp allowed his brothers and friends to violate the law but he enforced it against his enemies. The trouble started when Wyatt Earp pistol-whipped Tom McLaury for not checking in his gun, and before long the Earp brothers and Doc Holliday shot dead three cowboys who refused orders to turn in their guns.[940] Wyatt Earp and Doc Holliday were charged with murder, but the case was dismissed.[941]

The Tombstone homicides were not exactly an inspiring showcase for bans on carrying firearms. While folks evaded the ordinance by carrying concealed arms, Tombstone was not a violent town; there were only three homicides with firearms in town that year, and the decedents were the cowboys shot by the Earps and Holliday in the name of law enforcement.[942]

---

unlawful attack on his person." While the law was upheld again in *State v. Duke*, 42 Tex. 455, 458-59 (1874), the Texas Bill of Rights, § 13, only protected the right to bear arms "under such regulations as the Legislature may prescribe."

[939] Tom Correa, "Tombstone's Ordinance No. 9 Was Neither Fair Nor Equally Enforced," *American Cowboy Chronicles*, Aug. 8, 2014. http://www.americancowboychronicles.com/2014/08/tombstones-ordinance-no9-was-neither.html.

[940] Matt Jancer, "Gun Control Is as Old as the Old West" (Feb. 5, 2018). https://www.smithsonianmag.com/history/gun-control-old-west-180968013/.

[941] See Steven Lubet, *Murder in Tombstone* (New Haven: Yale Univ. Press, 2004).

[942] Correa, "Tombstone's Ordinance No. 9."

It could hardly be suggested that such carry bans did not violate the right to bear arms simply because judicial decisions about them are lacking. A poor cowboy riding into town who failed to check his firearm with the marshal in a timely manner, and whose pittance of wages was taken for the fine, would hardly even think of or be in a position to locate and to retain an attorney to appeal to the jurisdiction's highest court. Civil rights attorneys were hardly in abundance, and high-minded public interest law firms were not to be found in these dusty cow towns.

One commentator notes of Old West carry bans that "how well these laws were enforced and whether they were effective is difficult to say, and it is all but impossible to know precisely how prevalent they were."[943] Such laws were of dubious validity once the territories became states and thereafter adopted bills of rights.

Arizona territorial law restricted carrying of a firearm in town, but outside of town only restricted carrying a concealed firearm. As of 1901, it was an offense for a person "to have or carry concealed on or about his person, any pistol or other firearm," or "within any settlement, town, village or city within this territory" to "carry on or about his person, saddle, or in saddlebags, any pistol" or other weapon. There was a limited exemption for travelers.[944]

Admitted to the Union in 1912, Arizona's first Constitution provided: "The right of the individual citizen to bear arms in defense of himself or the State shall not be impaired, but nothing in this section shall be construed as authorizing individuals or corporations to

---

[943] Joseph Blocher, "Firearm Localism," 123 *Yale L.J.* 82, 118 (2013).
[944] Revised Statutes of Arizona Territory, Penal Code, Title XI, §§ 381, 385, 390 (1901).

organize, maintain, or employ an armed body of men."[945] The convention that drafted that provision rejected proposals authorizing the legislature "to regulate the wearing of weapons to prevent crime" and to "regulate the exercise of this right by law."[946]

Thereafter, the Arizona legislature reenacted its prohibition on carrying a concealed weapon.[947] That would eventually be upheld because "[t]he right to bear arms in self-defense is not impaired by requiring individuals to carry weapons openly. Appellants are free to bear exposed weapons for their defense."[948] The prior ban on carrying a pistol in a settlement or town would have been precluded by the constitutional provision, but does not appear to have been subject to any judicial review or decision.

In *In re Brickey* (1902), the Idaho Supreme Court reversed a conviction for carrying a loaded revolver in the city of Lewiston under an 1889 territorial act, on the basis of the Second Amendment and of the Idaho Constitution, which provided: "The people have the right to bear arms for their security and defense, but the legislature shall regulate the exercise of this right by law."[949] The court explained:

> Under these constitutional provisions, the legislature has no power to prohibit a citizen from bearing arms in any portion of the state of Idaho, whether within or without the corporate limits of cities, towns, and villages. The legislature may, as expressly provided in our state constitution, regulate the exercise of this right, but may not prohibit it.

---

[945] Ariz. Const., Art. II, § 26 (1912).
[946] *The Records of the Arizona Constitutional Convention of 1910*, 678–79 (John S. Goff ed., 1991
[947] Arizona Rev. Stat., Penal Code, Title XII, § 426 (1913).
[948] *Dano v. Collins*, 166 Ariz. 322, 323-24, 802 P.2d 1021 (Ariz. App. 1990).
[949] Idaho Const., Art. I, § 11 (1889).

A statute prohibiting the carrying of concealed deadly weapons would be a proper exercise of the police power of the state.[950]

In short, the Idaho court held that the legislature could ban concealed carry, but could not broadly ban all forms of carry. The above law violated the right to bear arms because it banned both open and concealed carry.

In some cases, carry bans would not be addressed by the courts for some time, but eventually were declared unconstitutional. New Mexico was a case in point. The Territory of New Mexico made it "unlawful for any person to carry deadly weapons, either concealed or otherwise, on or about their persons within any of the settlements of this Territory, except it be in the lawful defense of themselves, their families or their property, and the same being then and there threatened with danger...." Deadly weapons were defined to include pistols, but did not include rifles and shotguns.[951]

New Mexico's Constitution of 1912 provided: "No law shall abridge the right of the citizen to keep and bear arms for security and defense, but nothing herein shall be held to permit the carrying of concealed weapons."[952] New Mexico's constitutional convention rejected a clause that "the legislature may regulate the exercise of this right by law,"[953] which was seen as potentially negating the first clause.[954]

---

[950] *In re Brickey*, 70 P. 609 (Idaho 1902).

[951] Deadly Weapons, Act of 1869, Ch. 32, §§ 1, 2.

[952] New Mexico Const., Art. II, § 6 (1912).

[953] *Proceedings of the Constitutional Convention of the Proposed State of New Mexico* 81 (1910).

[954] "Convention on Home Stretch," *Santa Fe New Mexican*, Nov. 17, 1910, 1 (quipping that this version "consisted of two sentences which negatived each other.").

The town of Las Vegas, New Mexico, had a carry ban that was most often enforced against drunks who would wave their pistols wildly or fire them.[955] The New Mexico Court of Appeals eventually reversed a conviction under that ordinance on the basis that "an ordinance may not deny the people the constitutionally guaranteed right to bear arms...."[956]

The Kansas Constitution of 1859 provided that "[t]he people have the right to bear arms for their defense and security...."[957] A post-Civil War state law banned the carrying of a pistol by a person "not engaged in any legitimate business" or who "has ever borne arms against" the United States, i.e., unemployed persons and ex-Confederates.[958] Good citizens could carry at will.

Kansas adopted a state law in 1881 directing cities to "prohibit and punish the carrying of firearms, or other dangerous or deadly weapons, concealed or otherwise...."[959] The Kansas Supreme Court upheld application of such local ordinance to a person for carrying a revolver while under the influence of intoxicating liquor. The court held that the constitutional guarantee "applies only to the right to bear arms as a member of the state militia," without explaining how mandatory militia service could be a "right."[960]

---

[955] Donald Curtis Brown, *The Great Gun Toting Controversy, 1865-1910*, at 293 (New Orleans: Tulane University dissertation, 1983).
[956] *City of Las Vegas v. Moberg*, 82 N.M. 626, 627, 485 P.2d 737 (N.M. App. 1971).
[957] Kansas Const., Art. I, § 4 (1859).
[958] Kansas Statutes, 1868, 378; Robert R. Dykstra, *The Cattle Towns* 121 (N.Y.: Alfred A. Knopf, 1968).
[959] 1881 Kan. Sess. Laws 80, ch. XXXVII, § 23.
[960] *City of Salina v. Blaksley*, 72 Kan. 230, 83 P. 619, 620 (1905).

Dodge City, Kansas, fined any person who would "carry concealed, or otherwise, about his or her person, any pistol."[961] Typical enforcement involved drunks who were arrested for carrying pistols, jailed, released on bail, and fined.[962] Ultimately, the Kansas Supreme Court found a Junction City ordinance that prohibited the carrying of a firearm on the person off of one's property to be "unconstitutionally overbroad and an unlawful exercise of the city's police power."[963]

The Territory of Wyoming made it unlawful for a person "to bear upon his person, concealed or openly, any firearm or other deadly weapon, within the limits of any city, town or village."[964] When statehood was attained in 1890, the state Constitution included the provision: "The right of citizens to bear arms in defense of themselves and of the State shall not be denied."[965] Contemporaneously with the adoption of the Constitution, a law was passed more consistent with that guarantee by providing that "[e]very person, not being a traveler, who shall wear or carry" a dirk, pistol, or other specified weapon "concealed, or who shall carry or wear any such weapon openly, with the intent, or avowed purpose, of injuring his fellow-man, shall be fined…."[966]

In the Oklahoma Territory, it was unlawful to carry a pistol concealed on or about one's person.[967] Sherman Pender became Tulsa's city marshal in 1903 and would serve for almost forty years. He

---

[961] Dodge City, Kan., City Ordinances no. 16, § 11 (Sept. 22, 1876).
[962] Brown, *The Great Gun Toting Controversy* at 93 (citing Dodge City Times, Sept. 8, 1877).
[963] *Junction City v. Mevis*, 226 Kan. 526, 534, 601 P.2d 1145 (1979).
[964] 1875 Wyo. Territorial Sess. Laws 352, c. 52, § 1.
[965] Wyo. Const., Art. I, § 24 (1890).
[966] 1890 Wyo. Territorial Sess. Laws, c. 73, § 96 (11th Legislative Assembly).
[967] Wilson's Rev. & Ann. St. Okl. 1903, § 583, c. 25 (§ 2502).

recalled that even though pistols were carried in violation of the law, he and the mayor allowed it and experienced few problems with the practice except for drunken gun toters, who were punished.[968]

Such Old West territorial laws originated in the rough and tumble days when young cowboys fresh from cattle drives would come to town and potentially shoot up saloons.[969] These laws completely disregarded the interests of women. Annie Oakley, the renowned "Little Miss Sure Shot" who starred in Buffalo Bill's Wild West show from 1885 to 1901, personally taught 15,000 women how to shoot. "I would like to see every woman know how to handle [firearms] as naturally as they know how to handle babies," she stated[970] She encouraged women to carry pistols in their purses for self-protection.[971] Professor Mary Zeiss Stange has noted: "Annie Oakley felt a handgun was the appropriate firearm for self-defense – it could be neatly tucked away in a muff or parasol. Given her own history of apparent sexual abuse, she had good reason to take self-defense seriously."[972]

These laws were not representative of ordinary American town and city ordinances, which typically restricted the dangerous discharge of firearms but did not ban the carrying of firearms. The point is illustrated by a brief of the District of Columbia in 2015 defending its

---

[968] Brown, *The Great Gun Toting Controversy* at 415 (citing Interview with Sherman G. Pender, *Indian Pioneer Collection* (Oklahoma City: Oklahoma Historical Society), 39:333).

[969] While Hollywood has exaggerated the violence of the Wild West, there were periods of lawlessness in which constitutional rights were trampled. See, e.g, Genevieve Yost, "History of Lynchings in Kansas," 2 *Kansas Historical Quarterly*, No. 2, at 182 (1933).

[970] "She Personally Taught 15,000 Women How To Shoot," https://medium.com/ekko-forever/what-do-you-know-about-annie-oakley-9fd64b5a3e54.

[971] Ashlee Anderson, "Annie Oakley," *National Women's History Museum* (2018). https://www.womenshistory.org/education-resources/biographies/annie-oakley.

[972] "Annie Oakley: Legacy," https://site.nhd.org/13476035/Annie_Oakley.

ban on carrying firearms in the U.S. Court of Appeals for the D.C. Circuit. It claimed, "By the late 1800s, many cities completely banned public carrying."[973] However, of the ten examples cited, eight were not very populous, and most were "Wild West" towns in cattle-drive routes.[974] Only two of the cited cities with carry bans (Syracuse and Nashville) appeared in the Census Bureau's 1880 listing of the top one hundred most populous cities in the United States.[975] That left ninety-eight out of one hundred of the largest cities, from New York and Chicago to New Orleans and San Francisco, with no carry bans. To top that off, Nashville's ban on carrying a pistol was virtually identical to a ban in Chattanooga that the Tennessee Supreme Court declared in violation of the right of the citizens "to keep and bear arms for their common defense" under the Tennessee Constitution.[976]

When presented with the above ordinances by the District of Columbia, which were "almost exclusively from the frontier and Wild West," federal district court Judge Richard J. Leon wrote:

---

[973] Brief of the District of Columbia, *Wrenn v. District of Columbia*, No. 15-7057 (D.C. Cir., Aug. 27, 2015), at 43.

[974] Showing census figures from the late 1800s (compiled from http://www.census.gov/prod/www/decennial.html), they included:

Nebraska City, Nebraska (1870):	6,050
Los Ángeles, California (1880):	11,183
Salina, Kansas (1880):	3,111
Dallas, Texas (1890):	42,638
Rawlins, Wyoming (1890):	2,235
Checotah, (Oklahoma) (1890):	400 (est.)
Wichita, Kansas (1900):	24,071
McKinney, Texas (1900):	4,342

[975] Table 11. Population of the 100 Largest Urban Places: 1880, U.S. Bureau of the Census (1998), http://www.census.gov/population/www/documentation/twps0027/tab11.txt.

[976] *Glasscock v. City of Chattanooga*, 157 Tenn. 518, 11 S.W.2d 678 (1928) (quoting Tenn. Const., Art. I, § 26).

These laws…are needles in a legal haystack and come nowhere close to establishing a "universal and long-established tradition,"…of prohibiting the carrying of firearms in populated areas. They were in place in only an infinitesimal fraction of American jurisdictions, governed a minute portion of the Nation's population, and were found almost entirely in a particular, homogenous region….Nowhere do they argue that it is the norm in the United States *today* for the carrying of weapons in populated or public places to be prohibited….[977]

At bottom, carry bans in the "Wild West" were temporary expedients for tumultuous towns along the cattle-driving trails. When statehood replaced rough-and-tumble territories, the right to bear arms would adorn the new constitutions, and some of the old laws would be declared unconstitutional. The urban centers nationwide at that time had virtually no restrictions on the peaceable carrying of pistols.

B. Jim Crow Prohibition as "Reasonable Regulation"

The Fourteenth Amendment did away with actually naming African Americans in laws prohibiting the right to bear arms. To circumvent that in the Jim Crow era, facially neutral laws imposed prohibitive fees and restrictions on the poor and were selectively enforced in ways to deny the right of black citizens to possess and carry arms.

In 1892, Ida B. Wells wrote that a "Winchester rifle should have a place of honor in every black home, and it should be used for that protection which the law refuses to give."[978] She had in mind recent

---

[977] *Grace v. District of Columbia*, 187 F. Supp.3d 124, 139 n.14 (D. D.C. 2016), *aff'd*, *Wrenn v. District of Columbia*, 864 F.3d 650 (D.C. Cir. 2017).
[978] Ida B. Wells, *Southern Horrors: Lynch Law in All its Phases* 16 (1892).

events in Jacksonville, Florida, and Paducah, Kentucky, where well-armed blacks had thwarted lynch mobs.[979]

Perhaps not coincidently, a year later Florida made it a crime for a person "to carry around with him, or to have in his manual possession" a "Winchester rifle or other repeating rifle" without a license, which "may" be granted after posting a $100 bond.[980] That would be equivalent to $2,922 in 2021.[981] The average monthly wage for farm labor in Florida in 1890 was $19.35.[982] In 1901, the law was amended to add pistols to the list.

As noted in the Florida Supreme Court case of *Watson v. Stone* (1941), the law "was passed when there was a great influx of negro laborers in this State," and it was "for the purpose of disarming the negro laborers.... The statute was never intended to be applied to the white population...."[983] Moreover, it was estimated that "80% of the white men living in the rural sections of Florida have violated this statute," "not more than 5% of the men in Florida who own pistols and repeating rifles have ever applied" for a license, and that "there had never been...any effort to enforce the provisions of this statute as to white people, because it has been generally conceded to be in contravention of the Constitution and non-enforceable if contested."[984]

---

[979] Margaret Vandiver, *Lethal Punishment: Lynchings and Legal Executions in the South* 179 (New Brunswick, N.J.: Rutgers University Press, 2006); George C. Wright, *Racial Violence in Kentucky 1865-1940: Lynchings, Mob Rule and "Legal Lynchings"* 169-170 (Baton Rouge: LSU Press, 1990).
[980] 1893 Fla. Laws 71–72.
[981] "Why a dollar today is worth only 3% of a dollar in 1893," Mar. 12, 2021. https://www.in2013dollars.com/us/inflation/1893.
[982] George K. Holmes, *Wages of Farm Labor* 29 (USDA 1912). https://babel.hathitrust.org/cgi/pt?id=njp.32101050723756&view=1up&seq=745.
[983] *Watson v. Stone*, 148 Fla. 516, 524, 4 So. 2d 700 (1941) (Buford, J., concurring).
[984] *Id.*

In 1920, the Ohio Supreme Court upheld the application of a ban on carrying a concealed pistol to a worker living in a bunkhouse with other employees. Police entered the bunkhouse where he was sleeping, rolled him over, and a pistol fell out of his pocket.[985] A dissenting judge would have held the ban inapplicable to the home, commenting about the precedents cited by the majority: "The Southern States have very largely furnished the precedents. It is only necessary to observe that the race issue there has extremely intensified a decisive purpose to entirely disarm the negro, and this policy is evident upon reading the opinions."[986]

In Virginia, it was held lawful to carry a concealed handgun if it was not readily accessible, such as in saddlebags.[987] In a 1909 article, the editors of the *Virginia Law Register* criticized the decision with racist rhetoric:

> It is a matter of common knowledge that in this state and in several others, the more especially in the Southern states where the negro population is so large, that this cowardly practice of "toting" guns has always been one of the most fruitful sources of crime.... There would be a very decided falling off of killings "in the heat of passion" if a prohibitive tax were laid on the privilege of handling and disposing of revolvers and other small arms, or else that every person purchasing such deadly weapons should be required to register.... Let a negro board a railroad train with a quart of mean whiskey and a pistol in his grip and the chances are that there will be a murder, or at least a row, before he alights.[988]

---

[985] *State v. Nieto*, 101 Ohio St. 409, 424, 130 N.E. 663 (1920) (Wanamaker, J., dissenting).

[986] *Id.* at 430.

[987] *Sutherland v. Commonwealth*, 109 Va. 834, 65 S.E. 15 (Va. 1909).

[988] "Carrying Concealed Weapons," 15 *Virginia Law Register* 391–92 (1909).

In 1926, Virginia enacted registration and an annual tax of one dollar (the poll tax for voting, which "was born of a desire to disenfranchise the Negro," was $1.50)[989] for each pistol or revolver. Possession of an unregistered handgun was punishable with a fine of twenty-five to fifty dollars, and sentencing to the state convict road force for a period of 30 to 60 days.[990] Not surprisingly, "three-fourths of the convict road force are negroes."[991] The law functioned to prevent African Americans from having arms and to conscript those who exercised their right to bear arms for forced road work.

Despite all, on countless occasions African Americans managed to obtain, carry, and use firearms to resist lynchings, hate crimes, and gang violence. From the Jim Crow era through the civil rights movement of the twentieth century, they exercised their Second Amendment rights to protect themselves and their communities.[992]

Deprivation of the right to bear arms was not limited to black Americans. California historically "denied Chinese immigrants the right to bear arms."[993] The *San Francisco Chronicle* deemed California's 1923 law against arms possession by non-naturalized residents to be unconstitutional, but found that it had a "salutary effect in checking tong wars among the Chinese and vendettas among our

---

[989] *Harman v. Forssenius*, 380 U.S. 528, 543 (1965). See Va. Const., Art. II, § 20 (1902).
[990] 1926 Va. Acts 285, 286, repealed, Ch. 296, 1936 Va. Acts 486.
[991] Robert W. Withers, "Road Building by Prisoners," in *Proceedings of the National Conference of Charities and Correction* 209 (Ft. Wayne: Fort Wayne Printing Co., 1908).
[992] See Nicholas Johnson, *Negroes and the Gun: The Black Tradition of Arms* (Amherst, N.Y.: Prometheus Books, 2014); Charles E. Cobb, Jr., *This Nonviolent Stuff'll Get You Killed: How Guns Made the Civil Rights Movement Possible* (Durham, N.C.: Duke University Press, 2014).
[993] Assembly Concurrent Res. No. 42, Ch. 79, Relative to Chinese Americans in California (2009). https://leginfo.legislature.ca.gov/faces/billTextClient.xhtml?bill_id=200920100ACR42.

people who are of Latin descent."[994] Once again, denial of the right to bear arms to all members of selected minorities, rather than targeting criminal acts of specific individuals, functioned as a tool of oppression.

C. New York's Sullivan Law (1911): Disarming and Imprisoning Italian Immigrants

In the nineteenth century, New York was one of the freest states respecting the peaceable bearing of arms. A justice of the peace manual by John Dunlap published in 1815 stated: "It is likewise said to be an affray, at common law, for a man to arm himself with dangerous and unusual weapons, in such manner as will naturally cause terror to the people."[995] Other than that, one could carry at will.

Benjamin Vaughan Abbott, who had previously been involved in drafting the New York penal code, discussed the right to bear arms in his 1880 book entitled *Judge and Jury*. He recognized that "a citizen who keeps a gun or pistol under judicious precautions, practises in safe places the use of it, and in due time teaches his sons to do the same, exercises his individual right." But he denounced "carrying them carelessly in the pocket; toying with them at picnics, on board steamers, and in saloons; exhibiting them to curious girls...."[996]

Abbott's personal opinion was that "[c]arrying them [pistols] for defence, in the more settled parts of the land, savors of cowardice rather than of prudence; a well-behaved man has less to fear from violence than from the blunders of himself and friends in managing the

---

[994] "New Firearms Law Effective on August 7," *San Francisco Chronicle*, July 15, 1923, at 3.

[995] John A. Dunlap, *The New-York Justice* 8 (New York: Isaac Riley, 1815).

[996] Benjamin Vaughan Abbott, *Judge and Jury* 333 (New York: Harper and Brothers, 1880).

pistol he might carry as a protection."[997] While persons who carried pistols for self-defense in dangerous areas of cities would have disagreed, he recognized the legal trend in a number of states: "Carry a pistol if you please, but you shall carry it openly. Hang it in a belt, or hold it in your hand, or keep it in sight so that people can see you go armed...."[998]

As fate would have it, in 1881, the New York Penal Code for the first time restricted concealed weapons: "A person who carries concealed about his person any kind of firearms . . . such as is [*sic*] usually employed in attack or defense of the person, is guilty of a misdemeanor."[999] That same year, New York City made it an offense for a person to possess a pistol "concealed on his person, or not carried openly," without a permit, which would be issued to "a proper and law abiding person" "to carry a pistol for his protection."[1000] And in 1884, New York passed a law requiring a license for a person under eighteen years old to carry a pistol or other firearm in a public street, highway, or place of a city.[1001]

The Penal Code effective in 1895 showed the state ban on carrying concealed weapons to have been repealed.[1002] Then, in 1910, it became a crime for a person to "have or carry concealed upon his person in any city, village or town of this state, any pistol, revolver or other firearm

---

[997] *Id.* at 333-34.

[998] *Id.* at 337.

[999] N.Y. Penal Code § 412 (1881), in *People v. Raso,* 9 Misc.2d 739, 743, 170 N.Y.S.2d 245 (1958).

[1000] Elliott Fitch Shepard, *Ordinances of the Mayor, Aldermen & Commonalty of the City of New York, in Force January 1, 1881,* at 214-215 (New York: M. B. Brown, 1881).

[1001] Ch. 46, § 8, 1884 N.Y. Laws 44, 47. See *The Penal Code of the State of New York* 113 (New York: Banks & Brothers, 1895).

[1002] "§ 412. Carrying concealed weapons. – Repealed." *The Penal Code of the State of New York* 113 (1895).

without a written license therefor . . . ."[1003] "Thus for many years open possession of pistols and revolvers and all other firearms was permissible. The law only prohibited concealment of weapons."[1004]

Carrying a slung-shot, dagger, or similar weapon was originally a crime only if attempted to be used against another, but that was amended in 1905 to ban mere possession of such weapons. The ban was upheld because it only applied to "criminal" type weapons, not "those ordinary legitimate weapons of defense and protection which are contemplated by the [federal] Constitution and the [New York] Bill of Rights."[1005] (The latter copied the Second Amendment except for using "cannot" instead of "shall not."[1006])

But in 1911, the Sullivan Law was passed, the first law in any State (other than the black codes) to require a permit for keeping a pistol or other concealable firearm in the home. It made it a misdemeanor for a person to "have in his possession in any city, village or town of this state, any pistol, revolver or other firearm of a size which may be concealed upon the person," without a license. It made it a felony to "have or carry concealed upon his person" in the same places "any pistol, revolver, or other firearm" without a license.[1007] Under these provisions, open carry on the person or transport outside one's premises required a license to possess, not a license to carry.

Its sponsor, "Big Tim" Sullivan, was a state senator who has been described as a "Tammany Hall crook, a criminal overseer of the gangs

---

[1003] N.Y. Penal Law § 1897 (1910), in *People v. Warden of City Prison,* 154 A.D. 413, 139 N.Y.S. 277, 280 (1913).
[1004] *Raso,* 9 Misc.2d at 741.
[1005] *People v. Persce,* 204 N.Y. 397, 97 N.E. 877, 879 (1912).
[1006] New York Consolidated Laws, Civil Rights Law - CVR § 4.
[1007] N.Y. Laws 443, ch. 195, § 1 (1911).

of New York."[1008] The catch was that the law would be applied to law-abiding citizens, not to the Irish gangs that worked for Tammany, who intimidated voters at the polls. Rivals of Sullivan sewed up their pockets so the police couldn't plant pistols in them.[1009] Newly-arrived Italians and other unruly immigrants were not to be trusted.[1010]

The first person sentenced under the Sullivan Act was a worker named Marino Rossi, who was seen by a detective to be carrying a .38 caliber revolver in his hip pocket. The *New York Times* reported:

> Rossi explained that he was carrying the gun from fear of the Black Hand, and that his friends had warned him to do so in this city. He said that he was in fear of his life. He had no intention of using it wrongfully, and he was an honest working man and desired to know why it was that Black Handers were not arrested for carrying guns as well as law-abiding people.[1011]

Sentencing Rossi to one year in Sing Sing, Judge Warren B. Foster expressed no concern about the lack of protection for citizens from the threat of violence from the Black Hand criminal organization or other gangs. Instead the judge lectured Rossi on the bad customs of Italian immigrants:

> You can say you have had this gun for two years, and that it was the custom of yourself as well as your countrymen to carry guns. You say you did not realize that you were breaking the law in so doing.

[1008] Michael A. Walsh, "The strange birth of NY's gun laws," *New York Post*, Jan. 16, 2012. https://nypost.com/2012/01/16/the-strange-birth-of-nys-gun-laws/.
[1009] *Id.*
[1010] Lee B. Kennett and James L. Anderson, *The Gun in America* 177–78 (Westport, Conn: Greenwood Press, 1975).
[1011] "First Conviction under Weapon Law; Judge Foster Gives Marino Rossi One Year for Arming Himself Against Black Handers," *New York Times*, Sept. 28, 1911, 8.

It is unfortunate that this is the custom with you and your kind, and that fact, combined with your irascible nature, furnishes much of the criminal business in this country....

I and my colleagues on the bench intend to stamp out this habit, and with this end in view it is our object to let the community know that the violators of the Sullivan law are going to be severely punished.[1012]

The *New York Times* praised the one year sentence of Rossi, whose "hot-headed countrymen" customarily carried concealed weapons, adding: "The Judge's warning to the Italian community was timely and exemplary."[1013]

Another defendant on the docket that day was Gustav A. Kessler, a night watchman, who "had to work late at night in a dangerous part of the city, and wanted a revolver for protection against gangsters. He said he did not get a permit because he did not feel that he could spare $10 of his small wages to carry a $5 revolver."[1014] While his fate is unknown, it seems likely that Judge Foster berated him, too, and then sentenced him to Sing Sing for a year.

A test case was brought by a brave man named Joseph Darling, who notified the police that he kept a pistol in his home without a permit so he could be arrested and challenge the permit requirement.[1015] While recognizing that "the rights enumerated in the Bill of Rights...necessarily pertain to free men in a free state," the court

---

[1012] *Id.* Judge Foster would be investigated in 1912 based on a misconduct complaint that he gave a forger a lenient sentence when asked to do so by Big Tim Sullivan. "Judge Foster's Acts Now under Review," *id.*, May 18, 1912.

[1013] "The Rossi Pistol Case," *id.*, Sept. 29, 1911.

[1014] "First Conviction," *id.*, Sept. 28, 1911.

[1015] *People v. Warden of City Prison*, 154 A.D. 413, 419, 139 N.Y.S. 277, 29 N.Y. Cr. 66 (1913).

upheld the law but added: "If the Legislature had prohibited the keeping of arms, it would have been clearly beyond its power."[1016] A dissenting judge noted that "the professional criminal will generally violate the act and take his chances of discovery and punishment, while the law-abiding citizen will be obliged to disarm himself of his only effective protection against the predatory classes."[1017]

With his classic wit, H. L. Mencken wrote that the Sullivan Law required that "the Second Amendment had to be severely strained, but…the courts, as usual, were willing to sign on the dotted line." The result was that New York "is the heaven of footpads, hijackers, gunmen and all other such armed thugs.… Not one citizen out of a hundred that they tackle is armed for getting a license to keep a revolver is a difficult business, and carrying one without it is more dangerous than submitting to robbery."[1018]

A World War II-era decision established the rule that courts must defer to issuing authorities on whether an applicant for a carry license stated a "proper cause." *Moore v. Gallup* (1943) recognized that, while the right to bear arms "long ante-dated the adoption of the Federal Constitution," protected arms included "weapons of warfare to be used by the militia, such as swords, guns, rifles and muskets…but not pistols," which "are habitually carried by…gangsters."[1019]

[1016] *Id.* at 421–22.
[1017] *Id.* at 427 (Scott, J., dissenting).
[1018] H. L. Mencken, "The Uplifters Try It Again: Gun-Control Laws Deprive Reputable Citizens of Protection," *Evening Sun* (Baltimore), Nov. 30, 1925. https://fee.org/articles/the-uplifters-try-it-again/
[1019] *Moore v. Gallup*, 267 A.D. 64, 67–68, 45 N.Y.S.2d 63 (3d Dept. 1943), *aff'd.*, 293 N.Y. 846, 59 N.E.2d 439 (1944), *motion granted*, 294 N.Y. 699, 60 N.E.2d 847 (1945).

Yet the case was about a law-abiding citizen and Great War veteran who was appealing the denial of his previously-issued carry license.[1020] Amici curiae briefs were filed by gun clubs and by the National Rifle Association, represented by Karl T. Frederick,[1021] an Olympic shooter and Harvard Law graduate.

The dissent opined that the permit denial violated the right to bear arms.[1022] It noted the perceived threat of a foreign invasion, which demonstrated the "need of the citizens to become proficient in the use of firearms...."[1023] At that time, German U-boats had torpedoed numerous ships along the coast, including in New York Harbor, and landed saboteurs.[1024]

It bears recalling that no municipal liability existed in New York "for failure to provide special protection to a member of the public who was repeatedly threatened with personal harm and eventually suffered dire personal injuries for lack of such protection."[1025] That was the ruling in the infamous case of Linda Riss, who was repeatedly denied police protection against threatened harm and who was then viciously attacked. As the dissent pointed out, "in conformity, to the dictates of the law, Linda did not carry any weapon for self-defense.... Thus, by a rather bitter irony she was required to rely for protection on the City of New York which now denies all responsibility to her."[1026]

[1020] *Id.* at 65–66.
[1021] *Id.* at 64.
[1022] *Id.* at 71.
[1023] *Id.*
[1024] "Nazi U-Boats Attack New York Shipping!"
http://www.oocities.org/fort_tilden/uboats.html.
[1025] *Riss v. City of New York*, 22 N.Y.2d 579, 581, 240 N.E.2d 860 (1968).
[1026] *Id.* at 584-85 (Keating, J., dissenting).

Nothing had changed since 1911 when Marino Rossi carried a pistol for protection against the Black Hand, for which he was sentenced to a year in prison. For Ms. Riss, New York's assurances that no one "needed" to protect themselves were worthless.

"Under New York law, it is a crime to possess a firearm."[1027] So held the U.S. Court of Appeals for the Second Circuit based on New York's prohibition on possession of a handgun and the status of having a license being an affirmative defense which the gun owner must prove at trial.[1028] Thus, police officers who merely "see [a] gun" are "justified in seizing it because of its 'immediately apparent' incriminating character."[1029] The prohibition did not offend the Second Amendment because "the right to possess a gun is clearly not a fundamental right."[1030]

While the above decision was pre-*Heller* and pre-*McDonald*, the New York law has not changed one iota. Despite the *Heller* and *McDonald* precedents, the courts have continued to allow the police to decide if a person "needs" to carry a handgun, which effectively prohibits the bearing of arms and limits licenses to a privileged few.[1031] While the U.S. Supreme Court has not taken on the issue directly, justices have voiced concern about New York City's restrictions on

---

[1027] *United States v. Sanchez-Villar*, 99 Fed. Appx. 256, 258, 2004 WL 962938 (2nd Cir. 2004) (*per curiam*), *vacated & remanded*, *Sanchez-Villar v. United States*, 544 U.S. 1029 (2005) (for further consideration in light of *United States v. Booker*, 543 U.S. 220 (2005)).

[1028] *Id.* at 258, citing N.Y. Penal Law § 265.01(1) (crime), § 265.20(3) (exception for license); *People v. Washington*, 209 A.D.2d 162, 163, 618 N.Y.S.2d 32 (1994) (affirmative defense).

[1029] *Id.* (citation omitted).

[1030] *Id.* at 258 n.1, quoting *United States v. Toner*, 728 F.2d 115, 128 (2d Cir. 1984).

[1031] *Kachalsky v. County of Westchester*, 701 F.3d 81 (2nd Cir. 2012) (upholding law), *cert. denied*, 133 S. Ct. 1806 (2013).

transporting a firearm, albeit unloaded and inaccessible, from one's house to other places,[1032] and about "may issue" carry restrictions.[1033] The relevant cases are discussed in the next chapter.

* * *

The above examples of carry restrictions are historical aberrations that deviated dramatically from the predominant recognition in America's history and tradition of the right to bear arms. The Wild West had some towns that banned the carrying of arms, and some of these bans would later be ruled unconstitutional. The Jim Crow era saw laws with unaffordable, discretionary licenses that functioned to weed out African Americans. Big Tim Sullivan's law aimed to disarm Italian Americans and corruptly to issue carry permits only to the favored, and it continues to stymie New Yorkers from exercising the right to bear arms today.

That said, the right to bear arms has stood the test of time as a fundamental American liberty since the Founding. Other guarantees of the Bill of Rights have had disfavored moments too, but they continue to shine as distinctly American ideals. From free exercise of religion and freedom of speech, to rights against unreasonable searches and seizures and for due process of law, instances have occurred when minorities have been deprived of these rights. But in the big picture, the Bill of Rights—including the Second Amendment—has stood firm in the minds of the citizenry as a bulwark of American freedom.

[1032] *New York State Rifle & Pistol Association, Inc. v. City of New York*, 140 S. Ct. 1525, 1527-28 (2020) (Alito, J., joined by Gorsuch, J., & Thomas, J., dissenting).
[1033] *Rogers v. Grewal*, 140 S. Ct. 1865 (2020) (Thomas, J., joined by Kavanaugh, J., dissenting from denial of cert.).

Chapter Nine

FROM THE STATE COURTS TO
THE U.S. SUPREME COURT

A number of state court decisions from the twentieth century and beyond have recognized the right to carry arms in public under their respective state constitutional guarantees and the Second Amendment. Around the turn of the century, the U.S. Supreme Court rendered several decisions upholding the right to armed self-defense. In its path breaking *Heller* decision, the Supreme Court read the term "bear arms" simply to mean to carry arms, and it rejected an interest-balancing test that would balance away the right. And its *McDonald* decision reinforced that the right to bear arms is not a second-class right. Since those cases were decided, the Court has continued to buttress its methodology of interpreting Bill of Rights guarantees based on the public understanding at the Founding.

A) State Cases Recognizing the Right to Bear Arms

The following analyzes selected cases on the right to bear arms decided by state courts in the twentieth and twenty-first centuries. These precedents generally recognize the right to bear arms outside the home for lawful purposes.

Outright bans on carrying and possession of firearms and other weapons in public places or outside one's home were declared violative of the right to bear arms in Idaho, Tennessee, New Mexico, Colorado, Kansas, Oregon, and Delaware.[1034] The pertinent laws prohibited both open and concealed carry only in selected places, such as towns or state parks. Since bans on both open and concealed carry of handguns and other firearms, even in such limited places, are so rare in American history and tradition, most states have no judicial decisions on that issue.

In Vermont, a local ban on carrying a concealed pistol without a license, where "neither the intent nor purpose of carrying them enters into the essential elements of the offense," was found to violate the right to bear arms.[1035] In Ohio, a state ban on carrying a concealed weapon, to which "reasonable cause" was an affirmative defense, in the context where open carry would also lead to an arrest, was held violative of the right to bear arms.[1036] In West Virginia, a ban on carrying a weapon "for any purpose without a license or other statutory authorization" was found void.[1037] In Wisconsin, a ban on carrying

---

[1034] *In Re Brickey*, 8 Idaho 597, 70 P. 609 (1902) (carry ban violated Second Amendment and state guarantee); *Glasscock v. City of Chattanooga*, 157 Tenn. 518, 11 S.W.2d 678 (1928) (invalidating ban on carrying pistol on the person); *City of Las Vegas v. Moberg*, 82 N.M. 626, 627, 485 P.2d 737 (N.M. Ct. App. 1971) (ban on carrying weapons on the person void because "an ordinance may not deny the people the constitutionally guaranteed right to bear arms"); *City of Lakewood v. Pillow*, 180 Colo. 20, 22, 501 P.2d 744 (1972) (ban on possession of firearm except in one's domicile and on carrying firearm held "unconstitutionally overbroad"); *Junction City v. Mevis*, 226 Kan. 526, 534, 601 P.2d 1145 (1979) (ban on possession of firearm outside home or business held "unconstitutionally overbroad"); *State v. Blocker*, 291 Or. 255, 259, 630 P.2d 824 (1981) ("possession of a billy in a public place is constitutionally protected"); *Bridgeville Rifle & Pistol Club v. Small*, 176 A.3d 632 (Del. 2017) (ban on possession in state parks).
[1035] *State v. Rosenthal*, 75 Vt. 295, 55 A. 610, 610–11 (1903).
[1036] *Klein v. Leis*, 146 Ohio App.3d 526, 531, 535, 767 N.E.2d 286 (2002).
[1037] *State ex rel. City of Princeton v. Buckner*, 180 W. Va. 457, 462–63, 377 S.E.2d 139 (1988).

concealed firearms, as applied to one's business premises, was held violative of the right to bear arms.[1038]

The following two precedents are worthy of special note. One upheld the right to open carry without a license. The other rejected official discretion regarding an applicant's "need" in the issuance of a license to carry a concealed handgun. These illustrate variations in which exercise of the right to bear arms is recognized.

First, the North Carolina Supreme Court in *State v. Kerner* (1921) upheld the right openly to carry a pistol without a license.[1039] To the citizen, "the rifle, the musket, the shotgun, and the pistol are about the only arms which he could be expected to 'bear,' and his right to do this is that which is guaranteed by the Constitution."[1040] The right includes "all 'arms' as were in common use, and borne by the people as such when this provision was adopted."[1041] The court explained the urgent necessity of the right as follows:

This is not an idle or an obsolete guaranty, for there are still localities, not necessary to mention, where great corporations, under the guise of detective agents or private police, terrorize their employees by armed force. If the people are forbidden to carry the only arms within their means, among them pistols, they will be completely at the mercy of these great plutocratic organizations. Should there be a mob, is it possible that law-abiding citizens could not assemble with their pistols carried openly and protect their persons and their property from

---

[1038] *State v. Hamdan*, 264 Wis.2d 433, 665 N.W.2d 785 (2003).
[1039] *State v. Kerner*, 181 N.C. 574, 577–78, 107 S.E. 222, 225 (1921).
[1040] *Id.* at 576, 107 S.E. 224.
[1041] *Id.* at 577, 107 S.E. 224.

unlawful violence without going before an official and obtaining license and giving bond?[1042]

Second, in *Schubert v. DeBard* (1980), the Court of Appeals of Indiana held that the right to bear arms precluded the state police from exercising discretion as to whether an applicant had "a proper reason" for a license to carry a handgun.[1043] Such discretion "would supplant a right with a mere administrative privilege which might be withheld simply on the basis that such matters as the use of firearms are better left to the organized military and police forces even where defense of the individual is involved."[1044]

At the time of this writing, open carry requires no permit in thirty states, requires a permit in fifteen states, and is prohibited in only five states.[1045] Forty-one states and the District of Columbia are "shall issue" in the sense that permits to carry concealed are available to all law-abiding persons who meet training or other requirements. And several of those states have recently been considering dropping the permit requirement altogether.[1046] Vermont does not issue permits, but both concealed and open carry are lawful. Effective in mid-2021, at least twenty states have what some call "constitutional carry," meaning that both concealed and open carry without a permit are lawful.[1047]

[1042] *Id.* at 577–78, 107 S.E. 225.

[1043] *Schubert v. DeBard*, 398 N.E. 2d 1339, 1341 (Ind. App. 1980).

[1044] *Id.*

[1045] https://opencarry.org/maps/map-open-carry-of-a-properly-holstered-loaded-handgun/.

[1046] Lindsay Whitehurst, "States eye allowing concealed carry of guns without a permit," Associated Press (Jan. 24, 2021), https://apnews.com/article/us-news-utah-coronavirus-pandemic-tennessee-gun-politics-1b7a7bde0c1dfe87f4a24b2d10b0203a.

[1047] "There Are 18 Constitutional Carry States," Feb. 13, 2021. https://crimeresearch.org/2021/02/there-are-18-constitutional-carry-states/. In addition, Iowa and Tennessee also adopted constitutional carry in April 2021.

Only eight states are "may issue," i.e., government officials decide if a person "needs" to carry a firearm.[1048]

It is in that handful of "may issue" states where the question of whether the Second Amendment literally guarantees the right to "bear arms" is in litigation. The next chapter discusses the conflict in the federal circuit courts of appeals over the issue.

State cases upholding discretionary license issuance are largely pre-*Heller* and pre–*McDonald*. If they even mention the Second Amendment, they typically hold that it only protects a state power to maintain militias and not an individual right to bear arms, and even if it did protect such individual right, it is not applicable to the states. Such judicial decisions were often rendered in states that have no constitutional guarantee to bear arms.

A typical pre-*Heller* ruling in such states that recognize no constitutional right to bear arms is a New Jersey decision that the applicant who carried large sums of cash didn't "need" to carry a firearm. The police didn't know of any instance in which a person defended himself with a permitted firearm (not a surprise, no permits were issued), and thus no person other than a police officer was capable of defending himself with a firearm.[1049] It made no difference that most police officers retire without ever having fired a shot in self-defense.

Heller and *McDonald* changed nothing in such states. Some federal and state courts seemingly have waged a campaign of massive resistance against those decisions, reminding one of the resistance

---

[1048] https://www.usacarry.com/concealed_carry_permit_information.html. This source lists Connecticut as "may issue," but it is "shall issue."
[1049] *Siccardi v. State*, 59 N.J. 545, 550-51, 284 A.2d 533 (1971).

against the Supreme Court's 1954 decision in *Brown v. Board of Education*.[1050] Just one example: *McDonald* held that "the Second Amendment protects a personal right to keep and bear arms for lawful purposes," to which the Maryland high court responded: "If the Supreme Court, in this dicta, meant its holding to extend beyond home possession, it will need to say so more plainly."[1051] Apparently the term "bear arms" isn't very plain.

The next section addresses exactly what the U.S. Supreme Court has said about the right to bear arms outside the home and in public, from the turn of the century through the present.

B) U.S. Supreme Court Decisions on the Right to Armed Self-Defense

At the end of the nineteenth century, the Supreme Court, without specifically referring to the Second Amendment, recognized the common-law right of individuals to go armed with firearms in self-defense. The Court had jurisdiction over the cases because they arose in Indian Territory. In essence, it acted similarly to a state court of last resort. In the following cases, the Supreme Court generally ruled that the jury instructions given in murder trials failed adequately to explain the right to self-defense.

In one Supreme Court case, a large, strong man attacked a slight man, who "drew a small, bright pistol from his pocket," and shot the aggressor.[1052] Justice John Marshall Harlan wrote for the Court that if "the defendant had reasonable grounds to believe...that the deceased

---

[1050] *Brown v. Board of Education of Topeka*, 347 U.S. 483 (1954).
[1051] *Williams v. State,* 417 Md. 479, 496, 10 A.3d 1167, 1177 (2011), *cert. denied,* 565 U.S. 815 (2011).
[1052] *Gourko v. United States*, 153 U.S. 183, 14 S.Ct. 806, 807 (1894).

intended to take his life, or to inflict upon him great bodily harm, and, so believing, armed himself solely for necessary self-defense...the jury were not authorized to find him guilty of murder because of his having deliberately armed himself...."[1053] Justice Harlan was best known for his dissent in *Plessy v. Ferguson* (1896), in which the majority upheld the "separate-but-equal" doctrine allowing school segregation.[1054]

In another Supreme Court case, after being threatened, the defendant carried a Winchester rifle while riding on horseback along a road. He shot a man he believed was about to shoot him. Justice George Shiras, Jr., wrote for the Court that the jury should have been instructed that "the purpose of the defendant in arming himself was for self-defense."[1055]

In a further case in which Justice Harlan wrote the opinion, the defendant had "with him a shot-gun that he was in the habit of carrying, when absent from home" when he was attacked; he struck his assailant with the gun, killing him.[1056] The Court held that "a man may repel force by force in defense of his person, habitation, or property," and may "stand his ground and meet any attack made upon him with a deadly weapon" in a manner necessary to protect himself "from great bodily injury or death."[1057]

In yet another, the defendant, a Cherokee Indian, carried a pistol when he came to town with his wife to shop. He quarreled with a white man, who attacked him with a knife. As Justice Harlan wrote for the

---

[1053] *Gourko*, 153 U.S. at 191.
[1054] *Plessy v. Ferguson*, 163 U.S. 537, 552 (1896) (Harlan, J., dissenting).
[1055] *Thompson v. United States*, 155 U.S. 271, 275-76, 278 (1894).
[1056] *Beard v. United States*, 158 U.S. 550, 552 (1895).
[1057] *Id.* at 563-64.

Court, since "after deceased began cutting defendant the latter drew his pistol and fired," the defendant was entitled to a jury instruction of self-defense with no duty to retreat.[1058]

In a case where the Supreme Court had jurisdiction because a homicide took place on federal property in Texas, the defendant carried a pistol after prior threats and attacks by the deceased; he shot the assailant after being attacked with a knife. Justice Oliver Wendell Holmes famously wrote: "Detached reflection cannot be demanded in the presence of an uplifted knife."[1059]

All but the last of the these cases were decided in the 1890s. In *Miller v. Texas* (1894), in an opinion by Justice Henry Brown (author of *Plessy v. Ferguson*), the Court avoided deciding whether the 1871 Texas carry ban violated the right to bear arms.[1060] Franklin Miller had a shootout with Dallas policemen seeking to arrest him for carrying a pistol contrary to state law. He claimed that the two officers tried to kill him, but he returned fire and killed one of them. A newspaper account alleged that Miller had, just before that incident, been arrested for living "in open and notorious adultery with a young and greasy-looking negress,"[1061] which suggests that racist police may have been out to "get" him. After being nearly lynched while in jail, Miller was convicted of murder and sentenced to death.[1062]

[1058] *Rowe v. United States*, 164 U.S. 546, 547-48, 558 (1896).

[1059] *Brown v. United States*, 256 U.S. 335, 342-43 (1921).

[1060] *Miller v. Texas*, 153 U.S. 535 (1894).

[1061] "Foul Murder," *Dallas Daily Times-Herald*, June 17, 1891, at 1.

[1062] *Miller v. State*, 20 S.W. 1103 (Tex. App. 1893). For details, see Cynthia Leonardatos, David B. Kopel, and Stephen P. Halbrook, "*Miller versus Texas*: Police Violence, Race Relations, Capital Punishment, and Gun-toting in Texas in the Nineteenth Century – and Today," 9 *Journal of Law & Policy* 737 (2001).

A Texas appeals court rejected Miller's arguments that the trial was unfair and the jury instructions incorrect, and thus affirmed his conviction. Miller then sought a rehearing, arguing for the first time that the Texas laws prohibiting the carrying of a pistol and the authority to arrest without a warrant violated the Second, Fourth, and Fourteenth Amendments. The rehearing was denied, and he then sought review by the U.S. Supreme Court. Like its decisions on other guarantees in the Bill of Rights, the Court found that the Second and Fourth Amendments did not directly limit state action.[1063] The Court refused to consider whether the statute violated the Second and Fourth Amendments as incorporated into the Fourteenth:

> And if the Fourteenth Amendment limited the power of the States as to such rights, as pertaining to citizens of the United States, we think it was fatal to this claim that it was not set up in the trial court.... A privilege or immunity under the Constitution of the United States cannot be set up here…when suggested for the first time in a petition for rehearing after judgment.[1064]

Without ruling on the merits, *Miller* thus left open the possibility that the Second and Fourth Amendments would apply to the states through the Fourteenth Amendment. As for Miller himself, the governor commuted his death sentence to life imprisonment, and he would be pardoned in 1908.[1065] Perhaps it was thought he may have had a legitimate claim of self-defense after all.

Just three years after deciding *Miller*, the Supreme Court mused about exceptions to guarantees in the Bill of Rights, suggesting that restrictions on carrying concealed weapons did not violate the right to

---

[1063] *Miller v. Texas*, 153 U.S. at 538.
[1064] *Id.* at 538–39.
[1065] Leonardatos et al., "*Miller versus Texas*," at 756.

bear arms. *Robertson v. Baldwin* (1897) concerned whether the compulsory service of deserting seamen constituted involuntary servitude.[1066] Referring to the seaman's contract as an exception to the Thirteenth Amendment, Justice Henry Brown, who delivered the opinion of the Court, analogized via dicta:

> The law is perfectly well settled that the first ten Amendments to the constitution, commonly known as the Bill of Rights, were not intended to lay down any novel principles of government, but simply to embody certain guaranties and immunities which we had inherited from our English ancestors, and which had from time immemorial been subject to certain well-recognized exceptions arising from the necessities of the case. In incorporating these principles into the fundamental law there was no intention of disregarding the exceptions, which continued to be recognized as if they had been formally expressed. Thus, the freedom of speech and of the press (article 1) does not permit the publication of libels, blasphemous or indecent articles or other publications injurious to public morals or private reputation; the right of the people to keep and bear arms (article 2) is not infringed by laws prohibiting the carrying of concealed weapons....[1067]

The right to bear arms was thus recognized as having existed "from time immemorial" as part of "the fundamental law." It is true, as noted above, that in the decades after the Founding, a minority of states restricted concealed carriage. But prior to the Civil War, every state allowed either open or concealed carriage, and in fact, most states allowed for both. So while it is perhaps permissible for a state to ban concealed carry, it certainly cannot do so if it also bans open carry.

[1066] *Robertson v. Baldwin*, 165 U.S. 275 (1897).
[1067] *Id.* at 281-82.

There is no historical support—none whatsoever—for a complete ban on both open and concealed carry.

C) Of Arms, the Militia, and the People: Twentieth Century Supreme Court Decisions

The following analyzes four Supreme Court decisions in the twentieth century that offer insights into the nature of the right to bear arms. In a 1939 decision, the Court set the test for whether an arm is protected by the Second Amendment to be whether the arm has militia uses. A 1950 opinion held that German soldiers convicted by a military tribunal in Germany had no right to habeas corpus relief, just as they had no rights to free speech or to bear arms under American law. State control over the state militia was the subject of a 1973 decision, which impliedly precludes the argument that the Second Amendment is only a limited militia right. Finally, a 1990 decision found that "the people" in the First, Second, and Fourth Amendments were the members of the national community.

In *United States v. Miller* (1939), in an opinion by Justice James McReynolds, the Court reinstated an indictment charging that defendants transported in interstate commerce a shotgun having a barrel less than 18 inches in length that was not registered with the Treasury Department and that had no tax stamp, contrary to the National Firearms Act.[1068] Lacking evidence that possession or use of such a shotgun had a "reasonable relationship to the preservation or efficiency of a well regulated militia," the Court could not "say that the Second Amendment guarantees the right to keep and bear such an instrument." It was "not within judicial notice" that the shotgun was

---

[1068] *United States v. Miller*, 307 U.S. 174, 175 (1939).

"ordinary military equipment" or that "its use could contribute to the common defense."[1069] The issue was not whether Miller was in the militia, but whether it was factually proven in court that the weapon had militia uses.[1070]

Miller went on to say "that the Militia comprised all males physically capable of acting in concert for the common defense.... And further, that ordinarily when called for service these men were expected to appear bearing arms supplied by themselves and of the kind in common use at the time."[1071] The arms in common use, of course, were those that people carried for hunting, self-defense, and target matches, as well as for militia purposes.

As the Court would later remark in its *Heller* decision, the *Miller* opinion "did not even purport to be a thorough examination of the Second Amendment....The defendants made no appearance in the case, neither filing a brief nor appearing at oral argument; the Court heard from no one but the Government...."[1072] The definitive exposition of the Second Amendment would await another seventy years.

In *Johnson v. Eisentrager* (1950),[1073] written by Justice Robert Jackson (the chief U.S. prosecutor at the Nazi war crimes trials), the Supreme Court depicted Bill of Rights guarantees like free speech and bearing arms as being held by American citizens generally. The Court

---

[1069] *Id.* at 178.
[1070] That would not occur when the Supreme Court remanded the case to the district court, as Miller had been murdered by then and his co-defendant pled guilty and was sentenced to probation. Brian Frye, "The Peculiar Story of *United States v. Miller*," 3 *N.Y.U.J.L. & Liberty* 48, 68-69 (2008).
[1071] *Id.* at 179.
[1072]*District of Columbia v. Heller,* 554 U.S. 570, 623 (2008), citing Frye, "The Peculiar Story of *United States v. Miller*," at 65–68.
[1073] *Johnson v. Eisentrager*, 339 U.S. 763 (1950).

held that former German soldiers imprisoned in Germany after conviction by a military tribunal have no right to a writ of habeas corpus to test the legality of their conviction. Indeed, American soldiers are stripped of Fifth Amendment rights and may be tried by military tribunals.[1074] The Court explained:

> If the Fifth Amendment confers its rights on all the world except Americans engaged in defending it, the same must be true of the companion civil-rights Amendments, for none of them is limited by its express terms, territorially or as to persons. Such a construction would mean that during military occupation irreconcilable enemy elements, guerrilla fighters, and "were-wolves" could require the American Judiciary to assure them freedoms of speech, press, and assembly as in the First Amendment, right to bear arms as in the Second, security against "unreasonable" searches and seizures as in the Fourth, as well as rights to jury trial as in the Fifth and Sixth Amendments.[1075]

Justice Jackson and the Court thus included the Second Amendment in the "civil-rights Amendments," which guaranteed the "right to bear arms" and other freedoms to Americans. In no way did the Court imply that America's enemies were only limited to the "right to bear arms" in the militia.

In *Gilligan v. Morgan* (1973), an opinion by Chief Justice Warren Burger, the Court addressed a pertinent issue about the militia. The case arose out of the calling out of the National Guard by the Ohio governor at Kent State University in 1970, in which Guardsmen shot and killed four persons. Students sued the governor, seeking judicial oversight over the arming, training, and deployment of the National Guard.[1076]

[1074] *Id.* at 783.
[1075] *Id.* at 784.
[1076] *Gilligan v. Morgan*, 413 U.S. 1 (1973).

The students relied on the due process clause of the Fourteenth Amendment, but overlooked the power of Congress "to provide for organizing, arming, and disciplining, the Militia," reserving its training to the States.[1077]

The Court rejected the claim for judicial oversight over the Guard, explaining: "The complex, subtle, and professional decisions as to the composition, training, equipping, and control of a military force are essentially professional military judgments, subject *always* to civilian control of the Legislative and Executive Branches."[1078]

That reasoning eviscerates the argument that the Second Amendment somehow only protects a "right" to bear arms in a militia organized under state and federal authority. There is no "right" to join such militia, as its "composition" is based on military judgment, subject to laws and executive control. There is no "right" to carry arms in such militia, as the training, equipping, and control of the militia are also in the same hands.

In *United States v. Verdugo-Urquidez* (1990), the Supreme Court decided that "the people" in the Fourth Amendment does not include a foreigner whose house was searched by U.S. authorities in a foreign country.[1079] In an opinion by Chief Justice William Rehnquist, the Court explained:

"the people" seems to have been a term of art employed in select parts of the Constitution....The Second Amendment protects "the right of the people to keep and bear Arms," and the Ninth and Tenth Amendments provide that certain rights and powers are retained by and

---

[1077] *Id.* at 6, quoting U.S. Const., Art. I, § 8, cl. 16.
[1078] *Id.* at 10.
[1079] *United States v. Verdugo-Urquidez*, 494 U.S. 259 (1990).

reserved to "the people." See also U.S. Const., Amdt. 1, ("Congress shall make no law...abridging...*the right of the people* peaceably to assemble").... (emphasis added). While this textual exegesis is by no means conclusive, it suggests that "the people" protected by the Fourth Amendment, and by the First and Second Amendments, and to whom rights and powers are reserved in the Ninth and Tenth Amendments, refers to a class of persons who are part of a national community or who have otherwise developed sufficient connection with this country to be considered part of that community.[1080]

Once again, this confirms the obvious—"the people," not just an elite selected by the government, have a right to bear arms.

D) *Heller*: To "Bear" Means to "Carry"

In *District of Columbia v. Heller* (2008), in an opinion by Justice Antonin Scalia, the Supreme Court held that the right to keep and bear arms extends to individuals and invalidated the District's handgun ban.[1081] *Heller*'s analysis clearly recognized the right to carry firearms outside the home, presumably subject to limited exceptions.

Textual interpretation has a historical basis, in that the Constitution "was written to be understood by the voters," and its terminology was thus used in its ordinary meaning.[1082] Historical sources used "keep arms" to mean "an individual right unconnected with militia service."[1083] "At the time of the founding, as now, to 'bear' meant to 'carry.'"[1084] More specifically, to bear arms means to "'wear, bear, or carry...upon the person or in the clothing or in a pocket, for

---

[1080] *Id.* at 265.
[1081] *District of Columbia v. Heller*, 554 U.S. 570 (2008).
[1082] *Id.* at 576.
[1083] *Id.* at 582.
[1084] *Id.* at 584.

the purpose...of being armed and ready for offensive or defensive action in a case of conflict with another person.'"[1085]

Although "bear arms" may be used in a military context, there is no "right to be a soldier or to wage war," which would be an absurdity.[1086] In historical usage, "bearing arms" meant "simply the carrying of arms," such as "for the purpose of self-defense" or "to make war against the King."[1087] But limiting "bear arms" to an exclusive military usage is inconsistent with other purposes, such as for hunting. As the Court humorously wrote: "The right 'to carry arms in the militia for the purpose of killing game' is worthy of the mad hatter."[1088]

In his dissenting opinion, Justice Stevens rejected the "collective right" interpretation of the Second Amendment and agreed that "it protects a right that can be enforced by individuals." But it only guarantees "the right to use weapons for certain military purposes," not "to possess and use guns for nonmilitary purposes like hunting and personal self-defense...."[1089] In short, it "protects only a right to possess and use firearms in connection with service in a state-organized militia."[1090]

Justice Stevens did not explain how being compelled to bear arms in a state militia is a "right." Militia service was and is based on conscription and command, not on an enforceable "right" of an individual to join a state militia and to make decisions on use of weapons in a militia. How would that be enforced? A court is going to

---

[1085] *Id.*, quoting *Muscarello v. United States*, 524 U.S. 125, 143 (1998) (Ginsburg, J., dissenting).
[1086] *Id.* at 586.
[1087] *Id.* at 588.
[1088] *Id.* at 589.
[1089] *Id.* at 636-37 (Stevens, J., dissenting).
[1090] *Id.* at 646.

force the militia to let a person join, and order an officer to allow the person to "bear arms" when the officer ordered the soldier to peel potatoes?

After his retirement, Justice Stevens proposed that the Amendment be amended to read: "A well regulated Militia, being necessary to the security of a free State, the right of the people to keep and bear Arms *when serving in the Militia* shall not be infringed."[1091] Later, he advocated the outright repeal of the Amendment.[1092]

Heller found that the Amendment guarantees "the individual right to possess and carry weapons in case of confrontation," which the historical background confirmed.[1093] But the right is not unlimited.[1094] Since "all persons [have] the right to bear arms," "it can only be a crime to exercise this right in such a manner, as to terrify people unnecessarily."[1095]

At the Founding, "the sorts of weapons protected were those 'in common use at the time,'" but there was a "historical tradition of prohibiting the carrying of 'dangerous and unusual weapons.'"[1096] Preservation of the militia was the Amendment's stated purpose,

---

[1091] John Paul Stevens, "The five extra words that can fix the Second Amendment," *Washington Post*, April 11, 2014.

[1092] John Paul Stevens, "Repeal the Second Amendment," *New York Times*, March 27, 2018.

[1093] *Heller*, 554 U.S. at 592.

[1094] *Id.* at 595.

[1095] *Id.* at 588 n.10, quoting C. Humphreys, *A Compendium of the Common Law in force in Kentucky* 482 (1822).

[1096] *Id.* at 627, citing, inter alia, 4 Blackstone 148–149 (1769); 3 B. Wilson, *Works of the Honourable James Wilson* 79 (1804).

although most Americans valued the ancient right more for self-defense and hunting.[1097]

Heller also addressed the public understanding of the Second Amendment from just after its ratification in 1791 through the nineteenth century. That included post-ratification commentary, antebellum judicial opinions, Reconstruction legislation, and post-Civil War commentary.[1098] For instance, the Court discussed precedents upholding the right to carry arms openly[1099] and protection in the Freedmen's Bureau Act of 1866 for "the constitutional right to bear arms."[1100]

Based on the above, *Heller* declared the District of Columbia's ban on the possession of handguns violative of the Second Amendment. Recalling antebellum State court decisions that invalidated bans on openly carrying handguns as unconstitutional, the Court noted: "Few laws in the history of our Nation have come close to the severe restriction of the District's handgun ban."[1101]

However, the decision itself did not "cast doubt on...laws forbidding the carrying of firearms in sensitive places such as schools and government buildings," which are among the "presumptively lawful regulatory measures...."[1102] The obvious implication is that the

---

[1097] *Id.* at 598-99.
[1098] *Id.* at 589.
[1099] *E.g., Nunn v. State*, 1 Ga. 243, 251 (1846); *State v. Chandler*, 5 La. Ann. 489, 490 (1850).
[1100] See *Heller*, 554 U.S. at 614–15 (also citing S. Halbrook, *Freedmen, the Fourteenth Amendment, and the Right to Bear Arms, 1866–1876* (1998).
[1101] *Heller*, 554 U.S. at 629, citing *Nunn v. State*, 1 Ga. 243, 251 (1846); *Andrews v. State*, 50 Tenn. 165, 187 (1871); and *State v. Reid*, 1 Ala. 612, 616–617 (1840).
[1102] *Id.* at 626–27 & n.26.

right to carry arms in non-sensitive places outside the home is protected.

E) *Heller:* Rejection of Interest-Balancing

For Justice Scalia, the meaning of the Second Amendment was to be found in its text, history, and tradition. In his dissent, Justice Breyer would have relied on an "interest-balancing inquiry" which would defer to legislatures to decide if various interests outweigh recognition of a constitutional right.

Heller instead took a categorical approach and, without any consideration of legislative history or empirical studies cited in support of the ban, held:

> The handgun ban amounts to a prohibition of an entire class of "arms" that is overwhelmingly chosen by American society for that lawful purpose. The prohibition extends, moreover, to the home, where the need for defense of self, family, and property is most acute. Under any of the standards of scrutiny that we have applied to enumerated constitutional rights, banning from the home "the most preferred firearm in the nation to 'keep' and use for protection of one's home and family,"...would fail constitutional muster.[1103]

That the need for defense is "most acute" in the home presupposes that it is also acute elsewhere, such as on lonely streets or deserted parking lots at night. "Were it otherwise," wrote Judge Thomas Hardiman of the Third Circuit, "there would be no need for the modifier 'most.'"[1104]

[1103] *Id.* at 628–29 (citation omitted).
[1104] *Drake v. Filko*, 724 F.3d 426, 444 (3rd Cir. 2013) (Hardiman, J., dissenting), *cert. denied*, 572 U.S. 1100 (2014).

Heller rejected Justice Breyer's "judge-empowering 'interest-balancing inquiry,' that 'asks whether the statute burdens a protected interest in a way or to an extent that is out of proportion to the statute's salutary effects upon other important governmental interests.'"[1105] Relying on intermediate-scrutiny cases,[1106] Justice Breyer would have deferred to legislative empirical judgments based on a committee report and empirical studies.[1107] *Heller* responded:

> We know of no other enumerated constitutional right whose core protection has been subjected to a freestanding "interest-balancing" approach. The very enumeration of the right takes out of the hands of government – even the Third Branch of Government – the power to decide on a case-by-case basis whether the right is *really worth* insisting upon.[1108]

Since *Heller* was decided, disagreement has existed in the lower courts on what standards of review to apply in Second Amendment cases. Justice Clarence Thomas noted the application of two competing tests in the case that came to be known as *Heller II*, where the majority relied on levels of scrutiny—choosing intermediate over strict scrutiny—and the dissent by then-Judge Kavanaugh relied on text, history, and tradition.[1109] A number of cases since then have been decided against Second Amendment rights based on intermediate-

---

[1105] *Heller*, 554 U.S. at 634.
[1106] *Id.* at 690 (Breyer, J., dissenting), citing *Turner Broadcasting System, Inc. v. FCC*, 520 U.S. 180, 195–196 (1997).
[1107] *Id.* at 693, 696–99.
[1108] *Id.* at 634.
[1109] *Jackson v. City and County of San Francisco*, 576 U.S. 1013, 135 S. Ct. 2799, 2801 (2015) (Thomas, J., dissenting from denial of cert.), comparing *Heller v. District of Columbia*, 670 F.3d 1244 (D.C. Cir. 2011) (*Heller II*) (majority opinion) with *id.* at 1271 (Kavanaugh, J., dissenting).

scrutiny analyses akin to Justice Breyer's interest-balancing test, although others have rejected a tiers-of-scrutiny analysis.[1110]

F) *McDonald*: A Fundamental, Individual Right, Not a Second-Class Right

Next came the Supreme Court's decision in *McDonald v. Chicago* (2010). The plurality opinion by Justice Samuel Alito held that "the right to keep and bear arms is fundamental to *our* scheme of ordered liberty" and is "deeply rooted in this Nation's history and tradition," and thus that the Second Amendment is applicable to the states through the due process clause of the Fourteenth Amendment.[1111] Tracing the right through periods of American history from the founding through current times, the Court called the right "fundamental" at least ten times.[1112]

McDonald rejected the view "that the Second Amendment should be singled out for special – and specially unfavorable – treatment," to be treated as "a second-class right, subject to an entirely different body of rules than the other Bill of Rights guarantees...."[1113] It invalidated Chicago's handgun ban without according Chicago's legislative findings any deference or even discussion.[1114]

[1110] Compare *Drake v. Filko*, 724 F.3d 426, 440 (3rd Cir. 2013) ("justifiable need" standard for carry permit "withstands intermediate scrutiny"), *cert. denied*, 572 U.S. 1100 (2014), with *Wrenn v. District of Columbia*, 864 F.3d 650, 666 (D.C. Cir. 2017) ("So *Heller I*'s language and logic all but dictate that no tiers-of-scrutiny analysis could deliver the good-reason law a clean bill of constitutional health."), *reh. en banc denied* (Sept. 28, 2017).

[1111] *McDonald v. City of Chicago*, 561 U.S. 742, 767 (2010).

[1112] *Id.* at 767–91.

[1113] *Id.* at 780.

[1114] *Id.* at 750–51 (quoting Journal of Proceedings of the City Council).

Justice Thomas concurred with the end result of the plurality opinion, but would have held that the privileges or immunities clause, rather than the due process clause, of the Fourteenth Amendment protects the right to keep and bear arms from state deprivation.[1115]

In dissent, Justice Breyer objected that the decision would require courts to make empirical decisions such as: "Does the right to possess weapons for self-defense extend outside the home? To the car? To work?"[1116] He made no attempt to explain why the explicit right to "bear arms" did not answer those questions. The Court responded that judges would not be required "to assess the costs and benefits of firearms restrictions," given that "[t]he very enumeration of the right takes out of the hands of government…the power to decide on a case-by-case basis whether the right is *really worth* insisting upon."[1117] In short, it is not the role of a court to balance away a constitutional right.

G) The Meaning of Bill of Rights at the Time of Adoption

While the Supreme Court, at the time of this writing, has not resolved any substantial Second Amendment issues since *Heller* and *McDonald*, in 2006 it did issue a *per curiam* opinion related to whether stun guns are protected arms under the Amendment. Moreover, in 2019–20, the Court decided three cases on other Bill of Rights guarantees—the rights to jury trial, to free exercise of religion, and against double jeopardy—that resolved interpretative issues also applicable to the Second Amendment. These decisions are analyzed below.

[1115] *Id.* at 806 (Thomas, J., concurring).
[1116] *Id.* at 923 (Breyer, J., dissenting).
[1117] *Id.* at 790–91 (citation omitted).

A *per curiam* decision by the Supreme Court, *Caetano v. Massachusetts* (2016), reversed and remanded a decision of the Massachusetts Supreme Judicial Court that upheld a ban on stun guns.[1118] A stun gun is a non-lethal weapon designed to stun or immobilize a person by electric shock. The U.S. Supreme Court held that the Massachusetts high court erred in holding stun guns not to be protected on the basis that they were not in common use when the Second Amendment was adopted. That was contrary to *Heller*'s holding that the Amendment extends to "arms…that were not in existence at the time of the founding." It erred in concluding that stun guns were "unusual" because they are a modern invention, for the same reason. And it erred in asserting "that only those weapons useful in warfare are protected," a test that *Heller* rejected.[1119]

Justice Alito, joined by Justice Thomas, concurred in the judgment. The defendant Jaime Caetano got the stun gun for personal protection against her abusive former boyfriend. "By arming herself, Caetano was able to protect against a physical threat that restraining orders had proved useless to prevent."[1120]

It is noteworthy that Ms. Caetano carried the stun gun outside of her home, and indeed she was said to be "homeless." She displayed it to defend herself "one night after leaving work" when her ex-boyfriend threatened her. Police later arrested her for possession of the stun gun in the parking lot of a supermarket.[1121] If the Court thought that no right

---

[1118] *Caetano v. Massachusetts*, 136 S. Ct. 1027, 1028 (2016) (*per curiam*).
[1119] *Id.* at 1028.
[1120] *Id.* at 1029 (Alito, J., concurring).
[1121] *Id.* at 1028–29.

exists to bear arms for self-defense outside the home, it might just as well have denied certiorari and let her conviction stand.

Expanding on the *per curiam* opinion's statement that protected arms are not limited to those in existence when the Amendment was adopted, Justice Alito noted that such arms in common use today include revolvers and semiautomatic pistols. He added: "Electronic stun guns are no more exempt from the Second Amendment's protections, simply because they were unknown to the First Congress, than electronic communications are exempt from the First Amendment, or electronic imaging devices are exempt from the Fourth Amendment."[1122]

The Court has not decided any further Second Amendment cases on the merits. As discussed in the next chapter, Justices have filed dissenting opinions, in one case from the Court's decision that a case was rendered moot, and in other cases from the denial of certiorari. However, three cases on other Bill of Rights guarantees decided in 2019 and 2020 illustrate the Court's increased use of the interpretative methodology of text, history, and tradition.

In *Ramos v. Louisiana* (2020), in an opinion by Justice Neil Gorsuch, the Court held that the Sixth Amendment right to trial by jury requires a unanimous verdict, and that the requirement is incorporated against the states through the Fourteenth Amendment.[1123] The Court's analysis included three points relevant to the Second Amendment. First, the 1898 Louisiana constitutional convention "sculpted a 'facially race-neutral' rule permitting 10-to-2 verdicts in order 'to

---

[1122] *Id.* at 1031.
[1123] *Ramos v. Louisiana*, 140 S. Ct. 1390 (2020).

ensure that African American juror service would be meaningless.'"[1124] Facially-neutral restrictions on the right to bear arms, as discussed in chapter VIII of this work, also have a history in Jim Crow politics.

Second, rejecting the argument that the right to jury trial could be reduced to virtually no protections, the Court stated that "the promise of a jury trial surely meant *something* – otherwise, there would have been no reason to write it down." The Court imagined the term "jury trial" to mean "nothing but a single person rubberstamping convictions without hearing any evidence...."[1125] The same might be said about the term "bear arms," which must mean *something*, and that something must mean more than the government telling the citizens at large that they have no right to bear arms.

Third, as in *Heller*, the Court in *Ramos* rejected a watered-down test under which constitutional rights are or could be balanced away by judges:

[A]t the time of the Sixth Amendment's adoption, the right to trial by jury included a right to a unanimous verdict. When the American people chose to enshrine that right in the Constitution, they weren't suggesting fruitful topics for future cost-benefit analyses. They were seeking to ensure that their children's children would enjoy the same hard-won liberty they enjoyed. As judges, it is not our role to reassess whether the right to a unanimous jury is "important enough" to retain. With humility, we must accept that this right may serve purposes evading our current notice. We are entrusted to preserve and protect that liberty, not balance it away aided by no more than social statistics.[1126]

[1124] *Id.* at 1394.
[1125] *Id.* at 1395.
[1126] *Id.* at 1402.

The same could be said about the Second Amendment right to bear arms, which some courts have balanced away into oblivion.

Further, in *Espinoza v. Montana Department of Revenue* (2020), in an opinion by Chief Justice John Roberts, the Court found a state law that forbade financial aid to religious schools, but gave it to other private schools, to violate the First Amendment's protection for the "free exercise" of religion. The Court looked to "the founding era and the early 19th century," including "the early state constitutions and statutes," to find no "historic and substantial" tradition that supported the law.[1127] By the same token, the right to bear arms was recognized in the early state constitutions and was not abridged by statutes in the founding era and the early nineteenth century.

While "a tradition against state support for religious schools arose in the second half of the 19th century, as more than 30 States…adopted no-aid provisions," they reflected bigotry against Catholics, and "hardly evince a tradition that should inform our understanding of the Free Exercise Clause."[1128] Similarly, carry restrictions in a handful of states in the second half of the nineteenth century reflected bigotry against the powerless and African Americans, and should not inform our understanding of the right to bear arms.

Concurring, Justice Gorsuch noted that the free exercise clause "protects not just the right to *be* a religious person, holding beliefs inwardly and secretly; it also protects the right to *act* on those beliefs outwardly and publicly."[1129] Similarly, the Second Amendment

---

[1127] *Espinoza v. Montana Department of Revenue*, 140 S. Ct. 2246, 2258 (2020).
[1128] *Id.* at 2259.
[1129] *Id.* at 2275 (Gorsuch, J., concurring).

protects not just the right secretly to keep arms at home, but also the right to carry them publicly.

Finally, in *Gamble v. United States* (2019), an opinion by Justice Alito reaffirmed that the "dual sovereignty" doctrine allows a criminal defendant to be prosecuted under both state and federal law for similar substantive offenses without violating the Double Jeopardy Clause.[1130] The defendant had argued that the dual-sovereignty doctrine was inconsistent with the Constitution's original meaning, relying in part on a series of treatises "published after the Fifth Amendment was adopted."[1131] He attempted to defend this reliance on post-enactment evidence by pointing out that *Heller* "took treatises of a similar vintage to shed light on the public understanding in 1791 of the right codified by the Second Amendment."[1132]

But that argument, the Court explained, misunderstood the role that post-enactment historical evidence played in *Heller*: "the *Heller* Court turned to these later treatises only after surveying what it regarded as a wealth of authority for its reading – including the text of the Second Amendment and state constitutions. The 19th-century treatises were treated as mere confirmation of what the Court thought had already been established."[1133] In other words, post-Founding interpretations may rachet up the original public understanding, but do not change that understanding. This clarification of the interpretive role of post-Founding evidence in the Second Amendment context severely undermines those courts and commentators that have asserted that even

---

[1130] *Gamble v. United States*, 139 S. Ct. 1960 (2019).
[1131] *Id.* at 1975.
[1132] *Id.*
[1133] *Id.* at 1976.

"regulations from the early twentieth century" might be evidence of limitations on the Second Amendment's originally-intended scope.[1134]

* * *

The U.S. Supreme Court itself explained in *Heller* that "since this case represents this Court's first in-depth examination of the Second Amendment, one should not expect it to clarify the entire field," adding that it could "expound upon the historical justifications for the exceptions" to the right should they come before the Court.[1135] The scope of the right to bear arms and any exceptions thereto is a significant issue in need of clarification.

As discussed in the next chapter, the federal circuit courts of appeal and some state high courts have rendered conflicting decisions on whether the right to bear arms belongs to the people at large or only to privileged persons determined by state authorities to have a special need to exercise the right. Whether and how the Supreme Court resolves that issue remains to be seen, but the text, history, and tradition point in one direction only.

[1134] *Fyock v. Sunnyvale*, 779 F.3d 991, 997 (9th Cir. 2015).
[1135] *Heller*, 554 U.S. at 635.

Chapter Ten

TODAY'S LIMBO GAME: HOW LOW CAN THE STANDARD GO?

The game to see how low one can go under a limbo stick has long been a staple of children's birthday parties. It figuratively expresses the tendency of some courts to apply the lowest possible standard of review in deciding whether a prohibition on carrying firearms infringes on the right to bear arms. Despite the clear text of the Second Amendment and the Supreme Court's reading of the term to mean to carry arms, some courts find a way to nullify the right based on the judicially-created concept of so-called intermediate scrutiny.

The circuits are split on whether "may issue" laws, under which officials have discretion to decide whether a person "needs" to carry a firearm, violate the right of "the people" to "bear arms." Not unexpectedly, no significant litigation took place in the federal courts on that issue before *Heller* confirmed that the Second Amendment protects individual rights, and *McDonald* held the Amendment to apply to the states. The following discusses some of the leading opinions in the circuit split.

This chapter also addresses the judicial saga of a New York City ordinance making it a crime for a person holding a permit to keep a handgun at home ever to remove it from the home, even if unloaded, inaccessible, and locked away. That ordinance was upheld by the Second Circuit based seemingly on the lowest standard of review ever applied. When the Supreme Court granted review of that decision, the city scrambled to amend the ordinance, and the state legislature rushed to pass a conforming statute, in order to evade review by the Court.

A) The Post-*Heller* Circuit Split

There is a split among the federal circuit courts of appeal on whether the people in general have a right to bear arms in public. Some courts hold that they do, and others hold that government officials may decide who may exercise that right. The U.S. Supreme Court exercises its discretion on whether to review a case if federal circuit courts of appeal have rendered decisions in conflict, or if a federal court of appeals has rendered a decision that conflicts with a decision of the Supreme Court.[1136]

The following analyzes four of the primary decisions that represent the split among the federal circuit courts of appeals about whether the right to bear arms precludes government discretion over who may carry a firearm outside the home. The Seventh Circuit Court of Appeals invalidated Illinois' blanket ban that didn't even make licenses available, while the Third Circuit upheld New Jersey's law under which almost no one qualifies for a carry permit. The Ninth Circuit upheld California's discretionary licensing for concealed weapon permits, but refused to say whether the ban on open carry passes muster (it later held that it did). Justice Thomas dissented when the Supreme Court declined to hear that case. Finally, the D.C. Circuit

---

[1136] U.S. Supreme Court Rules, Rule 10.

held the District of Columbia's discretionary system violative of the Second Amendment.

Judge Richard Posner's opinion in *Moore v. Madigan* (7th Cir. 2012) invalidated Illinois' ban on carrying firearms, which did not even provide for discretionary licensing.[1137] Reviewing text, history, and precedent, the court concluded: "To speak of 'bearing' arms within one's home would at all times have been an awkward usage. A right to bear arms thus implies a right to carry a loaded gun outside the home."[1138] The right to self-defense is fundamental, and "a Chicagoan is a good deal more likely to be attacked on a sidewalk in a rough neighborhood than in his apartment on the 35th floor of the Park Tower."[1139] The existence of the constitutional right overrides policy arguments about whether "the mere possibility that allowing guns to be carried in public would increase the crime or death rates sufficed to justify a ban...."[1140]

By contrast, in an opinion by Judge Ruggero J. Aldisert, *Drake v. Filko* (3rd Cir. 2013) upheld New Jersey's discretionary carry license law.[1141] The majority held that the requirement to demonstrate a "justifiable need" to publicly carry a handgun for self-defense is a "presumptively lawful," "longstanding" regulation, and it thus "does not burden conduct within the scope of the Second Amendment's guarantee."[1142] Even if it did, it would be upheld under intermediate scrutiny.[1143]

[1137] *Moore v. Madigan*, 702 F.3d 933 (7th Cir. 2012).
[1138] *Id.* at 936.
[1139] *Id.* at 937.
[1140] *Id.* at 939.
[1141] *Drake v. Filko*, 724 F.3d 426 (3rd Cir. 2013), *cert. denied*, 134 S. Ct. 2134 (2014).
[1142] *Id.* at 429.
[1143] *Id.* at 430.

New Jersey enacted the "justifiable need" requirement for concealed carry permits in 1924, well over a century after ratification of the Second Amendment. The court found it not surprising that no legislative history existed with data to justify the requirement because it could not be anticipated that the Second Amendment would be held in *Heller* and *McDonald* to be an individual right applicable to the states.[1144] (The text of the Amendment recognizing the right to "bear arms" apparently did not suffice.)

In dissent, Judge Hardiman wrote that to restrict "bearing" arms to the home would conflate it with "keeping" arms.[1145] The ban was not "longstanding" in that, while need was required to be shown for a concealed carry permit under the 1924 law, open carry was not banned until 1966.[1146] No evidence existed to justify a ban on carrying by the typical citizen, the consequence of which was that the law was a "rationing system" that could be upheld only under rational basis review.[1147]

On the other coast, in California, the *en banc* majority in *Peruta v. County of San Diego* (9th Cir. 2016), authored by Judge William A. Fletcher, held that the Second Amendment does not protect a right to carry concealed firearms. The court refrained from opining on whether it protected open carry, although that too was banned.[1148] Carry permits were limited to persons with "good cause," excluding concern for one's safety.[1149] For tradition, the court recalled restrictions on the right

---

[1144] *Id.* at 437–38.
[1145] *Id.* at 444 (Hardiman, J., dissenting).
[1146] *Id.* at 448–49.
[1147] *Id.* at 453, 455.
[1148] *Peruta v. County of San Diego*, 824 F.3d 919, 924, 927 (9th Cir. 2016) (*en banc*), *cert. denied*, 137 S. Ct. 1995 (2017).
[1149] *Id.* at 926.

imposed by English kings, such as a statute that "limited gun ownership to the wealthy,"[1150] and antebellum state cases upholding concealed carry restrictions.[1151]

A dissent by Judge Consuelo Callahan, joined by three other judges, would have held that the right to bear arms was violated because the ban was on both concealed and open carry.[1152] "States may choose between different manners of bearing arms for self-defense so long as the right to bear arms for self-defense is accommodated."[1153] As to the county's unfettered discretion, "[s]uch discretionary schemes might lead to licenses for a privileged class including high-ranking government officials (like judges), business owners, and former military and police officers, and to the denial of licenses to the vast majority of citizens."[1154]

Another dissenting opinion, by Judge Barry Silverman, would have held that the law did not survive either strict or intermediate scrutiny. No evidence was provided that "preventing law-abiding citizens, trained in the use of firearms, from carrying concealed firearms helps increase public safety and reduces gun violence."[1155] In other words, California produced zero evidence that a "shall issue" law would increase crime.

[1150] *Id.* at 930.
[1151] *Id.* at 933–37.
[1152] *Id.* at 946 (Callahan, J., dissenting).
[1153] *Id.* at 946.
[1154] *Id.* at 955.
[1155] *Id.* at 957 (Silverman, J., dissenting).

When the U.S. Supreme Court denied certiorari in the *Peruta* case in 2017, Justice Thomas, joined by Justice Gorsuch, dissented.[1156] Based on *Heller*'s exposition of the right to "bear arms," Justice Thomas wrote that the Court "has already suggested that the Second Amendment protects the right to carry firearms in public in some fashion."[1157] He found it "extremely improbable that the Framers understood the Second Amendment to protect little more than carrying a gun from the bedroom to the kitchen."[1158] Given the historical evidence and precedents, the denial of certiorari "reflects a distressing trend: the treatment of the Second Amendment as a disfavored right."[1159] Justice Thomas concluded:

> For those of us who work in marbled halls, guarded constantly by a vigilant and dedicated police force, the guarantees of the Second Amendment might seem antiquated and superfluous. But the Framers made a clear choice: They reserved to all Americans the right to bear arms for self-defense. I do not think we should stand by idly while a State denies its citizens that right, particularly when their very lives may depend on it.[1160]

Having held that no right exists to carry a concealed weapon, the Ninth Circuit completed its work with its 2021 ruling in *Young v. Hawaii* that no right exists to carry a weapon openly either.[1161] Eschewing any analysis of the text—"the right of the people to...bear arms"—the decision by Judge Jay Bybee relied on

---

[1156] *Peruta v. County of San Diego*, 137 S. Ct. 1995 (2017) (Thomas, J., dissenting from denial of cert.).
[1157] *Id.* at 1998.
[1158] *Id.*
[1159] *Id.* at 1999.
[1160] *Id.* at 1999-2000.
[1161] *Young v. State of Hawaii*, 2021 WL 1114180, *3 (9th Cir. 2021) (en banc).

monarchial decrees and distorted readings of early American statutes to conclude that open carry is "outside the historical scope of the Second Amendment."[1162] For instance, the opinion claims that the 1836 Mass. Act "limited [public carry] to persons who could demonstrate their need to carry for the protection of themselves, their families, or their property," disregarding that to restrict carry, the Act required a complaint from a "person having reasonable cause to fear an injury, or breach of the peace."[1163]

Dissenting, Judge Diarmuid O'Scannlain, joined by three other judges, wrote that "the majority reduces the right to 'bear Arms' to a mere inkblot."[1164] He added: "Just as the Second Amendment does not protect a right to bear arms only as an on-duty militia member, it surely does not protect a right to bear arms only as an on-duty security guard."[1165]

Finally, *Wrenn v. District of Columbia* (D.C. Cir. 2017), in an opinion by Judge Thomas B. Griffith, invalidated the District of Columbia's restriction on issuance of concealed handgun licenses to those the police deem as having "good reason to fear injury."[1166] The analysis was based on the textual reference to "bear arms," the common law and historical tradition, and *Heller*. The court rejected the

---

[1162] *Id.* The monarchial decrees cited were medieval English except for a Hawaiian carry ban passed in 1852, when Hawaii was an independent monarchy. *Id.* (citing Act of May 25, 1852, 1852 Haw. Sess. Laws 19).

[1163] *Id.* at *24.

[1164] *Id.* at *48 (O'Scannlain, J., dissenting).

[1165] *Id.* at *68.

[1166] *Wrenn v. District of Columbia*, 864 F.3d 650 (D.C. Cir. 2017), *reh. en banc denied* (Sept. 28, 2017).

continuing relevance of the 1328 English Statute of Northampton in favor of the understanding at the Founding as follows:

> we can sidestep the historical debate on how the first Northampton law might have hindered Londoners in the Middle Ages. Common-law rights developed over time, and American commentaries spell out what early cases imply: the mature right captured by the Amendment was not hemmed in by longstanding bans on carrying in densely populated areas. Its protections today don't give out inside the Beltway.[1167]

Since the D.C. law was a total ban on the exercise of a right by the people at large, it was inappropriate to apply any level of scrutiny, strict or immediate. "Bans on the ability of most citizens to exercise an enumerated right would have to flunk any judicial test that was appropriately written and applied, so we strike down the District's law here apart from any particular balancing test."[1168] In sum, "[a]t the Second Amendment's core lies the right of responsible citizens to carry firearms for personal self-defense beyond the home, subject to longstanding restrictions" like licensing, but not bans on carrying without a special need.[1169]

In addition to the Third Circuit (*Drake*) and Ninth Circuit (*Peruta* and *Young*) decisions, discretionary licensing regimes have also been upheld by the First, Second, and Fourth Circuits.[1170] At the end of its

---

[1167] *Id.* at 661.
[1168] *Id.* at 666.
[1169] *Id.*
[1170] *Gould v. Morgan*, 907 F.3d 659 (1st Cir. 2018), *cert. denied*, 141 S. Ct. 108 (2020); *Kachalsky v. County of Westchester*, 701 F.3d 81 (2nd Cir. 2012), *cert. denied*, 569 U.S. 918 (2013); *Woollard v. Sheridan*, 712 F.3d 865 (4th Cir. 2013), *cert. denied*, 571 U.S. 952 (2013).

2019 Term, the Supreme Court denied petitions for writs of certiorari regarding the laws of New Jersey, Massachusetts, and Maryland.[1171]

Justice Thomas, joined by Justice Brett Kavanaugh, dissented from the denial of certiorari in *Rogers v. Grewal* (2020), a challenge to New Jersey's "may issue" law. Some states require a "justifiable need" or "good reason" for exercising the right to bear arms.[1172] Instead of deciding whether a law violates the right based on text, history, and tradition, some circuits have minimized *Heller*'s framework and "then 'filled' the self-created 'analytical vacuum' with a 'two-step inquiry' that incorporates tiers of scrutiny on a sliding scale."[1173] That "test appears to be entirely made up," as "the Second Amendment provides no hierarchy of 'core' and peripheral rights."[1174]

In Part II of the dissent (in which Justice Kavanaugh did not join), Justice Thomas wrote that "the right to carry arms for self-defense inherently includes the right to carry in public."[1175] On the historical side, "cases and treatises from England, the founding era, and the antebellum period confirm that the right to bear arms includes the right to carry in public."[1176] The Statute of Northampton in particular became "almost obsolete from disuse and prohibited only the carrying arms to terrify."[1177] "Finally, numerous Congressmen expressed dismay at the

---

[1171] *Rogers v. Grewal*, 2018 WL 2298359 (D. N.J. 2018), *summarily affirmed* (3rd Cir., Sept. 21, 2018), *cert. denied*, 2020 140 S. Ct. 1865 (2020); *Gould v. Morgan*, 907 F.3d 659 (1st Cir. 2018), *cert. denied*, 141 S. Ct. 108 (2020); *Malpasso v. Pallozzi*, 767 F. App'x 525 (4th Cir. 2019) (*mem.*), *cert. denied*, 141 S. Ct. 109 (2020).
[1172] *Rogers v. Grewal*, 140 S. Ct. 1865 (2020) (Thomas, J., dissenting from denial of cert.).
[1173] *Id.* at 1866.
[1174] *Id.* at 1867.
[1175] *Id.* at 1868.
[1176] *Id.* at 1869.
[1177] *Id.* at 1870.

denial of blacks' rights to bear arms when discussing the Civil Rights Act of 1866, the Freedmen's Bureau Act of 1866, and the Fourteenth Amendment."[1178]

Part III of Justice Thomas' dissent states that a handful of states ban the right of most citizens to exercise the right to bear arms, while the majority of states allow the carrying of arms to varying degrees. Granting certiorari would have allowed the Court "to provide lower courts with much-needed guidance, ensure adherence to our precedents, and resolve a Circuit split."[1179] It remains to be seen whether, or when, the Court will do so in a future case.

B) New York City's Ban on Transport Outside the Home

After a decade-long hiatus from taking on a major Second Amendment issue, in 2020 the Supreme Court was set to decide the validity of a restriction, that existed in no other jurisdiction nationwide, against taking a firearm out of the home. The jurisdiction with that one-of-a-kind ban, together with various interests that oppose any further word from the Court on the Second Amendment, pulled out all stops to keep the Court quiet on the issue. The following tells the backstory.

The U.S. Supreme Court granted a petition for a writ of certiorari in *New York State Rifle & Pistol Association v. City of New York* to review the city's rule providing that a person with a license to keep a handgun at one's dwelling may not take it out of the premises other than to a licensed shooting range within the city.[1180] The petition posed

---

[1178] *Id.* at 1874, citing Halbrook, "The Jurisprudence of the Second and Fourteenth Amendments," 4 *Geo. Mason L. Rev.* 1, 21–25 (1981).

[1179] *Id.* at 1875.

[1180] *New York State Rifle & Pistol Association, Inc. v. City of New York*, 883 F.3d 45 (2nd Cir. 2018) ("NYSRPA"), *cert. granted*, 139 S. Ct. 939 (2019).

the questions presented in part to be: "Whether the City's ban on transporting a licensed, locked, and unloaded handgun to a home or shooting range outside city limits is consistent with the Second Amendment...."[1181]

Upholding the ordinance in an opinion by Judge Gerard E. Lynch, the Second Circuit deferred to a declaration by a retired police official that allowing licensees to transport handguns to second homes or to competitions or ranges outside the city is "a potential threat to public safety."[1182] The court speculated that city residents could simply keep another handgun at a second home, or rent or borrow a handgun at out-of-city ranges or matches.[1183] Concluding that its review required "difficult balancing" of the constitutional right with the governmental interests, the court applied intermediate scrutiny and upheld the rule.[1184]

The Second Circuit's decision could well be the flimsiest application ever of intermediate scrutiny. An ex-official's declaration that it would be contrary to public safety merely to transport unloaded, inaccessible, locked handguns to other lawful places outside the home suffices to nullify and make a mockery of the constitutional right to keep and bear arms.

Then in 2019 the Supreme Court granted the Association's petition for a writ of certiorari. An array of interests desperately did not wish for the Supreme Court to rule that the right exists to take a firearm— even if unloaded, inaccessible, and locked away—outside of the home.

[1181] Petition for a Writ of Certiorari, *New York State Rifle & Pistol Association, Inc. v. City of New York*, No. 18-280.

[1182] *NYSRPA*, 883 F.3d at 63.

[1183] *Id.* at 57-58, 61.

[1184] *Id.* at 64.

They feared that this might be the first step toward a later ruling that the right to bear arms includes the right to carry arms in public. Moreover, the Court could be expected to expound on the standard of review in Second Amendment cases in a manner adverse to the seeming rubber-stamp approach of upholding any and all firearm restrictions under intermediate scrutiny.

So, the city filed repeated motions with the Court seeking dismissal of the case based on its intention to amend the ordinance. When the Court refused, the city sought delays in the briefing schedule to give it time to amend the ordinance before the case could be heard. The city then amended the ordinance, and the state legislature passed a law buttressing the new ordinance, which the governor promptly signed. Once again the Court denied the city's plea to dismiss the case and set a date for oral argument.[1185]

The city's grudging amendment to the ordinance allowed transport of a firearm directly to shooting ranges and second homes. The city then argued that the plaintiffs had received all the relief they asked for and thus the case was moot. Yet to transport a handgun to a second home, one would be required to obtain yet another premises permit from the issuing authority at that location.[1186] Transport to hotels or other temporary abodes would not be possible. The amended ordinance was almost as restrictive as the original one.

[1185] See Supreme Court docket entries of April 12–29, July 3–26, September 13, and October 7, 2019. https://www.supremecourt.gov/search.aspx?filename=/docket/docketfiles/html/public/18-280.html.

[1186] See Brief of Respondents, *New York State Rifle & Pistol Association, Inc. v. City of New York*, No. 18–280, at 5–6, 14–15 (2019).

Much of the oral argument in the Supreme Court concerned whether the case was moot; that the prior law had no real "public safety" value seemed to have been assumed. Justice Ruth Bader Ginsburg noted "one problem with the prior regulation, if you wanted to have a gun in your second home, you had to buy a second gun. And what public safety or any other reasonable end is served by saying you have to have two guns instead of one and one of those guns has to be maintained in a place that is often unoccupied and that, therefore, more vulnerable to theft?" Counsel for the city didn't even try to identify any.[1187]

In its *per curiam* decision, the Supreme Court found that the city's amendment allowing the petitioners to transport firearms to a second home or shooting range outside the city gave petitioners all the relief they sought, rendering the case moot. The Court vacated the judgment below and remanded the case for the district court to decide whether the new law permits routine stops for coffee, gas, food, or restroom breaks, and also whether plaintiffs may still add a claim for damages regarding the old rule.[1188]

Concurring with the holding that the case was moot, Justice Kavanaugh nonetheless agreed with the analysis of *Heller* and *McDonald* set forth in Justice Alito's dissent discussed below and shared the dissent's "concern that some federal and state courts may

---

[1187] Transcript of Argument, No. 18-280 (Dec. 2, 2019). https://www.supremecourt.gov/oral_arguments/argument_transcripts/2019/18-280_m64o.pdf.

[1188] *New York State Rifle & Pistol Association, Inc. v. City of New York*, 140 S. Ct. 1525, 1526-27 (2020).

not be properly applying" those precedents, a problem that the Court should address "soon."[1189]

Justice Alito, joined by Justice Gorsuch and Justice Thomas, dissented. "By incorrectly dismissing this case as moot, the Court permits our docket to be manipulated in a way that should not be countenanced." The city energetically defended its law until certiorari was granted, which "apparently led to an epiphany of sorts, and the City quickly changed its ordinance." And yet that did not render the case moot.[1190]

First, Justice Alito wrote, the new law did not give the licensees "*unrestricted* access" to ranges, competitions, and second homes outside of the City. Its requirements that travel must be direct, continuous, and uninterrupted left vague whether a person could stop for groceries, to pick up a friend to go to the range, or to visit a relative who lives near the range.[1191] Second, where constitutional rights have been violated, plaintiffs may be awarded nominal or compensatory damages.[1192]

On the merits, Justice Alito would have held that the old law violated the Second Amendment. As *Heller* stated, "'to bear arms implies something more than the mere keeping [of arms]; it implies the learning to handle and use them in a way that makes those who keep them ready for their efficient use.'"[1193] While sometimes a gun may be rented at a range, "the same model gun that the person owns may not

---

[1189] *Id.* at 1527 (Kavanaugh, J., concurring).
[1190] *Id.* at 1527–28 (Alito, J., dissenting).
[1191] *Id.* at 1533–34.
[1192] *Id.* at 1535.
[1193] *Id.* at 1541.

be available at a range, and in any event each individual gun may have its own characteristics."[1194]

Moreover, the city "points to no evidence of laws in force around the time of the adoption of the Second Amendment that prevented gun owners from practicing outside city limits." The city cited historical laws against the discharge of firearms within cities, but there was no showing that "municipalities during the founding era prevented gun owners from taking their guns outside city limits for practice."[1195]

Finally, Justice Alito wrote: "If history is not sufficient to show that the New York City ordinance is unconstitutional, any doubt is dispelled by the weakness of the City's showing that its travel restriction significantly promoted public safety. Although the courts below claimed to apply heightened scrutiny, there was nothing heightened about what they did."[1196] (This is part Part IV-B of the dissent, in which Justice Thomas did not join.)

The only factual basis offered by the city for its restrictions was the declaration of Inspector Andrew Lunetta, which made general allegations without any factual support. He basically claimed that the permit holders, who had all be vetted and approved by the police for their premises permits, would potentially become homicidal maniacs if they transported their unloaded, locked firearms outside of their homes.

Justice Alito reacted to the reasons Lunetta gave in support of the public safety argument as follows. First, "the travel restrictions discouraged licensees from taking their guns outside the home," yet "a

---

[1194] *Id.*

[1195] *Id.*

[1196] *Id.* at 1541–42.

reasonable opportunity to practice is part of the very right recognized in *Heller*...." Second, the restrictions prevented a person going to a range "from using it in a fit of rage after an auto accident," but that "does not explain why a person headed for a range outside the City is any more likely to engage in such conduct than a person whose destination is a range in the City." Third, police needed to check with ranges to ensure that a person was actually going to or from the range, but they could do that with ranges both in and outside the city. "[A] court engaged in any serious form of scrutiny would have questioned the absence of evidence, but no substantiation was provided or demanded below."[1197]

Justice Alito concluded that "the City's travel restriction burdened the very right recognized in *Heller*. History provides no support for a restriction of this type. The City's public safety arguments were weak on their face, were not substantiated in any way, and were accepted below with no serious probing. And once we granted review in this case, the City's public safety concerns evaporated."[1198]

* * *

Over two centuries passed between 1791 when the Bill of Rights was ratified and the Supreme Court's 2008 *Heller* decision. While the words of the Second Amendment have always been plain enough for Americans at large, *Heller* resurrected the Second Amendment from a certain judicial oblivion that began basically in the 1960s. As *Heller* noted, prior lower court decisions that stripped the Amendment of meaning "cannot nullify the reliance of millions of Americans (as our

---

[1197] *Id.* at 1542–43.
[1198] *Id.* at 1544.

historical analysis has shown) upon the true meaning of the right to keep and bear arms."[1199]

Yet despite the textual reference to "the right of the people to...bear arms" and *Heller*'s reading that in ordinary language "bear" means "carry," some lower courts brush that away and hold that banning this constitutional right is justified by judicial balancing tests that they devised.

Whether "the people" have a right to bear arms, or whether "the people" is a code term for a government-approved elite, should be definitively resolved by the Supreme Court. The Court took a small step in that direction by granting certiorari regarding the home-bound rule in New York City, which promptly fled the scene to avoid review. Petitioners from "may issue" states wait in line at the Court's door, knocking. It seems to be only a matter of time before the door is opened.

[1199] *Heller,* 554 U.S. at 624 n.24.

AFTERWORD

I n an ever-changing world, beset by natural and human disasters, constitutional rights ebb and flow, sometimes in unexpected, erratic ways. In normal times, the right to bear arms is debated and litigated in the courts, academia, and the public discourse. Articles are written, briefs are filed, and members of the public step up to the podium—or quietly buy firearms.

This work describes the origin and development of the Anglo American right to bear arms throughout several centuries. Like any similar study, it makes value judgments by selecting this very topic to study and by seeking to represent an accurate discussion of the text, history, and tradition of the Second Amendment. Scholars who denigrate the fundamental individual rights recognized by the Second Amendment also make value judgments, particularly that the right to bear arms is bad policy. But this book does not purport to debate the policy issue of whether the people should or should not have a right to bear arms. As the Supreme Court stated in *District of Columbia v. Heller*: "the enshrinement of constitutional rights necessarily takes certain policy choices off the table."[1200]

[1200] *District of Columbia v. Heller*, 554 U.S. 570, 636 (2008).

As described in this book, the Founders valued the right to bear arms for a number of reasons. The reasons included protection of life, liberty, and property from a variety of threats, including from criminals, hostile Indians, foreign invaders, domestic tyranny, and wild animals. The Founders also carried firearms for recreation, marksmanship, and hunting to put food on the table. They used firearms to win independence and to expand their new nation westward. To suggest today that carrying firearms outside the home in that great Founding epoch was severely restricted or even banned is simply to ignore history.

Some today suggest that the Second Amendment is obsolete and that the government may be trusted to protect everyone. Aside from the false assumption that the police can be everywhere and stop criminal attacks on victims, that false assumption ignores that the people may one day need to protect themselves from the government itself.

Insight into that issue was expressed by Alex Kozinski, who was born in Communist Romania of Jewish parents who were Holocaust survivors.[1201] The family escaped to the United States, where he became a judge on the U.S. Court of Appeals for the Ninth Circuit. When that court held that the Second Amendment was a "collective right" and not a right of actual individuals, he recalled how the Nazis and the Communists had perpetrated unspeakable crimes against unarmed people, adding:

> The Second Amendment is a doomsday provision, one designed for those exceptionally rare circumstances where all other rights have failed – where the government refuses to stand for reelection and

---

[1201] Shikha Dalmia, "Searching for Alex Kozinski" (July 1, 2006). https://reason.org/commentary/searching-for-alex-kozinski/.

silences those who protest; where courts have lost the courage to oppose, or can find no one to enforce their decrees. However improbable these contingencies may seem today, facing them unprepared is a mistake a free people get to make only once.[1202]

That has not occurred in the United States for the very reason that the people have retained their constitutional rights, however imperfectly and despite unwarranted governmental intrusions. Freedom of speech, the press and assembly, the right to bear arms, the rights to vote and to serve on juries, protection from unreasonable searches and seizures, and the array of rights of criminal defendants, all provide balance against the ever-growing bureaucratic state. Meanwhile, the debate continues in certain quarters in the United States on the basic right to carry a firearm.

There are ongoing debates about whether states with liberal carry laws and those with restrictive carry laws have more or less crime, and whether the carry laws are a cause of the higher or lower crime rates. Is the "more guns, less crime" thesis valid? When a state switches from a "may issue" to a "shall issue" licensing law, will there be a sudden avalanche of shootings by license holders? Do law-abiding citizens who carry firearms prevent or stop violent crimes in a meaningful way? Do soft targets such as schools where firearms may not be lawfully carried attract mass murderers? Do persons with handgun carry permits commit fewer crimes than members of the public at large and even

---

[1202] *Silveira v. Lockyer*, 328 F.3d 567, 570 (9th Cir. 2003) (Kozinski, J., dissenting from denial of rehearing en banc). See Stephen P. Halbrook, *Gun Control in the Third Reich: Disarming the Jews and "Enemies of the State"* (2013) (explaining how firearm registration and prohibition laws of the Weimar Republic were used by the Nazis to confiscate firearms from political opponents and the Jews); Stephen P. Halbrook, *Gun Control in Nazi-Occupied France: Tyranny and Resistance* (2018) (explaining how the French police collaborated with the Nazi occupation authorities to apprehend and execute gun owners).

police officers? Are criminals deterred by the existence of potentially-armed victims?

There are criminological studies with statistics aplenty on the above issues. But as the Supreme Court ruled in *McDonald v. Chicago*, it is incorrect to think that application of the Second Amendment to the states "will require judges to assess the costs and benefits of firearms restrictions and thus to make difficult empirical judgments in an area in which they lack expertise." That is because, "The very enumeration of the right takes out of the hands of government...the power to decide on a case-by-case basis whether the right is really worth insisting upon."[1203]

Today, the handful of states that prohibit the people at large from carrying arms are the distinct minority. They are ruled by mega-cities whose values sharply differ from those of the hinterland of the same states. Consider America at large. Open carry requires no permit in thirty states, requires a permit in fifteen states, and is prohibited in only five states.[1204] Forty-one states and the District of Columbia are "shall issue" states, which means that permits to carry concealed firearms on one's person are available to all law-abiding persons who meet training or other requirements. Vermont does not issue permits, but both concealed and open carry are lawful.

As noted, effective in mid-2021, at least twenty states have "constitutional carry," meaning that both concealed and open carry

---

[1203] *McDonald v. City of Chicago*, 561 U.S. 742, 790–91 (2010) (quoting *Heller*).
[1204] *Open Carry*, https://opencarry.org/maps/map-open-carry-of-a-properly-holstered-loaded-handgun/.

without a permit are lawful.[1205] Only eight states are "may issue," i.e., officials may issue a permit if they decide a person "needs" to carry a firearm.[1206] It is in those "may issue" states where the question of whether the Second Amendment literally guarantees the right to "bear arms" is in litigation, mostly in the federal courts.

In the absence of judicial resolution of the issue, some have advocated political solutions, including proposals in Congress to require states to recognize the carry licenses of other states. Such proposals are sometimes called "national reciprocity" or "national right to carry." Most states already have adopted reciprocity in the form of recognition of licenses issued by other states, similar to driver's licenses.[1207] Predictably, the "may issue" states, which do not recognize their own residents as having a right to bear arms, do not.

Should such proposals become viable, Congress could have two different jurisdictional hooks in the Constitution to enable it to pass such legislation. The most obvious would be the Second Amendment, which applies to the states through the Fourteenth Amendment, Section 5 of which provides: "The Congress shall have power to enforce, by appropriate legislation, the provisions of this article."

Alternatively, Congress may have jurisdiction to pass national reciprocity through its constitutional power "to regulate

---

[1205] "There Are 18 Constitutional Carry States," Feb. 13, 2021.
https://crimeresearch.org/2021/02/there-are-18-constitutional-carry-states/. In addition, Iowa and Tennessee also adopted constitutional carry in April 2021.
[1206] *Concealed Carry Permit Information By State*, USA Carry,
https://www.usacarry.com/concealed_carry_permit_information.html.
[1207] *USCCA's Concealed Carry Reciprocity Map & Gun Laws by State*,
https://www.usconcealedcarry.com/resources/ccw_reciprocity_map/

commerce…among the several states….”[1208] Courts have upheld many enactments on the basis that the regulated activity substantially affects interstate commerce and the right to travel. The federal Gun Control Act, with numerous regulations on the sale of firearms, was passed as an exercise of the Commerce Clause. Even its prohibition on possession of a firearm by a felon requires that the firearm has crossed state lines.[1209]

The Gun Control Act already includes provisions in favor of law-abiding citizens that preempt state laws. One provision states that, notwithstanding any state law to the contrary, a person is entitled to transport a firearm from one place where lawful to another place where lawful.[1210] Another provision authorizes an active or retired law enforcement officer to carry nationwide, without regard to state law, a concealed firearm that has been shipped or transported in interstate or foreign commerce.[1211]

Whether Congress will enact such legislation remains to be seen. While it has enacted various restrictions, it has also enacted protections of Second Amendment rights, from the Freedmen's Bureau Act of 1866, the Property Requisition Act of 1941, and the Firearms Owner's Protection Act of 1986.[1212]

The year 2020 saw three events that greatly impacted the environment in which the right to bear arms was perceived and exercised. The flipping of some state legislatures from Republican to

---

[1208] U.S. Const., Art. I, § 8, cl. 3.

[1209] 18 U.S.C. § 922(g).

[1210] 18 U.S.C. § 926A.

[1211] 18 U.S.C. § 926B & C.

[1212] See Stephen P. Halbrook, "Congress Interprets the Second Amendment: Declarations by a Co-Equal Branch on the Individual Right to Keep and Bear Arms," 62 *Tenn. L. Rev.* 597 (Spring 1995).

Democrat brought an array of bills to restrict or ban firearms in states that traditionally had few restrictions. The most dramatic example was the Commonwealth of Virginia, where numerous restrictive laws were passed. Nearly all counties and many municipalities declared themselves Second Amendment Sanctuaries where infringement on the right would not be enforced. The Virginia Attorney General declared that these resolutions had no legal basis.[1213]

On January 20, 2020, some twenty-two thousand or more citizens—many carrying handguns and rifles—peacefully protested against new restrictions in Richmond, Virginia, where the General Assembly was in session. Violence was predicted and the governor declared a state of emergency, but not a single incident materialized, and the protesters even picked up the trash at the end of the day.[1214] Despite such opposition, new restrictions on the right to bear arms were passed.

The second event to impact the right to bear arms was the arrival of the coronavirus. State and local governments shut down businesses and ordered citizens to stay at home. In most jurisdictions, gun shops were included with grocery stores as "essential" businesses that could remain open. In other jurisdictions, gun shops were deemed nonessential and ordered to close, in contrast to liquor stores which were considered essential.[1215] Fearful of the uncertainties that would

---

[1213] https://www.oag.state.va.us/files/Opinions/2019/19-059-Jones-issued.pdf. See Stephen P. Halbrook, "Virginia's Second Amendment Sanctuaries: Do They Have Legal Effect?," forthcoming in *Regent Univ. L. Rev.*, Spring 2021. https://ssrn.com/abstract=3735216.

[1214] "Thousands of armed U.S. gun rights activists join peaceful Virginia rally," https://www.reuters.com/article/us-usa-guns-rally-idUSKBN1ZJ15B.

[1215] See COVID-19 Information and Resources for FFLs (updated May 29, 2020). https://www3.nssf.org/share/PDF/COVID19-info-FFLs.pdf.

result from a breakdown in the economy, unprecedented numbers of persons bought firearms.

The third event in 2020 that prompted record firearm sales were the riots that were sparked in the aftermath of the death of George Floyd while being arrested. What began as peaceful protests against police brutality were hijacked by extremists intent on arson, looting, and attacks on law enforcement officers. Some cities abandoned any attempt to maintain order, the cry went out to defund the police, and record numbers of murders took place. Many citizens realized that they must provide their own protection.

Like the past, the future promises periods of normalcy interrupted by catastrophic events. Whatever the future holds, many citizens will seek to find security in the exercise of their Second Amendment right to bear arms, while opponents of that right will seek to impose further restrictions, enforced by the threat of imprisonment, on its exercise.

For well over two centuries, the Second Amendment still provides that "the right of *the people* to keep and *bear arms*, shall not be infringed." Those words were plain enough for the Founders, and they are plain enough today for persons who understand ordinary English. If some legislators and judges find those words too difficult to understand, it only reinforces that the Bill of Rights was ratified not just to forbid the government from violating the declared rights, but also to inform the citizenry of their liberties so they may take steps to preserve them.

About the Author

Stephen P. Halbrook holds a J.D. from Georgetown University Law Center and a Ph.D. in Philosophy from Florida State University. In law practice since 1978, he argued and won *Printz v. United States* (1997) and other cases in the U.S. Supreme Court, and represented a majority of members of Congress as amici curiae in the seminal Second Amendment case of *District of Columbia v. Heller* (2008). He has argued cases in almost all federal circuit courts of appeal.

Halbrook has testified before Congressional committees on the Second Amendment, firearm law issues, and Supreme Court nominees. A former assistant professor of philosophy at Tuskegee University, Howard University, and George Mason University, he is a Senior Fellow with The Independent Institute. See www.stephenhalbrook.com.

Made in the USA
Monee, IL
11 September 2021

76888468R00207